HOW TO AVOID

THE MOMMY TRAP

HOW TO AVOID

THE
MOMMY
TRAP

A Roadmap
for Sharing Parenting
and Making It Work

Julie Shields

CAPITAL BOOKS, INC.
Sterling, Virginia

Capital Books, Inc.
P.O. Box 605
Herndon, Virginia 20172-0605

ISBN 1-892123-88-6 (alk.paper)

Library of Congress Cataloging-in-Publication Data

Shields, Julie.
    How to avoid the mommy trap : a roadmap for sharing parenting and making it work / by Julie Shields.
        p.cm.
    Includes bibliographical references and index.
    ISBN 1-892123-88-6
    1. Parenting. 2. Fatherhood. 3. Sex role. I. Title.

HQ755.8 .S525 2002
649'.1—dc21
                                                    2002022410

Printed in the United States of America on acid-free paper that meets the American National Standards Institute Z39-48 Standard.

First Edition

10 9 8 7 6 5 4 3 2 1

For Elizabeth and Annie

CONTENTS

ACKNOWLEDGMENTS

Greatest gratitude goes to my husband, Ed Peartree, and my mother, Gail Shields. They read draft after draft and listened and talked to me way beyond the point where they could have any interest in the subject. They made it possible for me to write this book without sacrificing our children to the effort. Ed kept his promises and supported and understood my dream, even when it meant he had to put aside his for a while.

Thanks to my agent, Kristen Auclair, for all her hard work and patience. Ron Goldfarb also gave great advice that made the book more useful. Editor Noemi Taylor and publisher Kathleen Hughes at Capital Books have provided as much responsiveness and encouragement as any author could hope for.

Thanks to my dad, Larry Shields, for the material and his sustained interest in this and all my endeavors. Along with everybody I have spoken to during the past four years, Claire Cardone made wonderful contributions to my informal "think tank." Paula Mays, Allison Sofer, Whitney Warren, Sirina Tsai, Lise Schwartz, Don

Yannella, and Kit Johnston provided fresh eyes and intelligent com-
ments. Dave Driscoll and Granville Greene each helped me to get
my first break.

I am extremely grateful to the U.S. Trademark Office, and Debbie
Cohn in particular. If the Trademark Office hasn't implemented a
flexible work arrangement it's because it doesn't exist yet! Thank
you for hiring me back after three years away from the law and giving me a leave of absence to finish the book (and thanks also to Sid
Moskowitz for graciously tolerating my infrequent presence during
that time). Thanks to the Office of Plans, Policy, and Analysis in
the Bureau of Political and Military Affairs at the U.S. State Department for allowing Ed to work flexible hours.

The generosity and knowledge of Rhona Mahony, Michael Selmi,
Pamela Jordan, Carolyn Cowan, Jay Belsky, Amy Olson, Michael
McManus, Robert Wohlfort, Mary Ray, Fred Barbash, and Nancy
Kane added much to the book. A number of terrific teachers—
Natalie Wexler, Tim Wells, Noreen Wald, Rochelle Jones, and Mary
Collins—helped me a great deal as well. Finally, thanks to the families who opened their homes and hearts to me. I have changed their
names and, where requested, identifying characteristics of the couples. A few of the people I interviewed became composites for ano-
nymity or brevity's sake. But their statements and wisdom remain
true.

INTRODUCTION

As Elizabeth slept, the afternoon sun drifted through the window onto her soft cheek. I sat down in the study next to her room, in front of the computer. Her loud, rhythmic breathing punctuated the silence. All was safe.

I had just started a two-month leave of absence from my job as an attorney to take care of my ten-month-old daughter. My mother, who had baby-sat for Elizabeth for the past four months for twenty hours a week, had become ill and needed an operation. We knew that she would survive and that my legal career probably would not.

I relished the quiet, as any caregiver does when his or her sweet bundle of energy rests. At the same time, fear and anger swirled in my chest as I saw my previous existence about to end.

On my "second maternity leave," I had many hours to think—about what would happen if my mother couldn't baby-sit after her recovery, and, as I checked again on my angel, about how the world worked. She snored, in sweet ignorance of everything other than bodily needs, comfort, and love.

I wanted to tell Elizabeth everything. My parents had said I could be anything I wanted to be, same as they told my brother. I had just figured out that it wasn't true. I couldn't be a lawyer anymore, not the way we'd thought. I worked less and would probably quit in the near future (I did, seven months later, when my mother needed a second operation), though I didn't want to stay home full time.

I would have to find a replacement for my mother as caregiver if I wanted to continue to work. The desire to protect and nourish Elizabeth, the competence and warmth of Donna (the fairy-godmother "doula" who had helped us during the first few months), and my mother's highly engaged, loving care made it impossible to hand our almost year-old daughter to just anybody. But nobody like my mother, Donna, my husband, or me was available. We had looked. Elizabeth had grown accustomed to and deserved the best we could give her.

Up to this moment, I had envisioned the whole world out there for Elizabeth. Now, I wondered what we should teach her. Did we want to set Elizabeth up for this same thud of disappointment when she got older?

The house clean, I had nowhere to go and nothing to do. I started to type.

"To My Daughter."

In the world-weary voice of mothers across the centuries, I spilled my blood and soul onto the computer screen. This, sweetheart, is the way it is. You can't have it all; women have to choose; being a mother is the best thing in the world, but it aches to give up the rest of your identity.

I didn't know anything then.

As my situation, hormones, and understanding changed, the project evolved. I read a lot of books and found little in the way of solutions. I took notes after trips to the park, down the street, and to birthday parties. I talked to nannies, day-care workers, parents, grandparents, educators, single friends, employers, work-life counselors—anybody I could find—about parenthood, kids, work, and marriage.

Every day, I heard people take part in what I began to call "The Conversation": How do children thrive best? Why aren't things equal? Why didn't feminism take motherhood into account? Why do so many marriages flag once kids arrive?

I began to see light here and there. I met people who had solved the problem of how to create a happy, functional, modern family. I interviewed them. Situations where both parents worked and took care of their children with minimal or no substitute care interested me the most.

I learned that this was what I wanted in my own life, and began to take steps to make it happen. I decided to analyze what couples in contented situations had in common, to set out a roadmap for others, as well as for myself.

Patterns emerged. Most families with arrangements that differed from the norm had planned them in advance or set the stage in other ways for sharing parenting. Many mothers who stayed home because they thought it best for their children became mildly depressed. I met a few full-time moms thrilled to raise their children and tend the house. Mostly, their husbands earned lots of money so the women could hire household help and enjoy some personal time.

The mothers who worked and had traditional family roles seemed resigned to constant exhaustion and having no time for themselves. In various ways, over and over again, I saw smart, wonderful women trapped by the alternatives they believed available to them.

There must be some better way, I thought, though clearly not one way for all families. Everybody wanted something different.

Slowly, I stopped feeling as if life was happening to me, and created the existence I wanted. I used the examples I had sought out. They have power.

Most of us don't see many successful illustrations of how to practice the shared parenting we are attempting. We live in a different century than our own mothers did; we were raised with enhanced expectations of and for ourselves and our children. Yet we hang in limbo between 1950s family roles and new arrangements with no clear boundaries and rules.

Take this book as a guide for how to get to that new place. Parents can design the lives they want; marriages can thrive even after children arrive; fathers can have closer relationships with their children than their fathers had with them; and children can get the best love possible at the same time that mothers enjoy fulfillment apart from house and family.

Some of the ideas presented will seem too radical and others so obvious you'll wonder why you never thought of them. And when Elizabeth and her younger sister, Annie, take their turn at this, I hope they won't need this book at all.

Just the other day, Elizabeth, now five, told me she wants to be "everything in the whole wide world" when she grows up. I told her, and I believe, that she can.

IF IT'S BROKE,
FIX IT

There's Still a Long Way to Go, Baby 1

Even though things are supposed to be different today, one way or the other, I'm still responsible for all of the things my mother took care of when I was growing up. And I work, too.

—Lauren Martling, mother and graphic designer who works from home

SEVEN-THIRTY, MONDAY MORNING, AN AMERICAN CITY
Mary Clayton turns away as her husband Mark tries to kiss her good-bye. Resigned, he leans down to kiss their eight-month-old son, Jeffrey, instead. Mark has grown accustomed to Mary's resentment, which rises each day as he prepares to leave the house for work. Mary would like to walk out that door a couple of times a week to go to her own job but has not yet found a child-care situation she can trust.

Around the corner, Lauren Martling counts the minutes until her son's nanny will arrive. Dan woke up three times last night. Lauren can't wait to get out of her drool-laden pajamas and take a shower. She pours her third cup of coffee. With Dan on her lap, she sends her husband, George, an e-mail message, in capital letters, reminding him of his promise to baby-sit on Saturday when he returns from an overseas business trip.

Three blocks over, Ann King, a psychologist, hugs her husband, Mike, and giggling eight-month-old daughter, Maggie, good-bye. As

Ann walks downstairs to her office, she wishes that Maggie seemed sadder to see her leave, but appreciates that Mike makes Maggie's breakfast so much fun. At one o'clock, Ann will take over with Maggie. Mike will spend the afternoon drafting an architectural bid for a house renovation project and attending a meeting at city hall. For now, Ann looks forward to seeing her first client and spending time with Maggie later.

THE PROBLEM WITH NO NAME REVISITED

Mary Clayton's situation represents a new version of the same old story. Until giving birth to Jeffrey eight months ago, she held a tenure-track position as an economics professor at a state university. Now she takes care of Jeffrey full time. Before becoming a mother, Mary enjoyed committee work, running, and many friendships, in addition to her marriage. Her predicament depicts "the problem with no name," dressed up a bit for the twenty-first century.

In 1963, Betty Friedan gave the first chapter of *The Feminine Mystique* the title of "The Problem with No Name." The Problem with No Name describes the plight of homemakers matching slip-covers, eating peanut butter sandwiches, driving carpool, and lying in bed at night next to their husbands wondering, "Is this all?" The Problem with No Name was bad enough in 1963. It's even worse for contemporary women brought up to believe they could and should do it all.

If the lifestyle of the happy homemaker isolated mothers before, today it's even more isolating. Fewer people inhabit neighborhoods during the day. Entering a playground filled with nannies can lead at-home mothers to feel that few parents see value in spending time with their children. The stigma attached to staying home doesn't exactly make full-time moms feel valued. I have yet to meet a stay-at-home mother who hasn't expressed fear of being at a party and asked what she does.

Mary Clayton explains:

> The thing that's really hard is finding a new group of friends. All of my old friends work. A lot of the mothers I meet weren't committed to their careers and they actually seem to like being in the house all the time. I put a lot into my job, and I plan to go back. I don't have anything in common with these people.

My friends have not supported my choice to take this time off. My best friend told me she thinks I'm judging her. She has had problems with her son's day care. I said that's ridiculous, that I'm just trying to do what I think is best for my family, but we don't do anything together anymore.

Staying home to do the important work of raising children still has its drawbacks—the same drawbacks that led to the women's movement (namely, the desire for something beyond house, kids, and marriage), and others, including more isolation and social stigma.

Before Jeffrey was born, Mark and Mary Clayton had a lot of fun together. Now everything's changed, and not the way they expected. Every night when he comes home from his job as a software developer, Mark hopes Mary will be glad to see him. Instead, she hands the baby off and eagerly leaves the house for a walk. True, she'd called Mark a number of times from four-thirty on asking when he would be home, but apparently she wanted a break, not him.

When Jeffrey was a month old, Mary started looking into nannies and day care. She read articles and studies about child care, and asked every set of parents she knew about their arrangements. She visited day-care centers and interviewed countless nannies. Though she hadn't expected to, Mary concluded that Jeffrey would do best staying at home with his parents.

She has noticed that in some ways Mark takes better care of Jeffrey than she does, particularly with bathing and diapering. Far neater than Mary, Mark spends hours every night cleaning—vacuuming up soggy bits of teething biscuits and rewashing pots and pans smeared with crud even after Mary has tried to clean them. Though she finds it demoralizing to live with the mess she and Jeffrey create, Mary cannot fix it.

Mary doesn't want to quit her job. She needs to work to feel complete. She misses the adult interaction and stimulation of campus life. She asked for and received a year's sabbatical, and hopes to convince Mark to telecommute and work a compressed schedule so she can return to her very flexible job.

Mark has resisted making a career accommodation for what he views as Mary's decision not to place Jeffrey in child care. While he agrees they have not met any terrific nannies, and that Jeffrey should not go to day care at this age, thus far he has left things to Mary's sense of responsibility for their son. Mark wants her to keep the house neat, or at least neater, and show more interest in sex. They both adore Jeffrey, who is thriving, but are at an impasse with each other.

How did this couple get here? They didn't do their homework ahead of time. Failure to research and map out parenting roles[1] often defaults couples to the so-called "traditional" division of parental labor, where women nurture and men go out in the world to provide income.

Because she didn't look ahead, Mary Clayton fell into the Mommy Trap. She can (and as you'll see, will) get herself out, but only after passing through some rocky times first. Women contemplating getting married or becoming pregnant can avoid this situation with advance preparation.

THE TIRED SUPERWOMAN

In my interviews and while talking to friends and coworkers, I've noticed that many mothers employed outside the home have bags under their eyes. These women seem awfully tired. The feminist Naomi Wolf reportedly told Bill Clinton in 1996 that whichever candidate convinced American women that he understood their exhaustion would win the presidential election. A day in the life of Lauren and George Martling shows why.

Previously divorced, Lauren believes she must maintain her career in case things don't work out with George. She works as a graphic artist out of her home office. Pilar Arromoyo, a warm Bolivian mother of three, takes terrific care of the Martlings' eighteen-month-old son, Dan, from eight to four, Monday through Friday.

As soon as she hears the creak of Pilar opening the front door, Lauren jumps into the shower and heads upstairs to her third-floor office. She works straight through the day, sneaking downstairs for lunch when she knows Dan has fallen asleep. After Pilar leaves, Lauren takes Dan to the park and supermarket. She cooks and feeds him his dinner at six-thirty. While Dan eats, she makes dinner for herself and her husband, George.

George arrives home at seven o'clock. He and Lauren dine while Dan plays near them. George clears the table, leaving the dishes in the sink for Pilar the next morning, while Lauren gives Dan his bath and gets him ready for bed. George watches the news, then comes in to roughhouse with Dan (something Lauren has asked him not to do so close to bedtime) and kiss Dan good night.

George and Lauren flop down on the couch to watch television. She decides to get up the next morning at five-thirty so she can finish a brochure before Dan wakes up. She won't get it done before the ten o'clock deadline otherwise because Pilar doesn't arrive until eight, after seeing her own children off to school. Lauren dozes off, tired from the sleepless night before, working all day, spending time with Dan from four until now, and making two dinners. She wakes with a start, anxious to set the alarm before she conks out for good in front of the television, just as George says, "You know, it's so great having Dan. And he really hasn't changed our lives much at all."

Now, George isn't a bad guy. He actually is very nice. But he has no idea what Lauren does each day, or the toll it takes on her. He has never spent more than an hour or two alone with Dan, and then with much instruction. Lauren wants to throttle her husband after hearing his version of "Life with Baby," but laughs it off instead. She relates the story to a friend the next day.

> Sometimes I can't help feeling resentful of my husband. His life is basically unchanged. He loves Dan, but my life is so different now and his isn't. Everything I do is centered around Dan. The afternoons can be so long.

Tired all the time, Lauren has too many responsibilities. She knows that when Dan gets older things will get easier. Lauren has decided to have only one child so she does not have to disrupt her career and life again.

She doesn't give her husband as hard a time, or resent him as much, as Mary does Mark Clayton. But Jeffrey Clayton, who has just met Dan at the neighborhood park, will always seem to Lauren more content and more advanced than her son. She views her difficulty getting Dan to sleep through the night as the price she pays for maintaining an identity apart from her family.

Lauren believes she has proof that Dan would do better if she spent more time with him. The Martlings recently went on a two-

week vacation to California. Lauren noticed that Dan seemed happier and more confident during the trip. He seemed turned on, more
alive. Dan's eyes were brighter. He didn't wake up once at night.
Lauren explains:

> As good as Pilar is—and she knows so much more than I
> do—Dan prefers us. I know he would do better with his mile-
> stones, and sleep better, if I spent more time with him. But I
> also know that I would go out of my mind if I had to take care
> of Dan full time.

Many mothers have told Lauren about "Ferberizing," a method
for teaching a child to sleep through the night by allowing him or
her to cry for progressively longer periods of time. She's always felt
too conflicted about her absence during the day to impose strict
rules for Dan. Mary Clayton read Dr. Ferber's book when her son
was two months old, Ferberized him at three months, and has enjoyed eleven hours of quiet every night since.

As Lauren Martling sees it, she has only two choices: work, not
spend as much time with Dan, and suffer some consequences; or
stay home, spend more time with Dan, and become dependent on
her husband, and possibly depressed. In light of her disastrous first
marriage and her enjoyment of work, Lauren will not sacrifice herself completely to the family effort. Guilt, exhaustion, and a pre-
sumption that her husband should not make accommodations for
fatherhood have brought her into the Mommy Trap along with her
neighbor Mary Clayton.

When they became friends at the park, Mary Clayton and Lauren
Martling instantly engaged in The Conversation, where mothers,
fathers, child-care workers, grandparents, everybody, discuss the
seemingly impossible equation of parents, children, and work. Mary
envied Lauren's occasional lunches out and ability to work but also
noted with pride Jeffrey's confidence and mastery of his immediate
world. Lauren appreciated Jeffrey's exuberance and security, but
reveled in the knowledge that the next day at eight-thirty she would
do a creative project while Mary had no outlet. They didn't know
that in a few weeks they would meet Mike King at the sandbox, and
that he would greatly enliven The Conversation.

A LIFE OF BALANCE

For a glimpse of a brave new world, consider this evening at the Kings' house, four blocks over from Lauren and George. Ann, a psychologist, finishes her long afternoon seeing clients at her home office. She walks upstairs. Her husband, Mike, an architect, dresses their daughter, Maggie, for a visit to friends, an outing he has arranged.

Ann cooks the dinner, which the family eats together. The Kings talk about their day, basking in each other's company. After kissing her husband and daughter good-bye, Ann goes downstairs to her office to tidy up in preparation for her monthly book club. She prefers to entertain in the waiting room because it is clean and toy-free, and Mike is always working on a project or two in their living space upstairs.

Ann enjoys the evening immensely, and feels as if everything has come together. She adores being a mom, loves her work, and continues to expand her intellectual horizons.

Mike knows he'll work in the morning and play volleyball the next night. Maggie has had a good day with both her parents, having spent the morning with Ann and the afternoon and evening with Mike. Ann looks forward to her time with Maggie in the morning.

Both parents are keeping their careers alive. The Kings each work about thirty hours a week, including alternate Saturdays. Their daughter is thriving. The marriage is convivial, and they have a weekly date every Saturday night. That's balance.

The Kings have a lot less to say about their arrangement than Mary Clayton or Lauren Martling, because it works. All the talking comes when things don't function well. Highly satisfied with her situation, Ann says:

> I love my daughter and I love work. Sometimes, spending time with her seems like a vacation and sometimes work seems like a vacation. By dividing the day equally, my husband and I feel we have achieved the ideal balance. I have to have my time with my daughter and I have to work.

Lauren Martling and Mary Clayton will get to know Mike and Maggie King six months before they meet Ann King. When Ann becomes park-buddies with Lauren and Mary, Ann will never utter anything resembling a complaint about Mike, a unique quality. When other mothers mention they hardly have sexual relationships with their husbands anymore, Ann King will surprise them by mentioning her still strong and active lust for her husband.

Despite occasionally participating in activities of which few mothers would approve (like the six-foot-in-the-air infant toss), Maggie King will be no worse for the wear, and in fact, better. She will show exceptional curiosity, tolerance for novel experiences, and little fear. She'll also have a close relationship with the two most important people in her life. Affection will radiate to and from all three when they're together.

The Kings' example will send ripples throughout the neighborhood. Mary Clayton will pump Ann for information about how she and Mike arrived at their arrangement and how it works. To the disgust of fathers across town, mothers will invoke his name as an example of someone who does more than they do, of how their family's life could improve. Unlike her soon-to-be friends, Ann King did not fall into the Mommy Trap. Instead, she carefully created a situation that took everybody's needs into account and enabled her marriage to continue to grow closer.

THE WAY WE WHINE

Ann King's work-life arrangement depicts an increasing phenomenon, but situations like Mary Clayton's and Lauren Martling's still dominate the landscape for American mothers. I wish I had a dollar for every time I've heard a mother complaining about "him" and how little "he" does compared to her, or how much free time her husband has, and how little she gets. Countless studies documenting who does what in today's households show why mothers seem unable to stop grousing.

In the most famous study on the subject, University of California sociologist Arlie Russell Hochschild found that, compared to their husbands, employed mothers *work an extra month of twenty-four hour days a year at home* attending to their child-care and household responsibilities.[2] Hochschild calls the extra female workload the "the second shift," a phrase that has gained currency.

My friend Susan provides a good example of a working mother doing too much and talking a lot about it. Before the birth of their son, Susan's husband, Bob, seemed a fairly "sensitive" husband who often went grocery shopping and did nontraditional chores, such as making sandwiches for a weekend bike trip. After watching a Sunday night news segment about infant development, Bob turned to Susan and asked, "Are we doing enough to stimulate William?"

Susan spends more time with their son than Bob does, and would like Bob to do more at home. Deflecting resentment, she said, "I don't know."

"We should look into it," Bob replied, meaning *you*.

Susan objected to Bob's view of his parenting job description as consultant rather than principal. Without intending to, Susan had taken on the responsibility for childrearing. She vents:

> When did I become the brains of this operation? Before William was born, we split everything in the house. Now, even though Bob helps, I'm running the show. I'm the one who has to plan when things happen. What to bring. I make William's lunch and get him ready for day care. I decide what he has for lunch every day and make sure it's in the house. Bob doesn't even see William in the morning. I pick William up at day care, give him his dinner, and give him his bath.

It sounds as if Susan negotiated a poor situation for herself. But it's pretty darn common. Most women move into the executive ranks of parenting, regardless of whether they join the 45 percent of new mothers who stay home or the 55 percent employed outside the home. More than 60 percent of the men in the dual-income households that Hochschild studied performed between zero and 30 percent of the child care and household duties. Scores of other studies have yielded similar findings: Men do more than they used to at home but still do far less than women do.[3]

THE GLASS CEILING IS IN THE NURSERY
Who gets to see their friends, exercise, read the paper, or have kid-free fun? Not employed mothers working the extra month at home, and not most mothers who stay home, either. Research shows a

difference in both the amount and quality of leisure between new mothers and fathers. For example, a Social Policy Research Centre study of families in ten industrialized countries found that fathers spend less time with young children than mothers do, and a far greater proportion of their time playing than performing the work of child care.[4]

Fathers also have more pure adult leisure time. Because women have to grab free time where they can find it—in short intervals interspersed between self-care (things like taking a shower, sleeping, and getting dressed), work, and unpaid family work—they get less enjoyment out of the leisure they do secure. The numbers in Hochschild's study tell the same story. If a woman works full time and does 70 to 100 percent of the child-care and household duties also, she can't have anything left for herself.

But what about all that "balancing work and family" everybody always talks about? The existence of the second shift means that the majority of dual-income families balance only by *over-weighting the mother's side*. Because women take time for family and home, they remain behind men in the workplace, or leave altogether. An advertising executive and mother of two, who is considering cutting back at work or quitting her job so she can help her first-grader with his homework and school-related issues, says, "I see this issue for all the women with kids. It's plain in front of my face. I have to choose between my career and my family. How could you not choose your family?"

Thus, the vicious cycle continues, in which women as lower earners become the less valuable workers and the more important parent. And the buck doesn't stop there, because dads, marriage, children, and, ultimately, society suffer when one member of the family is overburdened and unhappy. Getting out of, or avoiding, the Mommy Trap requires changing to a concept of a *family* balancing comfortably, instead of plunking everything on the mother (or, to be fair, the mother taking on everything) from the start.

WHAT DID YOU EXPECT?

Two work shifts leave no play shift, no downtime, and not much sleep. That's one reason working mothers gripe so much. The job description for these moms provides a clue as to why so often women go part time or quit. Otherwise, women will likely suffer under an impossible workload. But there's something else going on here: frustrated expectations. *Until they gave birth, many of the women now performing 70 to 100 percent of child-care and household duties expected things to be 60/40, if not equal.*

Two definitive studies of the transition to parenthood found that the most unrealistic expectations pregnant women hold are those of how much their husbands will share in child and home care.[5] Despite changing women's opportunities outside the home, the women's movement left family roles basically intact. Yet, like my friend Susan, Mary Clayton, and Lauren Martling, many mothers don't anticipate that the childrearing workload will fall mostly on their shoulders (or how heavy or compelling it is). Then, boxed in by the seeming inevitability of what has happened, moms often see no option beyond resignation and complaint.[6]

Just as "You can have it all" became a catchphrase in the 1960s and '70s, everyday people utter a new, more downbeat mantra: "You can't have it all." It serves as a snapshot reference to the absurdity of a woman thinking she can have a fulfilling personal life or career, the best situation for her children, and a happy marriage all at the same time.

Hitting two out of the three categories now seems a more realistic goal. More realistic perhaps, but far from ideal, and by no means guaranteed. In later chapters, we will identify the tools that take the conversation beyond complaint, into happy solutions that make a trifecta possible for mothers, fathers, and children.

TERM LIMITS

Caught in their daily routines, the Clayton, Martling, and King families provide a tableau of the lives of working-, middle-, and upper-middle-class American mothers. While their experiences don't capture every possible situation, they stake out the outlines of the Mommy Trap, as well as a new family paradigm.

The Mommy Trap snares a mother whenever:

- she takes on parenting or household responsibilities that result in more unpaid work, and less leisure and personal time, than she would like, particularly in comparison with her husband;

- she does nothing to change the situation beyond expressing anger, complaint, and resignation;
- inherited preconceptions prevent her and her family from finding a solution to their problem—including those about what men and women can and should do, how child and household care should be performed, that the universe of work and child-care arrangements is rigidly predetermined.

The Mommy Trap occurs when a mother who feels guilty for spending time away from her children during the workday devotes every ounce of her energy in her spare time to her children. It snaps tightly around mothers who gatekeep, granting their husbands limited access to their kids, accompanied by critique and instruction. Women such as Mary Clayton, who end up at home, frustrated, because they assume that fathers provide income and mothers make career accommodations for the family, also reside in the Mommy Trap. So do stay-at-home moms happy to raise their children and not work for pay but who never get a break even to go out to lunch or the movies.[7] Those who plan months of maternity leave while their husbands take three days off after the birth of their babies, and who expect to share parenting equally (time to introduce myself!), constitute another large segment.

While I have researched what happens to women when they become mothers and can speak somewhat distantly about the experience, let me say up front that at different times I have been all of these women. I have made every mistake in the book more than once. That's how I know what they are. With time, I remedied some of my errors by talking to mothers who had set up better situations and by copying their methods. Whatever worked for them, I figured, could help me, too. I learned from couples who made up their own rules. I would love to pass their wisdom along to you.

I should make clear that the term "Mommy Trap" does not refer to giving birth and then having to take care of, or give up something for, your child. If I had the choice of becoming a mom and doing everything myself or not having children, I would pick my daughters without hesitation. But we actually have more choices than that, which can include many possibilities beyond those that expectant couples generally consider. More than anything else, the term Mommy Trap describes a failure to understand the wide range of options available to modern parents.

Let me also note that "traditional" roles work well for women who value domesticity. Nobody should fault mothers who like to stay home to do the difficult work of raising a family and taking care of the household. However, fewer and fewer women desire purely traditional roles. Post-women's liberation, most women want and expect something beyond house and family.

In a 1999 poll sponsored by the Pew Research Center for the People and the Press, only 25 percent of those surveyed agreed that "women should return to their traditional roles in society"; 48 percent completely disagreed with that statement and 23 percent mostly disagreed. Similarly, a survey of eight thousand women found that 80 percent believed men and women should be equal partners at home, and 68 percent wanted dual-income households.[8]

Later on, we'll look at research that shows that many women who think they (and their husbands) have moved past 1950s family stereotypes later find themselves in parenting roles that haven't changed much at all. Those who don't plan ahead like Ann King did wind up on the old road.

Follow me on a journey through the world of dating all the way to the joys of parenting teenagers. We will track Mary Clayton, Lauren Martling, Ann King, and others to see how to set up a personalized life-and-parenting allocation and learn how mothers already stuck can get out of the Mommy Trap. Wherever you fall along the continuum of life stages or hopes for paternal involvement, you will see yourself somewhere. If you're smart, like I wasn't, you'll have done some of the things our pioneering couples did. If you strayed, occasionally or often, you will find a way to right your course.

We will learn precisely how Mike and Ann King and other families with different arrangements created their satisfying situations. Not everyone will want to share equally. Nor can everybody afford to cut back on work hours to spend time with his or her young children. However, moving in those directions will start the end of our collective dysfunction—and the end of constant carping, endless cups of coffee, angst, and temper tantrums.

Women who do not have children and haven't selected their life mates yet have the greatest chance of sharing parenting more equally. Certainly, girls or women picking up this book before they become wives or mothers are ahead of the game. They can set up structures that allow them to do what seems nearly impossible: enjoy life and marriage after having children, and do a good job with all three, at the same time.

However, *there is hope for women who are already mothers.* First, we'll look at some common detours that lead to the Mommy Trap. Once we identify dead ends to avoid, we can trek on ahead to where we really want to go.

Why Quality Substitute Care Is Not a Complete Answer 2

I've read everything that says substitute care doesn't harm children, if it's of good quality and is not overused. But how much is too much? And how do you both work full time and have a life that isn't stressful all the time?

—Janey Berk, healthcare-policy consultant and mother of two

PARENTS MAKE THE BEST PARENTS

Like Lauren Martling in chapter 1 many women consider only two options when it comes to child care: doing it all themselves or buying substitute care. The Mommy Trap dictates that mothers can work and hire a mother replacement, or stay home if they don't like or can't find good substitute care. They may choose one or the other, or perhaps they can work part time and try for the best of both worlds.

These possibilities do not represent the optimum solution for many of today's families. As long as a working mother remains responsible for hiring and managing the help, and is the primary on-call parent, she'll still have too much on her plate (think of Lauren Martling's daily workload, even with a terrific nanny). But unless a mom has extremely traditional values and a community to support her, and odds are she doesn't, devoting all her efforts to house and family won't make her happy either.[1]

The standard routes bypass something crucial. *The best alternative to parenting by mother is parenting by father.* Given the chance, men make as strong, capable, and competent parents as they do strong, capable, and competent workers.

Women whose husbands take on primary parenting roles especially value knowing their children receive the same level of care moms would provide. Donna Diederle, a Foreign Service officer whose husband, Pete, stayed home for the first two years of their daughter's life, remembers:

> Leaving every morning was much easier because I knew I was leaving Kristy with her dad instead of with a nanny. That would have been very hard for me. It was easier for me to leave her with a caregiver because the caregiver was her father and I knew I could trust him and I knew that he would do all the right things. I could go to work feeling 100 percent confident that my child was well-cared for.

The nation continues to favor the ideal of parental involvement over hired child care for infants and small children, a logical preference that, combined with gender stereotypes, leads straight to the Mommy Trap. In a 2000 Public Agenda survey, 70 percent of parents with children ages five and younger said the best child-care arrangement during a child's earliest years is to have one parent stay at home. Fourteen percent preferred that parents work different shifts so one is almost always home. Just 6 percent said quality day-care centers were the best option, and 2 percent thought in-the-home baby-sitters best.

Why this persistent preference for parental care? Even the best day care or baby-sitter in the world doesn't reduce parents' desire to teach, do things with, and nurture their children, or diminish kids' interest in their parents' attention. Paid caregivers can never approach committed parents in love, interest, affection, continued presence in a child's life, and imparting a family's values.

Dr. Jay Belsky, a child development researcher who heads the Study of Children, Families and Social Issues at Birkbeck College in London, explains, "It's just easier for a parent to be committed because it is their child; it is not paid work."[2]

That is not to say that substitute care is always inappropriate (for my husband and me, it has been a lifesaver). When used judiciously, hired caregivers can nurture children wonderfully and help both kids and parents grow. Some people have no alternative but to use full-time child care. And children of parents unable to provide high quality care themselves benefit greatly from high-quality substitute care, begun early.[3]

However, research discussed below tells us that in the first three years of life children who are not at risk do better with part-time rather than full-time hours in substitute care. Since fathers can parent, too, we should not start from the assumption that mothers, and mothers alone, must choose whether to work, cut back, or hire a replacement caregiver. Instead, we can change our approach to seeking ways to provide babies the best start in life, at the same time giving mothers *and* fathers the best opportunity for happiness, individually and together.

JUST THE FACTS, MA'AM

We've heard a lot of debates—most of them obscured by emotion and politics—about the effects of substitute child care. Though media reports make it seem as if only controversy exists, some facts have emerged. We now know that dads parent as well as moms, and small children whose parents can provide high-quality care themselves do better with less than full-time hours in child care. For example:

- Children with highly involved fathers are more advanced, confident, sociable, and have a greater sense of control than other children have.[4]
- Care by fathers ranks highest in the areas of attachment and mothers' satisfaction of all nonmaternal care.[5]
- Children who have experienced substitute care, even high-quality care, for more than thirty hours a week starting in their first year of life, have less harmonious relationships with their mothers.[6]
- Even in high-quality care, more time in substitute care is related to more behavior problems, such as disobedience, noncompliance, and aggression.[7]
- Mothers who work full time and are not "at risk," that is, are not poor or depressed, are less involved with and sensitive to their children, have more negative interaction with them when they are together, and receive less affection from their children.[8]

- The pay in the child-care field is extremely low. Child-care providers tend not to be very educated or have high status. Each year about half of child-care workers leave their jobs.[9]
- Children more securely attached to their parents and caregivers do better socially, cognitively, and linguistically.[10]
- A child's brain grows most during the first three years of life than at other times in life. The brain develops through hearing words spoken in the child's native language by a live person, as opposed to a television or radio.[11]
- Caregivers with more education and of higher socio-economic status interact more with children, speak more often and more positively to children, and expose them to more words than caregivers with less education and of lower socio-economic status.[12]
- Positive caregiver-child interactions during the first three years correlate with better language abilities and cognitive development, and more school readiness.[13]

All these findings weigh in favor of parents who can provide high-quality care themselves, doing more with their children and using substitute care less. But few of us undertake much research about child development studies or fathers' abilities when making child-care decisions.

As a result of assuming full-time day care would work well for them, Janey and Ira Berk spent their first four years as parents rushing their children to and from day care, snapping at each other at night, and moving as fast as they could. They had little margin for error and no downtime. Their relationship deteriorated, and their stress level escalated. Most of their time at home involved some type of work or battle. Janey recalls:

> When we first had kids, we hadn't really talked about one of us staying home. Because we were both professionals, day care was a nonissue. It was just clear that our kids were going to go to day care. We didn't think about doing anything else.
>
> Letting them go to day care was really hard. We had good day care. And it was still hard, harder than I expected. We were both rushing all the time. When you try to get them to go somewhere quickly, it always turns into kind of a fight.

Like the Berks, many couples assume that someone else or some study has already determined that leaving infants for long periods of time to work two full-time jobs leads to a functional family arrangement. Ultimately, as we'll see later, the Berks decided that they and their children missed too much, and had too much stress, with both parents working full time. By searching for a way out of the Mommy Trap, the Berks created their own personal career and parenting solution, and all now enjoy a more satisfying existence.

THERE ARE NO MARY POPPINS

The Clayton family also learned after becoming parents that the standard Mommy Trap choices don't suit them. Jeffrey's pediatrician recommended first that a parent stay home, and second, a one-on-one arrangement at least until Jeffrey was eighteen months old. Most books Mary Clayton consulted made the same suggestions. Mary knew that she and Mark both wanted to continue to work so she discounted the idea that a parent stay home (which she interpreted to refer to her, not Mark). Instead, she looked for a nanny.

Mary had read that quality care occurs when caregivers talk often to and have frequent positive interactions with children. That came easily to her and Mark—they both loved to talk to, hug, and kiss Jeffrey. They couldn't keep their hands off his soft, warm skin, and he basked in their attention and touch. Mary noticed that other parents also kept up a constant patter and physical connection, while most of the nannies she saw did not. Still, two weeks before the end of her maternity leave, Mary hired Estella, the former nanny of a friend of a friend, on a trial basis.

One day, on returning from a short trip to the supermarket, Mary found her front door ajar, four-month-old Jeffrey alone in the living room, and Estella in another room making a personal phone call. The experience shook Mary's faith in nannies. Estella had seemed to understand everything Mary had said, and yet she didn't comprehend Mary's basic instructions about keeping the door locked, or share Mary's expectation that a caregiver stay physically close to Jeffrey.

Seeking expert advice, Mary met with a child-care consultant who, when pressed about how to avoid potential difficulties, advised hiring as little child care as possible. She also told Mary to install a camera if she hired an in-home caregiver, because "a nanny can have great references and surprise you amazingly."

Mary decided not to use another nanny while Jeffrey couldn't talk. She didn't want to hand over her dependent son, who couldn't tell her what happened when she was gone, and the idea of having to put a hidden camera in her son's nursery unnerved her.

After giving up on in-home care, Mary visited highly regarded day-care centers and family day-care homes. Upon walking into the first center, she understood the advantage of one-on-one attention. She saw that the time required to feed and diaper four infants means that babies in day care can cry without being comforted. The caregivers simply couldn't give the infants the type, amount, and variety of attention and experience Mary provided at home. And the babies didn't look very engaged or happy.

After doing her research, Mary made her choice. Ultimately, hiring a substantial amount of child care before Jeffrey was eighteen to twenty-four months old seemed like too much of a wager, with too much at stake. She and Mark had saved a good bit of money and could get by on one salary for a while. But Mary felt forced into staying home.

> There was no choice. I didn't find anybody I could leave Jeffrey with. My husband wasn't willing to make any kind of adjustment. There was no way I could go back to work. My son is still so little. When we come in to get him from his crib after his nap, he gives us this great big smile.
>
> It's really luck of the draw. The baby-sitters I saw, nobody would have hired them in any workplace. I didn't know them. How could I leave my baby with someone who didn't seem to have good judgment? I knew day care wasn't right for an infant. Mark just watched me go through all this. Somehow, it all became my decision.

The Mommy Trap says Mary Clayton has to choose: hire child care or stay home. However, after all her searching, she still can't find good care *and* she still wants a life outside the house. She yearns for a third way, one that can accommodate her need to do what's best for her son and for herself, and her desire for a parenting partner who's right there with her. For the Clayton family, as for many others with infants, the standard choices of nanny, day care, or mother at home exact high costs—from the child, the mother, and even the father (he gets distanced from his family, his marriage deteriorates, and he feels unappreciated).

QUALITY CARE IS RARE

Mary Clayton's inability to locate a good situation for her infant son represents the norm, rather than an exception. When advocates contend that substitute care adequately replaces parents, they always presuppose high-quality care. *But only 10 percent of American children in substitute care receive quality care, as these undisputed findings demonstrate:*

- 91 percent of family day-care homes do not provide adequate loving, stimulating, or beneficial care. (1995 Families and Work Institute study)
- 86 percent of day-care centers do not provide adequate loving, stimulating, or beneficial care. (1995 four-university study reported by the University of Colorado at Denver ["Denver study"])
- 74 percent of day-care centers provide care rated as *minimal,* meeting basic health and sanitary needs but providing children with little attention or educational encouragement. (Denver study)
- 40 percent of infant and toddler care is of *poor* quality, rated *less than minimal,* with poor hygiene, safety problems, babies not being held, and an absence of age-appropriate books and toys required for physical and intellectual growth. (Denver study)
- Just over 8 percent of day-care centers provide quality care for infants. (Denver study)
- Nanny care accounts for 2 to 5 percent of substitute care. Nannies appear to provide the same quality of care as day-care centers and family day-care homes. (National Institute of Child Health and Human Development [NICHD] study)
- The annual turnover rate in the child-care field is somewhere between 40 and 60 percent. (2000 Department of Health and Human Services [HHS] Executive Summary)
- Changing care arrangements disrupts children's development and attachment. Instability of care is considered a sign of poor child care. (National Childcare Staffing Study; 2000 HHS Executive Summary)

- Infants in poor-quality day-care centers (40 percent of infants in day care are in such centers) are vulnerable to more illnesses because basic sanitary conditions for feeding and diapering are not met. Day-care attendees suffer from far more respiratory infections, acute respiratory illness, outbreaks of acute diarrhea, and chronic ear infections than those who are cared for at home. ("Infectious Diseases in Children," July 1996; HHS Executive Summary 2000).[14]

As Mary Clayton discovered, the more we know about substitute care in the United States, the less we want to use it. *And even if we have to use full-time substitute care, most of us won't find a good arrangement.*

What about all those glowing reports of wonderful day-care situations and nannies? Some of them are accurate. Certainly, there are many great caregivers who can enrich children's and parents' lives. But researchers have consistently found that parents almost always report high satisfaction with the care their children receive, *without regard to the actual quality of the care.*[15] One study notes that while parents didn't demand a high quality of care in the day-care centers they used, the centers met parents' most basic need for a replacement that stayed open for ten to twelve hours a day, part time, before and after school, and in the summer.[16]

Forget ideas about optimal child development or whether parents know how to assess quality of care—the turnover rate in the child-care field often sends mothers back home. Statistics become reality awfully quickly. Diane Gordon, a former personnel director at a law firm, quit her job when her capable nanny left. She remembers:

> I just couldn't go through the whole nanny search again, and my job didn't allow me the time to do it right. You have to train the nanny and give her responsibility gradually so she can earn your trust and the kids' trust. And then what if the next person left again?

Should we interpret these statistics and experiences to mean that using substitute care is always a bad idea? Absolutely not. They illustrate the difficulties of finding quality care, or using too much of it, too early, and can help parents formulate their work and parenting plans. But no one would suggest there is anything wrong with hiring a trustworthy caregiver (for ideally no more than thirty hours a week, up until age three), or someone to help with household chores as often as possible. In fact, experts recommend that parents aim for neither full-time substitute care nor full-time parental care, but instead something in between.

QUANTITY AND QUALITY MATTERS

When parents come home from the hospital with their newborn, many consult Burton White, T. Berry Brazelton, Stanley Greenspan, and Penelope Leach for everything from how to get the baby to sleep through the night to when and how to potty-train. Not one of these trusted authorities favors full-time substitute care for infants up to age three, unless something is very wrong at home or a family has no viable economic alternative.

The experts don't view full-time care by one parent as ideal, either. For example, in the classic *The First Three Years of Life*, Burton White recommends four hours of baby-sitting a day, for up to seven days a week. That's twenty-eight hours a week, a substantial amount but two hours less than the threshold of substitute care at which problems seem to start. He notes that a respite from round-the-clock care gives parents a break from the stresses of continuous responsibility, and enables them to pursue outside interests: "Psychological relief, whether through outside work or relaxation, is very important for full-time parents."[17]

Attempting to take into account the needs of both children and parents, Drs. T. Berry Brazelton and Stanley Greenspan advocate a "four-thirds solution," where each parent works two-thirds time for the first three years of a child's life. That way, both parents can care for their child and pursue their careers. In this new paradigm, by sharing the workload at home, parents can minimize the time their children spend in substitute care. Brazelton and Greenspan also recommend that one or both parents (in combination) spend the first year with their babies to give them the best start.[18]

Ann and Mike King arrived at their own four-thirds solution. By spreading work over six days a week, they have avoided even the two days a week of substitute care that the four-thirds solution contemplates. They also created a year of parental leave by splitting their time at home. Ann explains why:

We knew we didn't want to use a nanny or day care. We both wanted to be involved, so we worked hard to find ways to make our marriage and kids primary in the beginning, so that we could give them both our best, when we knew it mattered most. The first three years are the most important. That's when everything gets turned on in their brains and secure attachment either happens or doesn't.

Penelope Leach, author of the influential *Your Baby & Child,* also advises parents to place priority on time at home during the early years, career demands notwithstanding:

In North America, especially, there is increasing pressure on parents not just to work while children are very young, but to work from a few weeks after they are born; and not just to work a few hours, but to work as if they were childless, including the commute, the after-work drinks and the expense-account travel. The snappy American term "quality time" tells parents that they can pack all the desirable interaction with their children into a single hour of each working day provided it is a *good* hour.[19]

According to a 1998 *USA Today* study, American women have rejected the once popular idea that children need quality rather than quantity time from their parents.[20] Nonetheless, some people continue to champion the cause of quality substitute care without giving any consideration to parents' desire for more time with their children and children's demand and need for their parents. For example, in *When Mothers Work: Loving Our Children without Sacrificing Ourselves,* Joan K. Peters suggests that a parent "frame" a child's day. Peters says that all mothers should work because they need only spend time with their children when they wake up and at bedtime.[21]

Reality paints a different picture. Couples who work long hours can find bedtime and the early morning hours problematic. In their study of new parents, psychologists Carolyn Pape Cowan and Philip A. Cowan observed that almost all of the dual-income families they visited had a hard time getting their children to bed at night.[22] Kids who see their parents for just an hour or two a day often seek their attention by acting out, waking up at night, moving slowly in the morning, or generally making things difficult whenever possible.

And, like Lauren Martling, many parents don't feel comfortable enforcing rules when they spend the workday away from their children, leading to more sleepless nights and less parental authority.

Sociologist Arlie Hochschild calls dealing with constant temper tantrums, aggression, and disobedience "the third shift."[23] The third shift describes the guilt and stress Janey and Ira Berk experienced rushing their children through the day, which they eliminated when they started putting quantity time into their household. On a personal note, my daughters act out and disobey me if I have not been available to them, behaviors they seldom exhibit when I've spent lots of time with them.

Once parents reject the idea of quality time, the Mommy Trap leaves most of the quantity time to mothers. But child-care experts point to new ways, like the Kings' situation, to accommodate children's needs and parents' desires for time with kids, happy marriages, and pursuits outside the home.

WORKING THE NUMBERS
In the real world, families confront economic constraints and often two sets of career and personal ambitions. Though it seems to be best for children to have their parents mostly available during the early years, not everybody can afford to, and being home full time might make some parents miserable. *But any effort parents make to spend more time with their children helps their children to feel more secure and to develop better, and enhances the family's experience.*

Developmental researcher Jay Belsky offers this guidance:

> We find a continuous dose-response relationship between time in care and problem behavior. The bad news is there is no magic number; the good news is that any reduction in time should yield some benefits. It is like dieting. There is no magic number of calories to consume, but eating less carries weight reduction benefits.

In urging parents and society to make young children their first priority, Stanley Greenspan suggests an "every little bit helps" approach.[24] Guy and Lynne Swanson have adopted this method in trying to "squeeze out that extra little bit of time" with their children whenever possible. By adjusting their full-time schedules, they try to drop their kids off at day care at nine-thirty in the morning and pick them up at four, making the Swansons usually the last in and the first out. Guy says:

> I think long days are hard for the kids, and the staff. I do things in the classroom, and the kids and the staff are tired at the end of the day, and I think it's a different kind of experience then. I think it's hard on the kids. I think that less is better.
>
> I didn't used to think that there was a value to kids spending a certain amount of time with their parents. I do now. It depends on the parents, but on average, I think the kids enjoy it better. I think the kids thrive more. I see how kids relate to the parents as opposed to their day care. And it's clearly different. With the parents, that's where they feel the security and the love. And I think they can get some of that at day care but it's always going to be less.

Lynn echoes her husband's sentiments:

> Overall, our work schedules mean that the kids, throughout their futures, won't have to be in day care for extraordinarily long days. And if one is sick or has a dance recital, we have the flexibility to accommodate it and not be stressed out about it. But that said, they are both enrolled full time.

Because both parents make accommodations, the Swanson children spend far less time in care than the fifty or sixty-hour weeks two full-time jobs might necessitate. Not everybody can provide the best possible caregiving situation for their children and at the same time ensure both parents' fulfillment or enough family income. But when parents consider the needs of every family member—rather than ignoring or denying the facts about substitute care or the effect of overloading mothers—they arrive at better, more balanced, and happier arrangements.

Research gives us targets to shoot for. We won't always make them. But common sense, expert advice, and overwhelming study findings suggest that parents who can provide high-quality care themselves try hard:

1. not to place an infant of less than twelve months in a day-care center. Infants need consistent one-on-one attention, and may be traumatized by turnover of caregivers and frequent illness.

2. not to place a child younger than three in substitute care for
   more than thirty hours a week (recommendations from Brazelton and Greenspan in *The Irreducible Needs of Children* and other
   sources).

So, we know enough to see that one Mommy Trap paradigm that
has developed—of full-time substitute care for forty to sixty hours
a week, starting from the age of six weeks—has some serious built-
in deficiencies. Because many mothers instinctively understand the
risks, they choose part-time work.[25] If they take the time for a longer
maternity leave, or from the workweek, women become more invested in their children, more sensitive to their needs, and less willing to place them in undesirable situations. But if their husbands do
not cut back, they remain less sensitive to their children's needs
and more attuned to workplace rules.

Which brings us back to that same old Problem with No Name.
As long as women alone attempt to remedy the deficiencies in the
new paradigm, whether by working and spending all their nonwork
time with their children, or staying home without relief, they run
into the deficiencies of the old paradigm. The homemaker and nurturer can't get fulfillment outside the house, if she can get out at all.

Fathers are the only actors who can provide balance in the equation for dual-income households. A father can make the difference
to his children and wife by giving up some leisure time and taking
time from work, just as mothers have been doing. Otherwise, if a
mom cuts back on her personal life and work to do the rest of the
child and home care, she may end up unhappy, complaining, and
overburdened, like Lauren Martling and Mary Clayton. Eventually,
her husband will find himself unhappy, too.

Fathers can make the difference for stay-at-home mothers as
well, by allowing them time for themselves. Dads remain the only
viable alternative for couples who make deep financial sacrifices to
have a parent at home or cannot locate acceptable child care. Later,
we will look to working mothers with "househusbands" for a new
family model that allows at-home parents psychological relief and
working parents' participation at home.

After the first three years, the negative effects of too much or
poor-quality substitute care seem to abate. Thus, parents who make
career or work-time accommodations can do so on a temporary

basis, redoubling their career efforts once their children need them less. Such a redirection of parenting would bring the United States more in line with the rest of the industrialized world. In countries such as Sweden, governments encourage and pay for more than a year of leave for new parents to spend with their infants, and subsidize time for parents at home during the first years. They enact these policies to foster the public interest in raising healthy, secure, productive members of society.

The cold truth about substitute care, particularly as it exists in the United States, forces hard choices. The Mommy Trap leaves the "choice" to mothers. However, couples can balance work and family more readily once men enter into the equation. The next chapter will dispel any doubts that they can do it.

Yes, Men Can, and It Will Be Good for Them, Too 3

> I do so much more to help out than my father
> ever did. Yet my wife gives me no credit. And at
> work, they don't understand when I want to
> take time off to be with my family.
>
> —Mark Clayton

PRACTICE MAKES PARENTS

Have you ever heard this one? "I don't know how she does it. It's much harder to take care of the kids than it is to work. I could never do it as well as she does."

Of course women are better at tending child and home—they've had all the practice! Most of today's mothers don't start out with much knowledge about taking care of babies. If they're like me, they bring their firstborn home knowing nothing about babies.

No God-given female instinct tells women how to change a diaper. As with any skill, mothers acquire the ability to tend children by doing it. And cooking and housework, which come with the territory, are not gender-based arts either.

The early days at home with a firstborn child frighten mother and father alike. Babies don't come with instruction manuals. My sister-in-law Karen had a pretty typical response during the early days of her oldest son's life. After our first daughter was born, she told us, "I couldn't believe the hospital let me take a baby home after two days and be responsible for him. I didn't know what I was doing!"

She'd always seemed very competent and all-knowing about her son Jonathan's moods, habits, and needs. It surprised me to learn that, like us, she hadn't had a clue about what she was doing at the beginning. Her husband, Tim, went back to work a couple of days after Jonathan's birth. Karen quickly became the expert through all of her on-the-job training.

Mothers often keep the uncertainties of the first days secret from the uninitiated, afraid their friends will look down on them for not knowing what to do and sometimes feeling lonely rather than blissfully happy. Only when I became a mother did my friend Susan tell me she had felt inadequate, because "All of the books said I was going to start recognizing what each cry meant. In the three months I was home with William, I never recognized a single cry."

Women's perceived superiority in childrearing turns out to be largely a matter of environment. Our current division of parental labor doesn't allow men to see how good they can get at taking care of their babies. Most dads stay home for a couple of days, maybe a week, and then go back to their jobs. I've heard about many fathers who didn't engage with their babies until they "got interesting and could do things." This lack of involvement occurs as a result of the way we structure our lives. It doesn't have to happen, as Marjorie and Jake Pappas discovered when circumstances forced Jake to take on the role of primary parent.

REAL MEN EAT PEANUT BUTTER AND JELLY FOR LUNCH
Jake Pappas was the last person anyone expected would become "Mr. Mom." An avid ESPN watcher, Jake had never been taken for a "sensitive man." But he lost his job during the eighth month of Marjorie's pregnancy. Her salary alone would not pay for both their mortgage payment and substitute care. Despite grave reservations on both their parts, they decided Jake would stay home with their baby, at least until he found a new job.

Feeling left out during breastfeeding, Jake initially ceded control to Marjorie. As the mother, Marjorie (a take-charge kind of person anyway) was supposed to know everything. When Marjorie went back to work, baby Benjamin cried all day. He had breastfed exclusively up until this time. Jake remembers:

The nightmare part of this was the day my wife went back to work. Benjamin screamed all day long. After three or four days of that, I said to my wife, "Honey? I'm gonna die." But you sit there, and you think, "I have to come up with ways to deal with it." I'd distract him. Or we'd go do things together.

Slowly, everything changed at home. Jake started to master baby care. Because he had no choice, he came up with ways to entertain and calm his son—taking him hiking, going to the park, and acting silly—methods Marjorie never developed because nursing had always done the trick. He bypassed the usual step of transitioning from breast to bottle, teaching Benjamin to drink from a cup at the age of six months.

Jake took great pleasure in seeing that Benjamin needed and enjoyed him so much. Five years later, he still takes care of Benjamin and baby brother Joe. Jake says:

> I can't imagine being the kind of guy who worked a nine-to-six job and didn't see his kids but two or three hours a day. It would just drive me nuts, now that I've done the other way. I feel like I'm really participating in their daily growth.

Marjorie Pappas agrees that Jake has developed more skill than she ever imagined he would.

> Though I don't like to admit it, Jake is probably better with the boys than I am. When Jake is playing with the boys, he's just playing with the boys. I'm trying to make dinner, call a friend back, or get something else done. He's really there in a way it's hard for me to be. I like to multitask if I can.

A study performed by Dr. Kyle D. Pruett, a professor and psychiatrist at the Yale University Child Study Center, demonstrates that fathers who are given the chance to nurture have similar experiences to Jake's. Over the course of ten years, Pruett followed eighteen families in which fathers served as the primary parent or shared child care with their wives. Some of the dads took on the role voluntarily, others reluctantly. All of the fathers formed deep reciprocal attachments with their children.[1]

At first when their babies cried, the fathers asked themselves what their wives would do. As they moved beyond the competence of the mother, the fathers abandoned the concept of the mother as a model. Then they figured out how to take care of their children. The fathers' caregiving styles emerged as they began to think of themselves as parents and not just mother substitutes. Ultimately, most of the men in the study continued to stay home or share in their children's care. Tending children causes parents—male or female—to want to spend more time with them and creates responsiveness, responsibility, and interest in the welfare of their offspring.[2]

JUST DOIN' WHAT COMES NATURALLY

Other research bears out fathers' capabilities. Take the first, and seemingly all-consuming, task with a newborn—feeding. Fathers get milk into a baby's mouth as efficiently as mothers. They also burp, soothe, stroke, and comfort a hungry baby just as well.[3] Physiologically, men respond the same way as women to upset babies, with quickened pulses, higher respiration, and alertness of the senses.[4] Why, then, do mothers complain, "It just doesn't bother him when the baby cries?" Conditioning.

Solo time in charge and societal expectations have conditioned mothers to know what the cry means, or if they don't, to do whatever they have to, *at once,* to find out. Societal roles condition dads to know what it means, too: Their wives will take care of it.

Allison and Howard Pearlman stayed home on maternity and paternity leave together for the first two months. As a result, they didn't experience the traditional conditioning of the mother becoming more in tune with their baby. Unexpectedly, they found that it bothered *Howard* more when the baby cried. At six weeks, Howard said, "I wasn't surprised that the baby cried but I was surprised by the way it affected me. It bothers me more when she cries so I'm just more creative and find ways to soothe her."

When men get the opportunity, they respond to the different cries. That's welcome information for those of us who may have yelled at our husbands during a dinner at a friend's house for not reacting quickly enough to our daughter's cries—I've been there, too.

Not surprisingly, babies who develop secure attachments to both parents thrive best.[5] Newborns show no consistent preference for one parent or the other.[6] Rather, they make first attachments to the person who holds, feeds, and stimulates them.

Babies protest the departure of their parents from a room on an equal basis, but not the departure of strangers. Later on, many children seem more invested in their mothers. Research done on the early days, observation, and the attachment formed between actively involved fathers and their children suggest that the common mommy preference occurs as a result of mothers' more constant presence. Babies learn from repeated experience that mom provides food, comfort, or whatever else they need, and so quite naturally they look first to and develop closer attachment with their mothers.[7]

But when fathers spend as much time as mothers at home, children develop equal (but different) attachments to both parents.[8] Sarah Stapleton-Gray and her husband, Ross, have always shared the care of their daughter, Kye, each working part time. She says, "I disagree that there is a biological basis to good parenting. Kye turns to either of us when she wants something and she bestows her attention and radiant smiles just as equally."[9]

At age five, Maggie King looks to whichever parent is closest to her when she needs assistance. At a recent party when she needed help strapping a birthday hat under her chin, she went over to her dad, holding out the hat to him. Wordlessly, Mike put it on, and Maggie skipped over to help her friend blow out the candles. Half a decade has given her unconventional conditioning: Both of her parents know her well, are likely to be present, and can anticipate and take care of what she needs.

WHAT A DIFFERENCE A DAD MAKES
Early father–child interaction translates into tangible results. Fathers allowed physical contact with their infants soon after birth need and miss their babies. In one study, every father who touched and held his newborn became absorbed, causing researchers to believe that physical contact causes dads to become engrossed in (that is, fall in love with) their infants.[10] Children with dads actively involved during the first eight weeks of life manage stress better during their school years.[11] Greater frequency of paternal visits to newborns in the hospital correlates with higher infant weight gain and, later, a more secure child.[12]

Pruett's study provides great ammunition for mothers seeking to share baby care. The more fathers do everyday repetitive tasks such as bathing, feeding, dressing, and diapering, Pruett found, the more socially responsive children become. The children in the study, and in many others tracking children of involved fathers, developed more advanced problem-solving, personal, and social skills than the norm. Researcher Norma Radin also observed a positive connection between children's verbal and math skills and the amount of contact they have with their fathers.

In my interviews of families with involved dads, many parents used almost identical words to describe their children's personalities. Their experience echoes the research results above:

- "My daughter is very friendly. She knows her alphabet at eighteen months." (parents both work part time)
- "She's extraordinarily verbal. She's very independent." (father stayed home for first year; now both parents work flexible full-time jobs and share child care)
- "My son is very outgoing. He's not clingy. He's not just focused on one person." (parents both work part time)
- "Inquisitive. Loves to play and laugh." (stay-at-home dad with a very involved mom)
- "He's a very outgoing, spirited boy, who transitions well from one thing to another." (stay-at-home dad whose wife works four days a week)

As I watched the children—regardless of their age—their independence *and* security struck me again and again. Because they got quality and quantity attention from two parents, these children exhibited interest in me as a new person and had no trouble occupying themselves for long periods of time, with little parental intervention. They developed well because they got the best of what both parents, and sexes, have to give. All the nontraditional families I interviewed cited having the influences of both parents as one of the benefits of involved fathering. For example, they said:

- "They learn so much about different aspects of the world. We are very different people." (mother of two who works part time and job-shares with her husband)

- "She's pretty much as comfortable with him as she is with me. Granted, when she's kind of cranky, she'll come to me first. I guess I'm more the lover and nurturer and he's more the play-mate and wrestler. So I think it's a nice balance." (mother who works four days a week and dad stays home)
- "No two people have the exact same set of parenting skills. So it gives the kids a fuller palate of parenting skills from which they can draw. It also gives them a greater sense of security to have both parents focusing on them. (father who works full time but stayed home for two years; mother then stayed home for two years, now works part time)

The benefits of paternal participation continue into adulthood. Research performed by Ross Parke, John Snarey, and others demonstrates that fathers' physical style of parenting teaches children emotional self-control and how to maintain strong social relationships as adults.[13] A Harvard University study found paternal involvement with young children the single strongest, parent-related factor in adult empathy.[14] Fathers who spend time alone with their children more than twice a week, giving baths, meals, and basic care, raise the most compassionate adults.

None of these findings emphasize the role of earning money (which has its value, too) but instead the daily hands-on caregiving by fathers. Active fathering also weakens some of the stereotypes that keep women responsible for the home. Being cared for by one's dad gives girls permission and encouragement to succeed in the world outside the home, and boys permission and encouragement to succeed inside the home.[15] Children of involved fathers don't make the assumption that women must nurture and men must work. One at-home dad recalls his son's question to him: "Can men be lawyers, too?"

Our sons and daughters will have more and better choices if men can do a little or a lot more today. We have all seen lists of societal problems caused by the absence of a father. Briefly, lack of father influence leads to poor control of aggression, difficulty in establishing gender identity, impaired intellectual and school functioning, depression, drug use, teen suicide, self-esteem problems, higher rates of divorce, and more teen pregnancy.[16] Children raised by involved dads do better and stay longer in school, have more self-confidence, explore the world more, commit fewer crimes, report higher job satisfaction as adults, and support highly engaged fathering as adults.[17] If we want things to be better for our children, we'd better find a way for them to enjoy all the great things fathers can do.

SO WHAT IF HE'S NOT MOMMY? THAT'S THE POINT

Fathers and mothers parent differently. Men tend to encourage babies' curiosity and urges to solve intellectual and physical challenges, and to foster children's sense of mastery of the outside world.[18] Fathering often involves more physical, roughhousing, unusual, and exciting play. Babies look to dads for fun—when their fathers approach, they greet them with a special look that says they expect a good time. Mike King loved nothing more than to throw his daughter, Maggie, in the air as high as he could and catch her. She giggled madly each time he did it.

Mothers usually prefer toy-oriented and otherwise mediated acts of play. They pick up children more, and like to keep them close.[19] Ann King liked to strap Maggie into a "bouncy seat" next to her while she worked. Every so often, Ann would jiggle the seat to keep it moving or stop and encourage Maggie to play with the toys attached to the seat.

Children with primary parenting fathers appear especially comfortable with stimulation from the external environment.[20] Exposed by their fathers to more opportunity for curiosity without mediation, children of involved dads gain extra mastery and confidence. They also feel more in control of themselves and the world around them, and take initiative and direct themselves more.[21]

Of course, another factor plays a role. Sarah and Ross Stapleton-Gray's daughter, Jake and Marjorie Pappas' sons, and the children in Pruett's study have two parents performing hands-on parenting, rather than just one. Mothers who are breadwinners generally give their children lots of attention and provide their stay-at-home or sharing husbands lots of support.[22] Children with actively involved fathers usually get more parenting overall and benefit from learning two effective approaches to life.[23]

Our current child-care arrangements, then, with mothers and other women doing the lion's share, do not give children the best possible upbringing. The division of parental labor that existed in agrarian societies prior to the Industrial Revolution, where fathers and mothers pooled their efforts, works better. The Information Revolution, which allows parents to bring work home again, and our changing understanding of fathering enable us to move forward to a better way of doing things.

IT'S NOT THAT GREAT FOR THE MEN EITHER

Back in chapter 1, we let women gripe a little bit. Now dads get to have their say. Men increasingly deal with two conflicting worlds and two sets of expectations that seem impossible to reconcile. They still want to provide for their families, and our society and culture continue to exert great pressure on them to do so. At the same time, today's fathers want more time with their children than their full-time work schedules allow. During a group breakfast at a Virginia country inn, the father of a strapping fourteen-month-old boy made a comment I have heard from many new dads, especially younger ones:

> Right now it's time I want, not money. I'd take less money in a heartbeat so I could be home more. Sometimes it's just too hard on my wife, and I miss too much with the baby.

Fathers are conflicted, too. A 1993 *Child* magazine poll found that both fathers and mothers believe that the most important quality for being a good father is daily involvement with their children, with supporting the family coming in a close second.[24] If parents acted in accordance with these beliefs, neither the second shift nor the glass ceiling would exist. Unfortunately, the workplace and societal norms, which idealize full-time workers (especially fathers) and fully available parents (especially mothers), collide with families' private beliefs. Fathers feel guilt for not doing more at home *and* anxiety to make more money, all at the same time.[25]

Under the status quo, many men see earning money as the one activity they must undertake to be "good fathers." Often a job change that requires more time at work soon follows. This thirty-seven-year-old father of two remembers:

> The baby changed my outlook regarding money. Before that I always was confident I could earn it at some vague point in the future, but not too concerned at the moment, and not making

much as a result. I started my own practice three months before my son was born and became somewhat fanatical about building it and tracking my profits. The baby lights a fire under a father's ass as nothing else can.

But many of today's new mothers don't want their husbands at work all the time—they want them home helping. A 1997 Families and Work Institute Study found that almost as many fathers in families with a mother at home (67 percent) experienced a great deal of conflict between work and family as fathers in dual-income couples (70 percent). Like my friend Jim, many dads, even those with a stay-at-home wife, report, "My wife is always yelling at me." And truth be told, too often women ridicule their husbands' efforts with their children at the same time they complain that they don't do enough.

James Levine, director of The Fatherhood Project, uses the term "DaddyStress" to describe the problem today's fathers have managing conflict between work and family. Levine emphasizes that DaddyStress remains largely unrecognized because fathers think they should not expose the conflicts they experience performing their double duties.[26]

Given the role models their fathers supplied, men such as Mark Clayton have difficulty reconciling their wives' demands to do more at home with their employers' time requirements. Mark's father, a great provider, left early in the morning, came home for a dinner made by his wife, and puttered around the house on the weekends. In Mark's view, he has done more than his wife, Mary, should expect because he takes charge of his son every day, as his father never did with him. Some part of Mark believes that he has failed because he cannot provide for Mary and Jeffrey as comfortably as his father did. He states:

I'm always borrowing from Peter to pay Paul. Either I'm not doing enough at home or I'm not doing enough at work. I can't put in the time at work I did when I was single. It pains me that I am not doing as good a job as I can, because I take a lot of pride in my work. I feel unappreciated at home and misunderstood at work, and I'm exhausted trying to satisfy both masters.

Trained from birth to succeed out in the world, many men often don't know how to switch gears. Many fathers express shock at the changes in their wives and marital relationships when they become parents. One dad in a highly conflicted marriage says, "After my son was born, I used to tell people that my wife was colicky, and I got many knowing smiles from other fathers. Who wants to be married to a shrew?"

Couples who at one time supported and understood each other end up feuding over matters that seem beyond their control. Dads can't act according to any script because they don't have one, and it often seems their wives find fault with whatever they do.

LOVE, AMERICAN STYLE

A big elephant has come to visit in many bedrooms. It's called sex. In households like the Claytons' and Martlings', where women are tired, resentful, or dissatisfied—and many of them exist—there's not a whole lot of sex going on. Sex, or the lack thereof, has become a huge issue in many of today's marriages.

A 1996 *Parenting* magazine poll found that having a baby dampened the fire in the sex life of 54 percent of new parents, and completely put it out for an additional 18 percent of couples.[27] While surveying a support group for stay-at-home mothers, I learned that some women trade sex for help around the house. One mother put it this way: "Clean house equals more sex." Intimacy, togetherness, and love can all disappear once pre-baby intimacy, togetherness, and love create a baby.

Sadly, few men get the chance to know what fun they could have if they spent more time with their children. In poll after poll, fathers say they want more involvement with their children.[28] At the same time, the outdated and misinformed Mommy Trap belief that men must work full time keeps millions of family arrangements less than harmonious. The workplace, which expects employees to work as if they had a full-time homemaker at home (or as if women still want to be housewives), can force fathers to make difficult choices as well.

Pruett sees a "yawning paternal emptiness which leaves men feeling uncertain, confused, and unfinished as men" caused by the systematic distancing of fathers from children. He calls this void "the father problem" or "fatherneed."[29] Fatherneed describes the feeling that Mark's father had, before he died at sixty, of not being close to Mark, and wanting desperately to be. Do you know a grandfather who never spent much time with his own children but will do anything, however ridiculous, for his grandchildren? That's fatherneed.

Let's not forget that the idealized 1950s yielded a generation of distant fathers who, after all was said and done, bemoaned the lack of connection with their children and their own fathers. This is not a desirable role model.

The second time around, Fred Barbash, a fifty-five-year-old dad, rejected the old way of fathering. He has always had a close relationship with his now-grown daughter, Carrie, whom he adores. But when she was little, he worked long hours and felt he missed too much. Fred retired early from his job as a *Washington Post* columnist to take care of his six-year-old son, Jack, from a second marriage. Fred made the choice to fulfill his own fatherneed and is having a ball. He says:

> I know there are lots of benefits to me. I must say, I'm doing this for me. I hope it benefits him, but the primary beneficiary at this time that I know of is me. I am having a sinfully good time. I do think he'll benefit from having a better relationship with his father.

Fred is right. Studies have consistently found that more father care leads to an improved relationship between father and child.[30] Dads who take time to parent in the early years stay more involved with their children later on, and end up happier, healthier, and wealthier at the end of their life.[31] Not coincidentally, women complain the loudest during the first few years.

WHAT A WONDERFUL WORLD IT WOULD BE

What would happen if every father found a way to give a little more time to his family? First, fathers' lives would improve. Touching, hugging, teaching, and loving one's children are some of the best activities in the world. What transcends the joy of a child reaching up to take your hand, and knowing you're there to kiss a "boo-boo," toss a ball around, or help deal with a friend's hurtful behavior?

Having a father give more time to his family has worked in my house. A few years ago, my husband switched to a flexible work schedule with alternate Wednesdays off. Although it wasn't easy to secure this arrangement, it wasn't all that hard either. Ed became the first employee, male or female, in his bureau at the State Department (n historical bastion of long hours) to work flexible hours. While the compressed work schedule policy had sat on the books for years, nobody had attempted to use it before.

Ed took over all of the child and house responsibilities during his "day off." He brought our younger daughter, Annie, to Gymboree class, which she loved. During naptime, he made phone calls he couldn't make from work. He started visiting a foot doctor, the girls in tow, something he had long needed to do but for which he had never found the time.

When circumstances later changed, I informed him I wouldn't object if he switched back to a regular schedule, but he didn't want to! Ed explained:

> I like my day off. I love my time with the girls. When I come home, I don't want to go back to work. I want to spend more time with them. And I'm more efficient when I'm at the office. My life is better now.

Mine is, too. Fathers who start doing even the smallest bit more get a break from all that complaining. Ann King *never* complains about her husband, Mike. By reducing his work time and taking care of their daughter when Ann works, he enables her to do a job she loves. She knows their daughter receives the best care in the world—real peace of mind not easily obtainable. Parents who share their double duties feel lucky, contented, and fulfilled, rather than angry, unappreciated, and exhausted.

Dads who do more child-care and household chores have happier marriages and are less likely to divorce.[32] Fathers who put in more time at home also have more sex. Both marital researcher Dr. John Gottman and psychologist Pepper Schwartz report that the more housework and child care a man performs, the better his marital sex life. Mike and Ann King say they have a lot of sex. Instead of strife, fathers who share the family workload will find gratitude at home, and even a reminder of what brought them together with their wives in the first place.

Once the parental load starts to balance, and it doesn't have to be equal, good things happen. People start to feel better. Couples can then approach the challenges they face together. Marjorie Pappas, whose husband has now stayed home for five years, says:

> It's much easier for Jake and me than it seems to be for our friends and siblings. We have only one problem: money. But you can deal with that. We're not fighting about who's doing what. We're in this together.

Fathers of the past who were kept away from their children through workplace dictates, and societal and maternal forces (we'll get to that later), never got to know the fun of just being with their children. When I showed my own father a draft of this book, he complimented it politely. Later, when pressed, he told me he couldn't agree with my premise. "It's unnatural," he said. "Men are meant to slay tigers, not tend the hearth."

I pointed out that no tigers run loose in modern America, that men and women can roughly equally put food on the table. I mentioned my law degree. My father conceded that men can adapt to the new world, sharing economic power with their wives.

Then I told him that when Ed comes home from work, he takes over, giving Elizabeth and Annie their bath. A 1950s-kind-of-guy, my father said, "I wouldn't want to come home from work and give kids a bath."

"But, Dad, it's fun to give them their bath."

Silence.

"It's fun? Well, you should tell them that," he advised.

I am telling you that. It's fun. You see, he doesn't know. You don't know if you don't do it. Kids are magical. Spending time with your children is wonderful, as in laugh-as-hard-as-you-ever-have and feel-as-good-inside-as-you-can wonderful. Baths are fun. You can even have fun changing a dirty diaper, though it's a lot harder.

Parents especially enjoy themselves when they share taking care of kids. Fathers can have the warm, close relationships with their children that their wives have had, and that they often realize only too late they crave. Mark Clayton, George Martling, Ira Berk, Mike King, and all of today's dads have a better chance to have it all than their fathers had. So do today's mothers and children. That's our opportunity. The rest of the book will help us make our opportunity a reality.

PART

2

BEFORE YOU SAY,
"I DO"

Negotiation 101

Before we got engaged, I gave him "the quiz." I told him I
wanted to share housework and childrearing, and he agreed.
We touched base again before deciding to get pregnant.
We've always assumed we would split all the
responsibilities and we always have.

— Rebecca Powell, Web-site designer who works three days
a week and whose entrepreneur husband works three
days a week and shares the care of their children

WE'RE TALKING ABOUT A LIFETIME PLAN

Like every other relationship, marriage involves negotiation. Yes,
love can make a huge difference and even provide some leverage in
"discussions," if you prefer, with your mate. But don't kid yourself.
Even when dating, people do all sorts of bargaining, both directly
and indirectly. Before getting engaged, most couples negotiate about
what their relationship and any resulting marriage will look like,
and even whether to get married.

At one time families arranged marriages and haggled over dow-
ries. The betrothed had little or no input. Today things have become more complicated. We no longer have any crystal-clear rules,
even for the first date. Before the women's movement, men were
supposed to make the first overture. Now women can, and do, ask
men out.

As the courtship progresses, couples might negotiate over whether
to sleep together, whether to have an exclusive relationship, whether

they will see each other all weekend or just on Saturday night, what restaurant to go to, what appetizer to share, whether to get dessert, or what movie to see. Every day, they will make decisions together as to what to do and what not to do. At any point, a romantic union can go in different directions, all of which require reconciling each person's interests and desires.

Modern parenthood also forces new choices about the use of time. Changing from two individuals with two jobs and no babies to being a family requires give and take from both partners. At one point, the rules for transformation had little elasticity. Women who got pregnant had to quit their jobs (if they had one). End of story. Now we can negotiate everything.

In fact, parents sometimes have difficulty seeing anything other than the bargaining aspect of marital relations. Who's going to have a professional or a social life? How will they pool their efforts at home? Who's going to come home early to relieve the baby-sitter? Who's going to call the baby-sitter? Who will take Susie to her much-loved ballet lessons, even though you both know she will never be a ballerina? Who can stay home with a sick child? Such is the stuff of life with kids.

A variety of factors will have an impact on the resolution of these large and small issues, only one of which is love. Rhona Mahony, the author of *Kidding Ourselves: Breadwinning, Babies, and Bargaining Power*, explains that, in marriage,

> Bargaining power is a big element of who gets their way. Relative income, relative earning potential, social status, physical size and strength, remarriageabilty, remaining years of fertility, and emotional attachment to the children all play a role. Men have more of all of these attributes than women, except for emotional attachment to the children.

Of course, marriage provides incentives to deal fairly with one another that do not exist in other situations. We're talking about two people who love each other, after all. Parents share a common goal that can lead to outcomes a "winner-take-all" negotiator would never accept. Yet looking at marital interactions through the prism of negotiating theory proves a surprisingly effective way to understand what goes on in marriage. The principles of bargaining provide the tools to change the status quo.

BEFORE YOU PASS GO,
RECOGNIZE YOU ARE IN IMPORTANT TALKS

Think I'm de-romanticizing and underestimating the power of love? Let's look at how a woman who doesn't know she's negotiating might fare. Then we'll see how a woman who understands she can bargain does in comparison.

Remember Mary Clayton, the professor who wants her husband, Mark, to work flexibly so she can resume her career? Before she stopped taking birth-control pills, Mary told Mark that if she got pregnant, she would work part time, or even stay home. The couple had been married for a year and a half, and both lavished much time on their careers. They cooked elaborate dinners together a few times a week, and took part in many activities and friendships, sometimes together and sometimes apart. Mary recalls:

> I had no earthly reason for saying I might stay home. I'd never been around babies. I guess I felt working full time wouldn't leave enough time for our baby. And that maybe motherhood would change me into another kind of person.
>
> I didn't expect him to go and rely on what I said, though. It was just talk. I was thinking out loud, more than anything.

Without realizing it, Mary had negotiated with Mark to stop using birth control. In some way, Mark had understood he was in a bargaining situation. He wanted to continue to work hard and thought they had agreed that, even after having a baby, he would be able to do so. As a result, it surprised him when Mary sought his presence at home after Jeffrey's birth. He says:

> She told me she was ready to have children. I wasn't. The idea scared me. Then she said she would either work part time or stay home and I would support the family. Since I was about to move to the next level at my job, I agreed to go along with the plan. I just assumed it would all get worked out without my being involved in a major way.

Mary made a number of errors that later put her in a situation she disliked. To start with:

- She didn't prepare in advance, think hard about what she wanted, or do any research.

- She didn't understand she was in a negotiation.
- She didn't realize her statements would have an impact on her future.
- She thought love would cause everything to come out all right and that her spouse would support whatever she decided do in the future, even if it differed from her initial expectations.

Mary did no research before formulating her position about having a child, one of the biggest decisions she will ever make. This is a huge no-no in negotiation, whatever the context. True, she felt a strong biological urge to have a baby. However, removed as we are from a state of nature, if we want to enjoy our long lives in civilization, we must look into our options before deciding whether, when, and how to have children. The women's movement and science have given us a new opportunity. *We can now choose the lives we want to lead.*

Rebecca Powell understood all this very well. A Berkeley graduate and professional activist, she had steeped herself in the history of feminism. After meeting Darrell Smith at a wedding and falling in love with him, she returned to California and he to New York. Before she agreed to see him again, she made sure Darrell would go along with her planned future. Rebecca states:

> I knew women who got all tied up in knots over the choice of whether to work or stay home. I figured whoever I married would split the duties. That way, it wouldn't be all this or all that. I knew I wanted to take care of a kid and to work. I wanted to share everything. I didn't want anything broken down by gender.

Darrell hadn't thought about these issues much. He had a close relationship with his mother and three sisters, which made him view women as equals. In the full flush of romantic ardor, he agreed in theory and even made a commitment to Rebecca's ideals, should the relationship progress as they thought it would. He says:

> I wanted to get married to Rebecca. And I wanted to have kids. I asked her to make a huge sacrifice and leave the Bay area to be with me. She would move to the East Coast only if she

knew I would be the kind of husband she wanted. I'm an open-minded person and what she said seemed fair, so I said, "Okay."

Rebecca laid the groundwork for achieving the life she desired. In contrast to Mary Clayton, Rebecca:

- knew what she wanted from marriage on her first date;
- viewed courtship conversation as a form of negotiation about the future;
- understood her mate would rely on what she told him; and
- knew marriage involved hard work, good communication, and planning, in addition to love.

Few of us have evolved as far as Rebecca has. She is the only woman I spoke to who came up with the idea of "the quiz" (brilliant idea, by the way; I wish I'd thought of it). When Rebecca became pregnant, she and Darrell checked in again with each other and proceeded with their plan to share child care, starting with maternity and paternity leave. Since their son Mac's birth, they have both worked part time, each taking care of their son while the other works.

After she became a mother, Rebecca might have found she wanted a different arrangement than she had anticipated. That would have worked out, however, because *she had put herself in a position of strength and could negotiate a different situation if she changed her mind.* It would be far easier to convince Darrell Powell to do less childrearing than he had bargained for than to convince Mark Clayton to do more than he had bargained for.

ASK FOR THE WHOLE ENCHILADA

Clearly, women collectively have not negotiated good deals for themselves. Mothers still do more, and fathers less, at home and with their children than women would like. Why is that? The most important reason is low *aspiration level.*

According to negotiations guru Chester L. Karras, "losers" in negotiations make substantial unnecessary concessions. *The most important factor in negotiations is aspiration level.* Those who ask for more get more. Those who ask for less get less.

A Karras study demonstrates the importance of aspiration level. In the study, 120 professional negotiators bargained over the award in a mock lawsuit between a drug company and a man who suffered eye damage after taking one of the company's products. In one scenario, the parties had an approximately equal balance of power. In the other, more legal precedent supported the plaintiff's claims. The negotiators with higher aspiration levels won higher awards, regardless of which fact pattern they used. Consistent with a large body of research, those who achieved better results started out wanting more and ended up with more.[1]

When dealing with people with high aspirations, those with low aspirations did poorly. *The negotiators who secured the lowest awards were always those who had made the largest concession in any single negotiation.* They also tended to make the first compromise.

Look at our examples once more. Mary Clayton started out presuming a small effort from her husband, Mark—and she got a small involvement from him. Mary made all the concessions, immediately. Mark made none. Is Mark a cruel, bad person who doesn't love his wife and means to oppress her? No. Without thinking much about it, Mark went along with the tide of tradition, as Mary had tacitly encouraged him to do.

Rebecca Powell asked for more and she got a large involvement from Darrell Smith. Neither she nor Darrell made a concession; instead, both accommodated their desires and beliefs. Does this mean Darrell is a wonderful, good person who loves his wife more than Mark Clayton loves his? Not necessarily. Rebecca asked for something different, used her strengths in a loving way, and Darrell responded positively.

Stay-at-home mothers who expect their husbands to help can also get lots of support. Jennifer, whose unpaid position as president of a volunteer humanitarian organization takes up hundreds of hours of her time a year, knew she wanted to stay home with her children. Unlike Mary Clayton, she also knew she'd like her husband involved from the start. Together, Jennifer and her husband, Joe, decided to share child-care and housework chores evenly. During the nine months she nursed her son, Alex, Joe did more housework and shopping than Jennifer did because:

> My philosophy has always been that my husband can do
> everything I can do but give birth and nurse. He never came

home and asked me why I couldn't keep the house clean. That was his job in the beginning.

Other parents besides professionals, artists, and the idle rich share childrearing. Deedee Rivera splits the care of their four children with her husband, Roberto. She works two part-time babysitting jobs and cleans houses on the side, mostly during the day. Roberto serves as banquet manager for a luxury hotel, working from three in the afternoon to eleven at night Tuesday through Saturday. Deedee sometimes brings some or all of their children to her jobs, but usually Roberto takes care of them in the late morning and early afternoon.

Though she comes from a Latin American culture that does not encourage dads' participation, Deedee made it happen. When I inquired if she had to ask Roberto to be highly involved, she laughed: "Of course, I did. Otherwise, men will just do what they want. He always helped since the beginning. We talked about it and realized because of our jobs this was the way we would have to do it."

This most basic primer on negotiation explains why women usually don't create comfortable post-baby roles for themselves. They become negotiation "losers" the moment they presume only mothers can nurture children and tend the household or that men's time outside the family has more value than women's time does. Women simply do not demand enough. Granted, this idea will initially come as a surprise to husbands doing all they can *within their framework of understanding*. However, raising women's aspiration levels will make men, women, and children happier, creating a "win-win-win" situation.

AVON LADY CALLING

To achieve more balance, women must alter their goals from mere delegated help ("Why can't you come home by six-thirty so you can give the kids their bath?") to substantial sharing of all mental and physical child-related tasks ("How can we best take care of this child and our own needs?"). At first, many men may resist requests to make any type of accommodation. Still, women have to start making different assumptions from the outset. At the very least, asking for a lot will bring about all types of more minor concessions.

Marital negotiations about work and child-care issues favor the "door-in-the-face" technique. Door-to-door salespeople have borrowed this one from social psychology, and we might as well pick it up, too. The door-in-the-face theory involves two steps. First, make a large, but objectively reasonable, request (metaphorically flinging the front door open wide). If the other side rejects it, make a smaller request. If your partner perceives that you have made a concession in reducing your proposal, compliance will almost certainly result.

The opposite technique—the "foot-in-the-door" request—achieves little in the context of determining child and work responsibilities. Nobody would change to a four-day work week to share the care of their children after being asked only to give them a bath. The foot-in-the-door approach does have its place, especially when used in conjunction with the door-in-the-face method (any parent can vouch for the success rate of constant large and small requests). And moms of school-age and older children who want to change their situations find the foot-in-the-door approach a great starting place, as you'll see in chapter 10.

Lynne Swanson used the door-in-the-face approach without knowing it. Her husband, Guy, wanted children. Lynne did, too, but she didn't want to sacrifice her career as a hospital administrator. She had seen too many friends lose ground at work or quit after becoming mothers. She didn't want to give up her identity in an attempt to have it all.

Lynne told Guy she would try to get pregnant only if he would stay home with their child. Guy declined. Then Lynne asked him to take on the role of primary on-call parent for the first two years. Guy agreed, and changed from a traveling sales position to management, so he could be available when needed. Both worked full-time, flexible hours, Guy from home when their children got sick and couldn't attend day care. He handled most of the child-related emergencies, including finding and monitoring their day-care situation. Later, when Lynne's new job position allowed her more involvement, they switched roles.

Having met and interviewed hundreds of women who have a husband who participates substantially with their children, I have found one common denominator: They asked for, or assumed, their husbands' substantial participation. Conversely, they did not presume that only women make time for family.

How to Raise Aspiration Levels in Premarital and Marital Conversations

- Think about what you want before you say anything.
- Prepare and investigate in advance. Do your research.
- Ask for the most of whatever you're talking about that you can objectively justify. You'll need it.
- Make any concessions slowly and carefully.
- Act as if you think well of yourself (even if you feel a pull of guilt or tradition when seeking time away from the house and children).

WHAT GETS IN THE WAY

This all sounds surprisingly simple. Women could adopt the proper stance and go through the motions and secure better situations. Yet they might well backslide without an understanding of why women don't ask for more and why they don't see all the possible solutions. We are not talking only about an individual predicament but also a collective, societal condition.[2]

I don't mean to suggest we have not started to make some inroads. Change has begun. I see far more fathers with children at the supermarket on weekdays (surely the best indication of men doing more grunt work) than I did even five years ago.

Still, if all they need to do is ask, why don't more women do it? Like Mary Clayton, many of us have unconsciously absorbed some or all of the following beliefs:

- Women must choose whether to work for pay or do the best job they can with their children.
- If they work for pay, mothers must balance work and family, hopefully with some help from their husbands.
- It is impossible for mothers to balance work and family.
- Fathers do not nurture or parent as well as mothers (or, the father is a bumbling incompetent best kept on the golf course).
- For families who want to make parental care of their children their first priority, the only option is to have the mother cut back at work or stay home.

Years ago, I attended a child-care fair sponsored by my employer that perfectly crystallized society's expectations. My daughter Elizabeth was then seven months old. A month before, I had returned to my job as an intellectual property attorney for twenty hours a week. My mother took care of Elizabeth from nine to three on the days I worked. I got up at five in the morning, waking Elizabeth to nurse before I left. Then I put her back in her crib and rushed into the office so I could get back as soon as possible. Ed went into work late, to reduce the time Elizabeth spent away from her parents and to give my mother a break.

When I arrived home, I took care of Elizabeth until Ed returned. I felt like half a mother and half a worker, without the benefits of doing either full time. By nine every evening, I had fallen fast asleep.

I knew my mother loved and took wonderful care of Elizabeth, and my husband helped. I maintained but did not advance my career. I had lunch with my friends two days a week. And yet balanced was the last thing I felt. A more accurate description would be twisted like a pretzel. I was in constant motion, like a wind sock, always poised for the work or home breeze to blow me in a new direction. I had become a human yoyo and it didn't feel all that great. I hoped the experts would have some answers about how to work and parent well and have a life, all at the same time.

All the seminar leaders at the fair were female. Women exclusively attended all the sessions. Dr. Melinda Salsbury, a licensed clinical social worker, prefaced her talk about "Balancing Work and Family Life" with an anecdote. She had asked her best friend, a junior-high-school teacher with two children, what advice to give women interested in balancing work and family. The response?

"Don't do it."

My heart sank. Salsbury had subverted anything about to follow by informing us her program had no value. In effect, she told us that attempting to work and raise children at the same time either cannot be done or is so difficult it is not worth attempting. She, and all the women present, had the same understanding: that balancing is a female issue.

Salsbury described the prevalent situation of working mothers as household administrators, with all the mental responsibility for the welfare and care of their children and the home. She analogized their dual work and home responsibilities to that of a tightrope walker juggling children, a household, and a job.

Wait a minute. Does that sound good to you? Except for the Flying Wallendas, you don't hear about many people clamoring for a turn on the high wire. Few can walk a tightrope at all, and the activity itself carries some danger. One difference between working mothers and tightrope walkers: while tightrope walkers have a safety net underneath them for protection, many working mothers do not.

Back at the high-wire juggling and balancing tutorial, I raised my hand. Noting that no men had come to the session, I asked whether the stresses she described affect working fathers as well. She replied, "I wondered whether there would be any men on my way over. Men feel these stresses but are not likely to go to a child-care seminar. They get to be forty, forty-five, and they regret that they didn't spend as much time with their kids as they could have, and that they're not close with their children."

My stomach had gnarled as I listened to what my lawyerly brain perceived as illogic. I said, "You're recommending little things women can do to have a better balance—finding five minutes to exercise, searching for the best child care you can find, cutting back on expectations of ourselves at work and at home. What if our husbands took on half the household administration?"

Salsbury paused, then answered, "I just regard it as a given that women are the household administrators. Nobody's talking about men taking on half of that responsibility or child care. I counsel a lot of people, and I don't know of one equal marriage. If you can think of a way to get your husband to do it, go ahead."

Here's a tip: *Don't regard it as a given that women manage households and children.* Start talking about men taking on half of that responsibility, or however much of that responsibility you want them to have. Remember our Negotiation 101. As long as you keep your aspirations low, your achievements will be low (and your workload too high).

The seminar leader's well-intentioned advice illustrates the assumptions keeping women from seeking better arrangements. But *we* already know those assumptions are wrong. The stories of women like Rebecca, Ann, Lynne, and Jennifer show what altering preconceptions can do. The new, and improved, presuppositions:

- Women can have it all and like what they have, as long as men have it all, too. "All" can include child and household administration.
- Dual-income couples can balance work and family if both fathers and mothers enter into the equation. Balance can include men making career accommodations and time adjustments.
- Fathers and mothers can balance work and family if they devise solutions together.
- Fathers nurture as well as mothers. It is in the interest of society, mothers, fathers, and children for dads to participate.
- Families who make parental care of their children their first priority have many options, including having the father use flexible hours, cutting back at work, or staying home.
- Stay-at-home mothers can have a life outside the house and family.
- Families may decide that a stay-at-home mother's "job description" includes less than all the home and childrearing duties.

If couples who actually do balance work, life, and family gave a seminar, they would offer the above precepts. Take them to heart, and you will either avoid or get out of the Mommy Trap.

BATNA: A GIRL'S BEST FRIEND

It would be nice if asserting a moral or correct position would ensure success in negotiation. Life doesn't work that way. Issues of fairness can play a huge role, particularly between lovers. But a negotiator must have some sort of power as well. Some truisms about negotiation:

The impatient actor pays. Women more eager to get married or have babies than their mates put themselves at a disadvantage later on.
Those who earn more do better. All the mothers we've met who persuaded their husbands to do more than the norm had the ability to make money. Dividing childrearing and home care involves the use of time. Those whose time has more quantifiable value have more sway.

Education builds bargaining strength. Aside from the independently wealthy, most people acquire earning potential from schooling. Quitting or scaling back on careers (the "throwing-the-diplomas-in-the-trash-can" move) constitutes a large concession when determining whose desires will win out in a marriage.

In family negotiations, the person most committed to the relationship gives up power.[3] The more women give up on their jobs and education or fail to stay abreast in their professions, and the more effort they put into their family, the more dependent they become in their relationships with their husbands. The standard childrearing arrangements cause women to cede power at the starting gate.

These realities bring us to the all-important BATNA (Best Alternative to a Negotiated Agreement). Never heard of it? Negotiation theorists use the term BATNA to describe the alternative to agreeing, the standard by which one measures any proposal.[4]

Say I want to buy a purse from a street merchant in Florence. If he gives me a price I know to comport with fair-market value, I will buy it. If he refuses to budge from a price $10 higher than a vendor around the corner, I won't buy the purse from him. Ultimately, whether we agree to any proposal will depend on our alternatives to agreeing. That's BATNA.

In negotiations of any type, those with better BATNAs get more of what they seek than those with lower BATNAs.[5] Those with strong BATNAs have little incentives to agree. Those with weak BATNAs may have no choice but to agree. If I know the purse I want is on sale two stalls over for $10 less, and my merchant knows it, too, and I can walk, I will get the price I desire. If, on the other hand, my arms are overflowing with delicate vases and nobody else in the city sells a bag that can hold them as well, and we both know it, I will pay whatever he asks.

The most effective option for women who want more equal marriages is to develop their own BATNA.[6] Modern parents have an obvious alternative to agreeing: divorce. Whether consciously or not, and whether we like it or not, the specter of divorce looms over marital discourse.[7] Dr. Robert Wohlfort, a psychologist and director of the Pastoral Counseling Institute, explains.

In the past, there was a strong sense of "You give your word, you keep it, no matter what. You're not happy—so what? You just stick it out." Now, I think there's less sense of that. It's more, "It's got to get better; if we don't work it out, I'll find somebody else."

Even if they have no intention of ever leaving their marriage, moms must create potential sources of independence from their husbands. This seems a smart move anyway, in a country where half of marriages end in divorce. That doesn't mean mothers should leave their husbands or threaten to do so. But creating a strong position will enhance women's ability to get what they (along with their children) need and want.

Women must consciously develop their strengths. If they raise and use their BATNAs, they can create a new world of mutual support, love, and nurturing. The next chapter will show how to begin, from the first date forward.

Think about Work and Family Issues before Angling for the Ring 5

I broke up with my college boyfriend when we graduated even though we really loved each other. He didn't believe in mothers working. As a chemical engineer and child of divorce, I didn't believe in staying home.

—Katie, happily married, working mother of two

DUE DILIGENCE DATING

We all thought Katie was crazy when she broke up with Rob, the only guy who had ever treated her decently. They spent all their time together, and seemed to be in love. I now realize Katie was much smarter than we gave her credit for. Although it seemed premature to think about children during our senior year, it wasn't. Katie didn't angle for an engagement ring, either. She tried to set up the future she wanted, and she succeeded.

After taking a job at Westinghouse, Katie met a man there who also treated her well. Her new boyfriend's mother had worked. He appreciated the idea of not having to support his family by himself. They got married and had two children and remain happily together.

Not everybody realizes the implications of their youthful actions. For change to occur, women must approach dating and premarital conversation more consciously.

USE IT OR LOSE IT

Katie made the most of what she had, when she had it. A woman's bargaining power soars highest before she marries and ebbs lowest

---

▍ ## Before Getting
Too Serious

- Know (or find out about) yourself.
- Learn what your partner thinks and believes.
- Communicate expectations and desires as early as possible.
- Discuss and tentatively resolve potential conflicts before getting engaged.

---

just after she gives birth.[1] That explains why Mary Clayton found it difficult to convince her husband to share parenting responsibilities during her maternity leave. It all boils down to BATNA (Best Alternative to a Negotiated Agreement; see chapter 4).

Think of a mother holding a newborn. She will tolerate far more undesirable behavior from her man than an undergraduate at a fraternity party would. The college student has many options, including walking two steps to another guy she finds attractive. In contrast, a nursing mother has great incentives to stick with her marriage, and to go along with her husband's desires, even if she has just learned that they don't agree with her own. She won't divorce him without a fairly spectacular reason. Her BATNA is pretty poor.

Most likely no handsome swain lurks anywhere nearby. Possibly no prospective beau would take on someone else's infant child. In addition to her emotional attachment to the marriage, the mother may have no means of financial support other than her husband. She has little leverage if she hasn't already chosen her spouse wisely and put herself in a good position. For many reasons, she may have to remain in her current situation, even if she doesn't like it.

Men, even loving, wonderful husbands, start out with higher BATNAs than women have. They have more status and probably make more money. Pregnancy, nursing, tradition, and societal expectations give women what author Rhona Mahony calls a "head start" in emotional and physical attachment to their children.[2] When trying to divide child care, mothers' higher investment in their offspring generally lowers their BATNA. Because they have more involvement with their children, and because they know a divorce would place mother and children in an undesirable situation, women will put up with a lot more than they might otherwise accept.

As time goes by, men's BATNA rises as women's plunges. Women earn less. As they age, they can't or don't want to procreate again, and society views them as less attractive. In general, mothers don't see their stock rising in the marriage market. Fast forward, and we find our perky college student now forty, with three kids, fading looks, an expanded waistline, and breasts "previously owned" by hungry infants.

Men make more money as they get older and can procreate until the day they die. They have fewer responsibilities at home and bear fewer effects of child care and housework. Unlike women, older men are more attractive as remarriage prospects.

These facts highlight the points at which women can control their lives and the times where they may run into trouble. *Women must use their strong premarriage bargaining power by thinking about and addressing work and family issues before agreeing to marry.* If necessary, they can end long-term incompatible relationships, as Katie did, or forge a beneficial understanding while they have the greatest ability to do so. Women can make their preferences known as soon, and as often, as possible. But first they must find out what they are.

WHAT'S YOUR GENDER IDEOLOGY?

Beliefs about family roles may lay dormant for years of happy dating and marriage, only to spring up at the most inopportune moment: after a baby is born. Wise women ascertain views about sex roles, including their own, before getting too far ahead of themselves. Obvious as this may seem, few couples hash out parenting roles before they marry.

I don't mind admitting that my husband and I did not identify and talk about our preferences until our first child was a few months old. I can also tell you we could have saved ourselves great turmoil had we thought about them before.

Three current types of "gender ideology" describe the way individuals define appropriate paternal and maternal behavior: traditional, transitional, and egalitarian.[3] Traditionalists—for example,

Katie's long-lost boyfriend Rob—believe women should tend the home and children while men provide for the family and that men should have more power in the relationship. Egalitarians—examples include Mike and Ann King, and Rebecca Powell and Darrell Smith—believe each gender has roughly interchangeable abilities and should share work, family responsibilities, and power equally. Most people fall into the transitional category, a hybrid area between those traditional folk and the egalitarians.[4]

As Katie sensed, when couples hold different gender ideologies, they experience great discord after they have children. If at all possible, do not marry or have children with someone with a different gender ideology.

The concept of gender ideology explains why some women are happy with a night out once a year and others insist on daily time for themselves. It also shows why a one-size-fits-all approach does not work. Every person has unique needs, experiences, and desires.

▮ How to Spot His Gender Ideology

- A traditional man brings laundry home to Mom or asks you to do it, eats food sent lovingly by Mom or asks you to cook it, never cleans his apartment, and views his primary family role as income provider.
- An egalitarian objects to the term "obey" in marriage vows, probably comes from a nontraditional family, may have some domestic skills, may have a "low-key" personality, and is far rarer than you think.
- All others are transitional, which means they're confused. They can hold views closer to the traditional or egalitarian ethos. They may see men and women as equals in theory, and also view men as primary breadwinners and women as responsible for the children, the house, and for making career accommodations.

Find out what you want, ask for it, and avoid entanglements with men whose views do not mesh with your own.

TRADITIONAL + TRADITIONAL = NO PROBLEM

Clearly, some women don't want careers: They revel in motherhood and domesticity. Both my sisters-in-law are traditional. Thankfully, so are their mates.

Nobody thought my husband's sister Karen would return to work after she became a mother. Although she had a good job, she did not display a high investment in it. Karen *likes* and derives personal satisfaction from cooking and taking care of the house. She performs these activities very well. Her house looks beautiful, she can seamlessly entertain four different sets of family over Christmas, and she and her husband are raising three lovely boys.

After marrying at twenty-one, Jill, my brother's wife, earned a master's degree in art history and did a little student teaching before having her first baby. Three others followed in quick succession. In recent years, Jill has taken up interior decorating, part time, for stimulation and some income. While cooking does not play a large part of her repertoire, her house always looks perfect, no child who enters ever wants to leave, and she and my brother have reared four great kids.

My sisters-in-law prefer household responsibilities divided by gender, with men going out in the world to provide the main family income and women taking on the primary role in and their identity from tending the household and children. When they became mothers, they shed their jobs without a second thought. They do not feel trapped at home. They love being there. It is good for them, their children, their husband, and society that they can do what they want.

That said, even traditionals today expect and ask for more help with child care than their grandmothers did. Karen respects her husband's need to run six miles on Saturdays and Sundays, as long as he brings their youngest son with him in a jogging stroller. Jill sleeps in on the weekends while my brother takes their four kids out to breakfast. Both have gone on "girls' vacations" with their friends. Solicitous as they are of their husband's recreational and work lives, neither has any compunction about occasionally taking time for herself or making demands of her husband during his non-work time.

My sisters-in-law wisely secure occasional assistance from their husband, house-cleaners, and baby-sitters. While traditionals do not have great conflict over their roles, mothers in such marriages often become exhausted doing 90 percent of everything at home.[5]

EGALITARIAN + EGALITARIAN = LOOKING GOOD

Ann and Mike King embody egalitarianism. They believe in shar-ing, and they do share, everything. They never entertained the idea of Ann giving up her career, or Mike his. The oldest daughter in a Catholic family of six children, Ann developed a strong interest in the helping professions. She took care of her siblings as they grew up. Her mother suffered from a depressive disorder, which cemented Ann's passion for finding ways to improve people's lives and to become a psychologist.

Mike also has a strong commitment to his livelihood. He loves to solve spatial-relations problems and has great interest in buildings, so he became an architect. Mike's mother died when he was five. His father never remarried, giving Mike a role model of involved fatherhood. Though Mike holds conservative political views, he is most definitely an egalitarian when it comes to gender roles.

The Kings live above Mike's studio in a ramshackle two-hundred-year-old building that also houses Ann's office. Ann and Mike met in a church study group for Washington singles. On their first date, they talked about the movie *Dead Poet's Society*, exploring the rami-fications of suicide. Ann appreciated Mike's willingness to analyze interpersonal relations. She knew she had found a good fit: a devout, sensitive, open to discussion, and nontraditional man. She explains:

> You have to ask, "Will he do therapy with you? Will he work on growth and change?" If you're in it for the long haul, there will be times you won't be able to fix it yourself. If he won't get help, don't get married. None of the other guys I dated would have done any of the stuff Mike has done.
>
> We're both from nontraditional families. My mother always worked. His did, too. She was the brains behind the business.

His grandmother was a lawyer and ran for president of the United States. After we got married, we used our nontraditional role models to help figure out how things should be.

As a result of their agreement about parental roles and the value of talking (and therapy), this couple has not had a high level of conflict since becoming parents.

TRANSITIONALS TOGETHER = TROUBLE BREWING

Unfortunately, few people fit within either the egalitarian or traditional rubric.[6] Having absorbed conflicting messages, many men, and plenty of women, too, think they're egalitarian but are in fact transitional. These misconceptions can hold firm until a couple has a baby.

When they marry each other, transitionals often disagree about what each spouse ought to do.[7] Transitional couples have as much conflict over the division of family labor and who makes work accommodations as spouses with different gender ideologies do.[8] The gap between traditional and egalitarian can accommodate many different beliefs, which may fluctuate at any given moment. As a result, transitionals (and most of us fall under that label) have a hard time creating arrangements that feel right. Consider this family.

Jason Marx, a New York City public school teacher, doctoral candidate, adjunct professor, and aspiring writer, married Theresa, a nurse of Mexican descent. He looked like an egalitarian. The son of a female rabbi, Jason held liberal views, valued art and relationships more than money, and took great interest in children. Though she came from a conservative family, Theresa also seemed egalitarian. Neither demure nor submissive, she had fallen into a lucrative career. During the eight years they lived together in her rent-controlled Greenwich Village apartment, they shared their expenses equally. Before getting engaged, they never discussed how they might divide parenting responsibilities if they had children.

Four years after the wedding, Theresa's biological clock started to tick loudly. Both enjoyed playing with relatives' and friends' children, and were happy when Theresa got pregnant. Jason's career as a freelance writer had recently taken off. Feeling burned-out from dealing with inner city kids and the hassles of the world of adjunct professorship, Jason decided he would take care of their baby. After giving birth, Theresa switched to three twelve-hour shifts a week and, once a month, four twelve-hour shifts in five days.

Jason thought he was egalitarian, and that he'd have lots of time to write. He was wrong on both counts. Fourteen months after the birth of their daughter, Jason explained:

> Any man who stays home feels the pressure, unstated or whatnot, that you should be out there being the main bread-winner. It's just hotwired into our psyches. I feel okay with the fact that my wife makes more than I do and then I don't. But I think parenting should be split, just because I've experienced what it's like to take care of my daughter and it's a ball. It surprised me how much love I had in my heart. As soon as I saw my daughter, I just melted.

Jason has given us the transitional man in a nutshell, albeit one who sits a lot closer to the egalitarian camp than some others—on Mondays, Wednesdays, and Fridays, anyway. Note that Jason talks about men who stay home. But he is not a "househusband"—Jason labors hard at, and makes money from, his writing. Yet he views himself as if he stays home full time, or as he imagines his neighbors see him. Despite his attachment to his daughter, some part of Jason believes that dads must work full time outside the home and bring in more income than their wives do.

KEEP WITHIN YOUR COMFORT ZONE

Jason Marx has run into trouble because he performs 60 percent of the child care in his house when his gender ideology has a comfort level of 40 percent or less. Even though he recognizes the value of caring for his daughter, Jason doesn't feel like a whole man in the eyes of the world. His gender ideology won't let him. If Jason held pure egalitarian beliefs, he wouldn't mind what others might think.

For example, Rebecca Powell's husband, Darrell Smith, didn't care when his father asked when he was going to get a real job instead of working part time from home and tending his son three days a week. "It didn't bother me. He's a traditional-roles person.

I'm surprised at how few dads I see with their kids. I see more moms, and they all say what I'm doing is great."

Darrell is okay with it. Jason is not. Also, Jason doesn't get the encouragement from Theresa that he needs. With her support, Jason might reconcile his egalitarian and traditional sides (we can change our gender ideology with self-awareness and vigilance, as we'll see in chapters 11 and 12).

But as it turns out, Theresa is not egalitarian either. Every day, she critiques the way Jason does things: if their daughter slips while climbing a ladder or Jason forgets to bring a snack for an outing. An egalitarian mother would recognize Jason's style of childrearing as equally valid. *A transitional mother thinks she knows better.*

Theresa's carping makes Jason feel unappreciated. Since becoming parents, the Marxes have fought frequently and without resolution. Jason can't relinquish baby duties, as a father in a traditional arrangement will do when his wife criticizes his efforts. So he has stopped listening to Theresa. Jason's unresponsiveness infuriates Theresa, prompting greater and louder invective. Because the Marxes did not ascertain their gender preferences before getting married or having children, they did not make life choices that could accommodate their beliefs.

After the birth of their second child, Jason and Theresa swapped roles. Jason took over the teaching schedule for a professor on leave for a year, making him the primary income earner. Theresa switched to private-duty nursing, reducing her work hours and the length of her shifts. Jason still takes care of the kids when Theresa works, but because he works outside the house and brings in more money than she does, he feels better. Now doing 60 percent of the child care, and exerting more control over how things are done at home, Theresa feels better, too. Having found an arrangement that supports both of their gender ideologies, they fight less and appreciate each other more. And they're both crazy about their children, who are developing beautifully.

TRANSITIONALS AND THE MOMMY TRAP

Let's check in with Lauren Martling, our coffee-guzzling, e-mail–complaining, working mom. She occupies a spot on the continuum close to the traditionals, in some ways. Lauren believes men should provide income and women should work if they like or have to. She derives her identity from her work. At the same time, she thinks children do best with more parental involvement, which puts her in a bind.

George Martling's salary would allow Lauren not to work if she so chose. But she worries about BATNA, and divorce, having experienced one already. She has this to say about her life:

> Sometimes I think about quitting and devoting more time to Dan. But then I couldn't justify having Pilar. I'd feel too much like a maid if I had to look after him and feed him and clean up all the time. I wasn't raised to do that. George makes more money than I do. His job is less flexible. Since I have a home office and control my workload, I am the one who takes over when Pilar leaves. If he did a little bit more that would be okay with me. If he did too much, I wouldn't feel like "the mother" at all.

Lauren has a mixed-up gender ideology, neither one thing nor the other. This type of transitional thinking often leads to the Mommy Trap high-wire juggling act. George also has a transitional mind-set, bordering on traditional. He would gladly make more time for his son *if Lauren asked him.* George views his parenting role as "helper" rather than "partner."

Hearkening back to negotiation theory, Lauren has a relatively low aspiration level in terms of George's involvement. But she's kept her BATNA pretty good by working full time and going to the gym. For the most part, this family has created a transitional arrangement that comports with their gender ideologies. Consequently, they have not experienced a high degree of conflict about who does what, although they have had some disagreements related to George's travel. Lauren *is* unhappy, but doesn't know why and has not yet expressed that fact to herself. Once she begins to break out of her gender ideology (and I promise that she will), she will find a better balance and take herself off the tightrope.

HOW DO YOU KNOW?
Where does gender ideology come from? People develop ideas about gender roles from society, their parents' behaviors, and their own

experiences, needs, and desires.[9] For example, as I was growing up in the early 1970s, my parents and the predominant culture told me girls could do anything boys could do. My mother stayed home with my brother and me until we entered third and fourth grade. Then she went to law school and, two and a half years later, began to work full time. My father practiced medicine, taking the proverbial Wednesdays off, when he sometimes took us to play golf with him.

Most of the school year when I was in junior high and high school, I played on athletic teams. One of my parents would pick me up after practice or a game. Between sport seasons, in the summer, and during vacations, I became a "latch-key" kid, which I didn't like at all. As a result of these influences, I have a strong belief in equality of the sexes, a preference for parental care for infants and young children, a deep commitment to career and athletics, and an unwillingness for my children to come home from school to an empty house. Knowing these preferences and matching them with my husband's (or potential husband had I known what you know now) would enable me to honor them to the extent possible.

My modern ideals do not allow for a cookie-cutter approach. I hold egalitarian views *and* I favor parental care for young children, which makes traditional work schedules impossible. For me to find a situation that makes me happy, I would have to marry a man with the same expectations and desires that I have *and* we would have to work hard together to set up an unconventional arrangement. As you know by now, we did not devise a nontraditional situation in advance, and we had a devil of a time for a while. The sooner couples understand and reconcile their gender ideologies, the better.

WARNING: HANDLE TRADITIONAL
DATING TACTICS WITH CARE

Most of what we read and see about romantic love stops at the altar. Jane Austen's novels, along with so many movies and all those fairy tales, lead up to that magic moment of declaration of love and then marriage. They say nothing about how to live happily ever after. The message: Make yourself beautiful and good, fall in love, and the rest will come. Mary Clayton's and Lauren Martling's experience shows us that for transitional and egalitarian women, the idea that love will cause everything to come out all right needs some fine-tuning.

As long as both spouses desire a traditional division of efforts, courtship rituals and marriages based along the old beliefs will work very well. *However, those seeking a different arrangement must take another road to get where they want to go.* If you want a more equal effort at home, look to the dating styles of my college-friend Katie, Rebecca Powell, and Lynne Swanson. Lynne remembers:

> When we were dating, I decided all these guys were going to be worried about the biological clock and all that. So I would go out on dates and say, "I know you think I'm worried about my biological clock. I am. I'm looking for a husband. I'm sort of on a search. I'm not going to date anyone exclusively. I'm not going to live with this guy for six months or three years and then find out that he doesn't work out." So Guy knew at least at the early stage of our dating that I was dating several men at the same time. Rather than running away, I think they all were attracted to my being so up-front about it. It was really against all the stuff they say to do. I knew what I wanted: to get married, have kids, and have a partnership. I was very clear.

This may sound extreme. But since Lynne wanted an egalitarian marriage, she had to find a different way to achieve it. Guy understood he was getting a woman who knew about BATNA and might use it if she had to. Women who desire nontraditional marriages adopt traditional methods at their peril. If they use the tactics of Cinderella and Snow White, they will probably not receive much more effort at home from their husbands than a wealthy, handsome prince—even a kind one—with hundreds of servants might put forth.

Rebecca Powell instinctively understood some of the issues marriages face. She spent six weeks on the telephone between the time she met Darrell and their second date, finding out about him. Each night they spoke for an hour. They had forty-two conversations about their expectations and their beliefs. She went over her "mental checklist" of what her ideal relationship would look like, without interference from the emotional and physical aspects of relationships that can prevent talking about the future.

In describing "the quiz," Rebecca says:

> I asked him everything. I got his view of marriage. First I said, "If I move out there, will you move back to San Francisco when we have kids? Will you share the housework and cooking? Will you share childrearing?"
>
> We talked about how we spend money. We determined that we had the same approach. We were both savers, not spenders. We prefer to have money in the bank rather than a nice car.

Rebecca and Darrell have far less stress than other parents. Why? They worked it out in advance, have the same spending profile, the same gender ideology, and planned and prepared the work–life situations they wanted. In contrast, before getting married, Jason and Theresa Marx never discussed parental roles. They didn't put much thought into what their responsibilities would be. As a result, they experienced great disharmony.

▌ Questions to Consider

- How important is having a career to one or both of you?
- Will one of your jobs take precedence? Would either of you move geographically to support the other's career?
- How will you split the responsibilities when you have children?
- Will one partner have more control over decisions? All decisions or just some?
- Who should do what household tasks?
- Who should do child care? How much?
- Do you have a reaction to someone other than the two of you taking care of your child?[10]
- Will you use substitute care? How much?

This is not meant to be an exhaustive list. Just start thinking and talking about your preferences and expectations.[11]

Dr. Pamela Jordan, coauthor of *Becoming Parents: How to Strengthen Your Marriage As Your Family Grows,* cautions:

> Somehow, we all carry the expectation that our expectations will just become reality without planning or blood, sweat, and tears. Not so! It takes work! . . .
> We seem to expect our partner to be able to look in their crystal ball and read our minds and know exactly how much we expect them to be involved in dealing with household things and how much we expect them to be involved with a child. Yet we typically don't communicate that, verbally get those things out on the table.

The rest of the population—those of us not as on the ball as Lynne Swanson, Rebecca Powell, and Ann King—would do well to make use of the many resources available. Make up your own quiz. or talk to marital therapists, clergy, and happily married parents about how to identify areas of potential disagreement. Tentatively resolve them before getting too serious.

MIRROR, MIRROR, ON THE WALL

Ideas about gender roles start with one's family. "Genograms" provide a great jumping-off point for determining gender ideology, whether one's own or someone else's. Family therapists use genograms when taking a patient's history. They give a thumbnail sketch of a person's background, tailored to specific areas of interest, such as relationship patterns, education, and the ways decisions were made.

Draw a family tree, going back at least two generations. Also, move forward to the children or grandchildren of the key person or people involved.[12] Think about how the mothers and fathers depicted on the tree divided their responsibilities, and whether they conformed to the gender stereotypes of their time. Does the relationship map tell you anything about the flexibility or inflexibility of gender roles allowed within the families?[13] What do you like about what you see there, and what would you like to change?

Identify any unspoken messages about gender roles your (or his) relatives may have passed on. Do you agree or disagree with them? Keep your preferences, and those of your boyfriend, in mind when mulling over whether to get married. Talk about them, looking for potential conflicts. See whether your parenting visions match. If you can't resolve your differences now, rest assured that this particular disunity will not dissipate years later when the baby cries for his or her three A.M. feeding and somebody gets the tiredness (and rewards) that come with providing milk and comfort.

THE ALL-IMPORTANT VISIT HOME

Why do we get so nervous the first time we meet a beau's family? For one thing, it screens the coming attraction of our life's movie. Will it be a love story, horror show, comedy, or a tragedy? The visit will reveal his expectations of marriage. Your life may well look like what you see there if you don't take an active hand in designing a future that fits your predilections.

Don't worry only about whether they will accept and like you. Think hard about whether you want to spend the rest of your life with or being these people.

Rachel, a happily married, fifty-two-year-old mother, knew her husband would make a good father when she visited his family. She says, "I liked what I saw there. It was how I always pictured family would be, ideally."

Learn how you want your life to be, and pick someone who has the same vision. Then you won't end up scrambling to fix unforeseen problems in the middle of your happily-ever-after.

Marital Calisthenics: Building a More Perfect Union **6**

> We didn't know if we should get married, so we went to couples therapy. We learned what to do when our fights started to escalate. After the baby was born, we used the same tactics, which were automatic by that time. It made it a lot easier to get what the other was saying and kept us from arguing like a lot of our friends did in the beginning.
>
> — Kecia Johnson, mail carrier and mother of two

A DAY TO REMEMBER, ONE LIFE TO LIVE

Look on a bookstore shelf sometime and see just how few serious resources engaged couples have. Hundreds of manuals describe the perfect dress for imperfect figures, the right hairdo for the occasion, appropriate yet fun gifts for the bridesmaids, and other crucial matters. Checklists outline every possible detail of the wedding festivities. Books in all shapes and sizes cover everything from setting a date to planning the honeymoon, and who should do each task.

And yet at my local library, sandwiched between countless guides about childrearing and even more about divorce, I found one slim tome titled *Before the Wedding: Look before You Leap*. On page one, author Michael E. Cavanagh points out with startling truth that "Many couples spend much more time preparing for their wedding (a one-day event) than they do for their marriage (a lifelong commitment)."[1]

The standard path to the altar doesn't provide much help in getting ready for a challenging, new, supposedly permanent role.

Marriage has a lower pass rate than even the hardest bar exam or medical boards. Forty to 50 percent of American marriages end in divorce. About 35 percent of engaged couples take part in some sort of premarital counseling, usually because their church requires it.[2] Look at the contrast between the success rate of marriage and the number of people who train for it, and the success rate of say the California bar exam (about 50 percent) and the number of people who take courses and study for it (100 percent).

We have stumbled onto another significant common disconnect between statistics and behavior. Nothing could be more important than crossing all the "t's" and dotting all the "i's" before getting married. However, most of us solicit and receive more advice about and instruction for getting a driver's license than we do before obtaining a marriage license.

My father offered the only guidance my husband and I received. As the wedding approached, he took us aside and said, "It'll be hard."

Well, I thought, is that a crack about my sometimes-difficult personality? Ed responded, "I know. I'll be in graduate school, Julie doesn't have a job, we're moving to a new state, and we won't have any money."

"No," my father said, "that'll be the easy part."

Years later, I appreciate my dad's wisdom. Marriage, especially after motherhood, turned out to be more difficult than I ever imagined. When I started investigating why some parents had an easier time of it, I found almost all of them had done a lot of prep work on their relationships (or sometimes themselves) before getting married and having children. Just a few had amazing role models or similar family, religious, or cultural backgrounds that seemed to make things smoother for them.

Learning marriage skills early on enables couples to approach the vicissitudes of life together. Timing is key. Addressing differences, particularly for the first time, gets much harder after having children. Lack of time, fatigue, upset expectations, and higher stakes present obstacles that don't exist for most engaged couples.

THE ABCS OF GETTING HITCHED

It's no accident that the most contented set of parents I've met, with the most vibrant relationship, consists of a psychologist and her spouse. Professional licensing requirements caused Ann and Mike King to attend dozens of couples and personality enhancement workshops before and after their marriage. As you may recall, the Kings like to talk things out. When they showed up for their pre-marital inventory for Catholic pre-Cana classes, the course leaders thought the Kings had cheated, because they had already pondered every issue in the program! Ann remembers:

> We discussed everything. We talked about in-laws, money, how to save, spending, kids, how to live, work, what our priorities were. We read and talked about a book called *The Hard Questions*. We also did an Engaged Encounter, a Pairs workshop, a "Getting the Love You Want" workshop, and have become a mentoring couple for our church's marriage programs.
>
> We are always working on our relationship. We use the Harville Hendrix imago intentional dialogue with everything, whether it's where to put the dishwasher in our kitchen, how to change our work schedules, or talking to our daughter about her fear of thunder.

Sound like overkill? The thing is, it works. Sample at least some of the Kings' methods (towards the end of the chapter we'll talk about the imago dialogue Ann refers to here). In contrast, Mark and Mary Clayton considered only whether they loved each other before making their match.

Mary remembers:

> I didn't think about anything after that day, other than moving into our new apartment, getting the electricity turned on, that sort of thing. We didn't get married in a church or a temple, because we didn't want to favor either side.
>
> We had gone to counseling earlier in our relationship, when we ran into trouble during the courtship. But we didn't do anything before getting married. When Jeffrey was born, everything fell apart. We started arguing all the time. I thought that if Mark really loved me, he'd help me go back to work. By the time we got to a marriage counselor, I was regularly threatening to leave. If it weren't for our son, I'm sure Mark would have been happy to see me go.

If Mary and Mark had gone to premarital counseling or read a book like *Before the Wedding*, they could have talked about and reconciled their differing expectations regarding work and family. They would have either reached an agreement or decided they were incompatible. '

Better timing would have allowed them to deal with the conflict inherent to two careers and parenting calmly and without urgency, as the Kings and Smith-Powells did. Instead, Mary felt unloved and alone at a traumatic period in her life. Her threats to leave deeply unsettled Mark. As a result of Mary's parents' divorce, she held an unrealistic view of marriage. She hadn't watched the effort or restraint that spouses put in over time. Their relationship suffered for a long time.

The Claytons' story represents one version of the Mommy Trap. Modern woman doesn't investigate or design her life options, love for child surprises her, lack of good child-care options frighten her, her husband doesn't consider making a career accommodation, and she and her marriage become miserable. Fortunately, as you'll see in chapter 10, Mary became friendly with Ann King, who directed her to a colleague who helped the Claytons find a more harmonious arrangement. If you put yourself in a better position to start out with, you can sooner create the parenting roles you desire, and save yourself some heartache, if not prevent a divorce.

MODERN ROMANCE

Why am I talking about marriage and divorce, and babies, parental labor, and conflict? It certainly seems unromantic. But according to psychologist and minister Dr. Robert Wohlfort, romantic love dies anywhere from twenty-four hours to one year after the wedding. Then, he says, growth or a power struggle takes over.

The success of long-term relationships depends not only on love but also requires mutual compromise, commitment, communication, and conflict-resolution skills.[3] And while unlovely, divorce floats all around us. When choosing their mates and before deciding to have children, women ought to appreciate the possibility of divorce. That way, they can increase their BATNAs (Best Alternative to a Negotiated Agreement) and their chances to create nurturing, happy families that will grow closer and more supportive over time.

Most divorces occur within seven years after the wedding. Not coincidentally, people usually have children in the first seven

> ### ▌ Some Facts about Marriage, Divorce, and Babies
>
> - Couples from different religions divorce more frequently than couples who have the same religion.[4]
> - Dual-income families have a higher rate of divorce than single-income families.[5]
> - Most divorce occurs during the first ten years of marriage, with a median marriage duration of seven years.[6]
> - A third to a half of new parents experience as much marital distress as couples already in therapy for marital difficulties.[7]

years of marriage. *Having babies can send marriages into a tailspin.* In fact, according to marital researcher Dr. John Gottman, "Parenthood is really the beginning of the end of a marriage for many couples."[8]

Mike McManus, columnist, author, and founder of Marriage-Savers, a program that has drastically reduced the divorce rate in cities such as Modesto, California, explains why today's parents seem to have so much trouble:

> The key to the issue of working out parenting roles is learning how to compromise. Our culture screams the absolute opposite, "You're an individual, you're sacrosanct, the most important thing in the world, do your own thing, if someone else gets in your way, run over him. Look out for number one." We never hear "look out for number two."

Today's partners must accommodate many pressures and interests unheard of in the past, providing more opportunities for compromise or conflict. Job and geographic mobility pull people far from where they began, providing less security and community support than the previous one-employer career model did. Interfaith and cross-cultural marriages pose a new set of dilemmas. Few couples have a culturally or society-prescribed, mutually understood set of expectations.

The same reasoning applies to parenting and employment. The entry of women into the workforce provided the biggest jolt to old-fashioned matrimony.

SHARE THE HAPPINESS OR SUFFER WITH INEQUALITY

Arguments over gender ideology and the second shift led to a number of divorces in Arlie Hochschild's famous study.[9] Even when couples stayed together, the unevenness of family efforts exacted a cost in addition to the mothers' exhaustion and heavy workload: Women lost their "un-ambivalent" love for their husbands, and began to resent them.[10] In the happiest two-job marriages Hochschild observed, the couples shared, and valued, child and home care.[11]

Similarly, both at-home and working mothers in the Cowans' study of new parents became dissatisfied when fathers didn't share the joys and burdens of parenting and housework. Carolyn Cowan explains:

> It's a bit of a challenge whatever way you do it. Working outside of the family, even if you have good child care, doesn't necessarily solve it. And there is the slight danger that mothers at home will be somewhat depressed—especially if they don't have much support from other people. In our studies, mothers who stayed home to care for their babies reported more symptoms of depression than mothers who returned to school or work. It doesn't mean they're clinically depressed. They may be worried about or feeling badly about what they're doing professionally, or just lonely. So, that's why it's kind of complicated.

As did Hochschild, the Cowans found that men's involvement with their children has an impact on marital happiness. The less involved a father becomes with baby care, the more likely that he and his wife will become disenchanted with their relationship.[12] Dads who do more with their children feel better about themselves, as do their wives, and both are more satisfied with their marriage.[13] *The Cowans found that how the partners negotiated their arrangement and how both partners felt about the outcome made the greatest difference to marital happiness or unhappiness.*[14] If partners approach the process of transforming from a couple into a family collaboratively, marriage can flourish in exciting new ways.

HAPPY TRAILS

Until children arrive, marriages generally have few problems accommodating two adult lives. Overnight, everything changes. Today's couples truly have more to argue about than our parents did. *Gender roles constitute the number-one cause of argument for new parents.* New parents argue most about the Big Two:

1. Who does what with the children and in the house?
2. Who makes the career accommodation, that is, which partner, if any, should work, stay home, cancel a meeting, or pick up a child from day care?[15]

These issues have a pervasive effect because of the frequency with which they manifest themselves. A mother can be reminded of her desire for her husband to change or feed their baby twenty times a day. Instead of feeling "We can handle anything together, as a team," many women unexpectedly see themselves as on their own, with views that conflict with their husbands'.[16]

As a result, flexibility regarding work and commitment to sharing family responsibilities are now the most predictive areas of marital happiness for parents. For example, in Life Innovations' nationwide study of twenty-one thousand couples, parents with the greatest elasticity with respect to work and the greatest commitment to sharing family responsibilities were the most content.[17] Parents with the least flexibility at work and the smallest commitment to sharing responsibilities had the most conflicted marriages. Parents who perceive their roles as traditional had the least happy marriages.[18]

Happy couples:

- are committed to sharing family and household responsibilities; and
- have flexibility at work.

This is new. Previously, roles satisfaction did not predict marital satisfaction. Amy Olson, who conducted the Life Innovations study, told me:

> We were surprised by the overall finding initially with respect to flexibility. But then, we said, "Of course that makes

sense." Flexibility ties into roles, and parenting at this particular point in time. Parents today need to negotiate more and to be more flexible. The strengths in the roles relationships we saw were where both partners were equally willing to make adjustments in roles, and they were both satisfied with the division of housework. In equal relationships you're going to have happier marriages. Even when you look at couples who aren't reporting necessarily that they're not happy about their roles, you see that the more equal a partnership is, the happier they are. Even if they're not aware of what is making them unhappy, you still see it.

That explains why Ann and Mike King, Rebecca Powell and Darrell Smith, and Lynne and Guy Swanson report greater satisfaction as parents than so many others do. Note, too, that both partners need to be satisfied with their division of responsibility and the way they arrived at their arrangement. In addition to the Hochschild, Cowans, and Life Innovations studies, a vast amount of research supports the findings that modern marriages thrive when dads share child and house care, and languish or combust when they don't.[19]

AN OUNCE OF PREVENTION

Now we see that marriages can run into trouble after children arrive, and we've begun to understand why. As Ann and Mike King did, we can preempt these problems, and prevent their escalation by tackling them before the wedding. Here, BATNA and marital research converge. Marriage preparation advocate Mike McManus has observed that providing training and counseling after years of marriage doesn't work as well as teaching couples skills beforehand.

> The longer you wait, the harder it is. Because then you have all these self-rationalizations built up in your mind.
> The usual problem in divorce is that the couples haven't learned to make the relationship work. They don't know how to resolve conflict. That's the heart of the problem. We can teach those things.

Premarital inventories can predict with almost 90-percent certainty whether affianced couples will divorce. Many marriage-preparation efforts use a questionnaire called PREPARE. A 125-item inventory, PREPARE identifies relationship strengths and weaknesses in the areas of realistic expectations, personality issues, communication, conflict resolution, financial management, leisure activities, sexual relationship, children and marriage, family and friends, "equalitarian" roles, and religious orientation. Other programs use a similar, more religion-oriented test called FOCCUS.

When doing the inventories, each partner fills out the questions individually. For example, participants answer "disagree," "strongly disagree," "agree," or "strongly agree" to the following items dealing with work and family:

- We are in agreement about how we will combine both careers and childrearing. (FOCCUS)
- In a marriage, the husband should be as willing to adjust as the wife. (PREPARE)
- If a couple has young children, the wife should not work outside the home. (PREPARE)

After a computer scores the responses, identifying areas of agreement and disagreement, a counselor or clergy member helps the couple discuss the zones that need improvement or communication. *Ten to 15 percent of couples who do PREPARE or FOCCUS call off their engagement.* The tests highlight important topics people fail to talk about or explore fully—such as work and parenting and gender ideology—either because they know they will cause conflict or they have no awareness of their importance. All engaged couples should do a PREPARE- or FOCCUS-based evaluation, so they get a realistic picture of themselves, each other, their relationship, and marriage itself.

Because of their religious, professional, and educational backgrounds, Ann King and Rebecca Powell had their agendas well set. Most of us don't. Premarital inventories strip off the rose-colored glasses created by a lifetime of watching Hollywood movies and reading romance novels. Married Catholics who participated in pre-Cana efforts most valued the preparation they received in communication, commitment, and conflict resolution.[20] A friend remembers:

> I loved it and thought it was very good for John, who was basically forced to talk about important issues: how many kids did we want to have, what were our long-term goals, how did

we feel about money, managing it, etc.? We, of course, had talked about things like this but it forces you to sit down and really discuss these issues up-front well before you face them.

At the time, we both wanted five children—ha! I think pre-Cana teaches a good form of communication. I remember a role-play where the wife was offered a great job with a great salary and the husband was offered a job across the country—not as much money. They had to decide what was best to do for the family. In that particular role-play, the husband decided to stay home with the kids so the wife could take the job.

Those who use marital enrichment programs report 70 percent greater satisfaction with their marriages than those who don't.[21] Of course, couples who participate in these efforts may self-select, and might be highly informed, low-risk pairs. But in extreme cases such "interventions" can prevent marriages that should never take place. A woman who wants to make sure her husband becomes the kind of father and partner she desires increases her chances by:

- Choosing her man carefully.
- Talking to him about the terms of her lifetime contract, before she signs it.
- Double-checking her instincts with PREPARE (which can be done with a lay professional for those who are not religious, or have different religions) or FOCCUS.
- Setting a precedent for and providing a forum for addressing important topics with a third party.
- Gaining a realistic expectation of her relationship, as well as marriage itself.

Use the tools available, when they will have the greatest effect. A few years down the road, you will prefer to spend the night at Ann King's house rather than in the Mommy Trap, and so will your children and husband.

THE BABY BOMB

Many have analogized the birth of a first child to a small explosion going off in one's home. Almost nobody makes the transition from childless couple to cooing parents without disruption, Ann and

Mike King included. In a recent study, 84 percent of married couples agreed that having children had reduced their marital satisfaction,[22] and 68 percent of the parents polled said that the father was not involved enough with the children.

Few expectant parents realize their marriage has more than a four-in-five chance of deterioration after a baby's birth. In one study, Arizona State sociologist Mary Benin found that marital happiness plunges steeply after a first birth, returning to pre-baby levels of satisfaction only after the children leave home.[23]

No one tells us at our baby showers that the first weeks and months after giving birth can breed conflict. Female hormones rage. Unbroken sleep becomes a distant and cherished memory. Tempers and time are short. Newborn babies require round-the-clock care. If you're not a mother yet, that last sentence means nothing to you. To an involved parent of even a three-day-old, it explains the whole history of the world. Or half. The love he or she feels for that precious warm bundle explains the rest.

Despite what expectant mothers may think, maternity leaves are not relaxing. Just ask Kerry Beard, who felt like hitting her husband each morning of her maternity leave when he showered and left the house and her. Or my coworker Rudy, a doting father who confided he felt lucky to get away from his two-month-old daughter and his wife everyday.

The explosion of a baby's arrival displaces the previous order by removing at least one adult from the outside world and unexpectedly polarizing parents. It sends women home, where they've not spent much time, and into unexpected incompetence. Men rush back to "provide for the family" with new vigor. Each embarks on a consuming love affair with the baby, making couple time scarce.

In a landmark study, Jay Belsky analyzed 250 couples to determine how a first child changes a marriage.[24] He found the best predictor of how a couple weathered the transition to parenthood was if they had learned how to resolve conflicts prior to their child's birth. Consistent with other researchers, Belsky found that couples who didn't know how to address their differences experienced terrible disunity. Couples who knew how to disagree productively became closer.[25] *The ability to manage conflict without escalation constitutes the most important skill of the transition.* Learning how to communicate positively and to attempt to reconcile competing interests and desires will prove more important than even that infant swing everybody will say you must have.

Before getting married, and certainly before having children, couples should:

- learn how to talk about and resolve conflict;
- create a cohesive "we" identity together;
- provide space for and support individual interests; and
- gain a realistic expectation of life as parents.

Couples who bypass these steps and don't hold traditional views may well find themselves arguing, as the Claytons did, about their roles. They will have fallen into the Mommy Trap.

I HEAR YOU

How partners deal with whatever comes their way determines the success or failure of their relationship, including whether they achieve work flexibility and a commitment to sharing family responsibilities. Specific methods exist for dealing with common problems modern parents face. The later a couple learns these methods, the less chance they will stay together. If they divorce, the wife will likely have even more house and child-care responsibilities, and less money.

Techniques taught by therapists, marriage counselors, families, workplaces, and negotiators all share the same concept: listening. One way or the other, experts of all types recommend some form of intentional dialogue or active listening. Ann and Mike King use the Harville Hendrix imago-based dialogue, one of many existing variations. All forms of active listening have the following components:

- Instead of waiting until your partner finishes speaking so you can rebut what he or she has just said, you have to repeat what your partner said, validate it, and show empathy for his or her position.
- You must agree to make an "appointment" (set aside time to give your undivided attention) within a reasonable amount of time, say twenty-four hours, to discuss an issue your partner raises.
- If things get out of control, you can call a time-out and regroup.

- Later on, or at a different time, brainstorm together to think up ways to fix the problem.

The dialogue causes partners to listen to and hear each other, something couples in trouble do not do. It may not be sexy but it works. Dr. Wohlfort explains:

> The dialogue lowers reactivity in conversation. The couple will be more fully connected to one another, which makes it much easier and faster to come to mutual respect and mutual decisions. It's a communication skill, and it's essentially much more than that. It is a disciplined way to welcome each other into one another's lives and it breaks up the idea that "you ought to think as I do." Instead, your point of view, your way of seeing things, your opinions are every bit as valid as mine.

Tom and Kecia Johnson benefited a great deal from this principle. They had dated for seven years, spending every night together and paying rent on two apartments. Kecia wanted to get married, and Tom couldn't commit. At forty-one, he loved Kecia, depended on her, and enjoyed their wonderful relationship. His father had left his family when Tom was eighteen months old, and his mother had never remarried. Tom couldn't bring himself to make the next step. Two weeks after he proposed, he had asked for the ring back.

Kecia told Tom she couldn't hang in limbo anymore. After a week of a torturous breakup neither wanted, they went to a couples' therapist. Ten years later, Kecia says:

> We'd been stuck for so long. Once we got there, the conversation got real safe for Tom. I was able to understand why he had such fear of marriage, and separate his feelings from my own desire to get married. We learned to get to the bottom of our arguments instead of skimming the surface. Since then, whenever we've started to have any trouble, we've always gone back to the dialogue. When our son was born, we'd push him in the stroller, and do the dialogue while he slept. A lot of problems got easy for us, because we knew how to disagree without things turning ugly, and to find a solution we both could live with. Even when we can't find an answer, it just makes me feel better to know he heard me and understood what I said. We both know we're trying. Sometimes that's all I need to know.

How do you learn to listen? Some people just know how, but not many. Marriage counselors or therapists can teach a new way of discourse, and provide a good place to practice. Workshops and many excellent books outline steps for disagreeing pleasantly (see the Resources section in the back of this book for some recommendations). The dialogue provides an effective mechanism to use when requesting male participation in child and home care and flexibility at work. Consider it an insurance policy for times when debates get heated and compromise involves more sacrifice than going with a chocolate dessert when you really would prefer something with fruit in it—that is, once baby comes along.

WHILE YOU'RE STILL JUST THE HAPPY COUPLE

Look before You Throw 7
Away the Birth Control

Before we decided to get pregnant, we baby-sat for my
sister's two kids for twenty-four hours. We talked about who
would stay up at night, who would change diapers,
and we knew we would both need a break.

—Lynne Swanson, working mother of two who trades off
primary parenting responsibilities with her husband

GET IT RIGHT THE FIRST TIME

As a relationship therapist, Ann King had an intimate awareness of
the details that create discord, as well as great amounts of work,
for new parents. Much as she wanted to have a baby, Ann did not
get pregnant until she and her husband had put everything in place
for sharing. First, Mike built a home office for her. Then Ann secured licensing for private counseling and developed a strong client
base. The Kings consciously set up the roles and situation they
desired. Ann explains:

> I never intended on not working. I knew very well that stay-
> at-home mothers get depressed if they have no life for them-
> selves. We tried to set good boundaries with other people and
> our work so we could have enough left for the family.

Rebecca Powell negotiated a part-time schedule with full-time
benefits while pregnant with her first child. At the same time, her
husband, Darrel Smith, started his own home-based computer con-
sulting business. After doing research about substitute care and

visiting a number of day-care centers, they determined that, at least for the first year, they would take care of their child themselves. They planned to revisit the issue when their baby turned one to see what they wanted to do then.

Both these couples set the stage well before childbirth for their post-baby arrangements. Mary Clayton didn't convince her husband, Mark, to change his schedule so she could go back to work until their son, Jeffrey, was three. Lauren Martling's husband, George, did not start pulling more of the parental load on the weekends and evenings until their son, Dan, entered kindergarten and his nanny, Pilar, left for a new job.

You probably know what I'm about to say. *Most of us spend more time planning the baby's clothes and nursery than investigating what life with baby will be like.* We spend more time talking and worrying about labor and delivery, at most a twenty-four-hour process that we cannot control, than learning what skills we will need as parents. As a result, we walk right into the Mommy Trap.

The biological urge to procreate may instill a state of hopeful ignorance in prospective parents. I wouldn't want to take the fun of buying gorgeous little things from anyone. But do some serious research as well. Couples find it far easier to erect the proper foundation at the outset than to tear down or renovate once children already exist.

Dr. Pam Jordan, founder of the Becoming Parents Program (BPP), notes:

> Most couples think about getting through pregnancy and getting through labor and birth and they don't talk about how it's going to be when the baby's there. That's really when it's all beginning—that's when the rubber hits the road. And yet that's the part that nobody prepares them for. . . .
>
> It's very important that they at least discuss their expectations before they have a baby. Otherwise everything happens in crisis mode. Instead of the anticipatory guidance of having a "heads up," of gee, that's probably going to become an issue after the baby comes, then all of a sudden things hit you from out of left field. You feel totally out of control and you're dealing with them at the worst possible time—when you're exhausted and frustrated.

Jordan designed her twenty-one-hour class for expectant couples to fill in the vast gaps left by childbirth preparation. Usually, a BPP group meets six times during pregnancy and once after birth, tackling such issues as communication, conflict resolution skills, how to articulate expectations, infant behavior, self-care, jealousy and anger, and an "owner's manual" for babies. At the six- to eight-week postpartum booster session, the instructor reminds the new parents, who have just begun to feel grounded again, that their baby's behavior will likely change to extreme irritability for the next month or so. Parents check in with one another, and gain great comfort in learning that others are having the same experiences.

Unfortunately, most people do not have access to a program like BPP. If a similar program is not available to you, do anything you can to promote a more realistic understanding of life as parents in the twenty-first century. The assumption that mothering and working or just plain mothering comes naturally, or that acquaintances have chosen the best way to do things, leads to all sorts of problems prepared women can avert.

I KNOW WHAT I'M TALKING ABOUT

I will never forget shopping with my mother at a French children's boutique in northwest Washington, D.C. After three hours, we narrowed down the possible going-home-from-the-hospital outfit to three tiny beige, white, and red unitards and two gender-neutral sweaters (I still love to think of how new and perfect they were and I still have them). Head bobbing precariously, on the fifteen-minute ride home from the hospital, Elizabeth slept in and slobbered on her beautiful garb. Her sister, Annie, donned the Tartine e Chocolat clothes a few years later. Between the two of them, they wore the European finery maybe ten times.

I will never forget Elizabeth's second night home, either. She shrieked all night. At two in the morning, I got through to the pediatrician, who listened to the cries and pronounced them angry rather than hurt or pained. We walked through the house. We rocked. We sang. We paced. I cried.

We contemplated going to the emergency room. Every time I offered my breast, Elizabeth refused to nurse. Frantic, my husband said, "You read all those books. What did they say?"

"I knew what I was supposed to eat and when to get an epidural," I replied. "They don't say anything about a baby crying all night."

We paged through *What to Expect When You're Expecting*, which had a section on the first six weeks, and *What to Expect the First Year*, because we'd thought ahead. Nothing. At our eight o'clock appointment the next morning, the doctor asked me whether I had pumped my breasts during the night to release all the pent-up milk. I had procured a breast pump, and had even set it up. Yet I had not understood that my size 40, double-E breasts would get so engorged the baby couldn't latch on.

"Breastfeeding problem," Dr. Ballistreri wrote. "Go home and pump a little and she'll eat and sleep just fine."

"And stop crying?"

"Yes, and stop crying."

I've let my hair down so you can see how someone who made sure the nursery looked sweet and rented a breast pump could have no idea why nursing mothers might need breast pumps. And that was just day three. What I didn't know could fill a book.

Ed and I had spent a beautiful summer weekend inside at George Washington University Hospital in one of those childbirth classes. We sat uncomfortably on the floor with other pregnant couples and learned to breathe. (I worried that he seemed to catch on better than I did.) Statistics on this one don't look too good either. Few women experience natural childbirth. I thank God I didn't. My labors happened so fast that I never used the breathing exercises.

Some women take breastfeeding classes, too. I did not, believing I would instinctively know what to do. A few baby-care classes exist. *Take one—both of you!* It can start the process of acquiring a real understanding of what the next few months to eighteen years will bring.

If you have some extra cash, consider hiring a postpartum doula to give correct information, encouragement, and support to Mom and Dad. Our family couldn't have had a better, kinder, more educational introduction to babies and parenting than that given to us by Donna Karabin, a doula sent from heaven via a present from my dad. Unfortunately, she didn't start coming until day four!

REALITY SPITS UP

An adorable, chortling baby dressed in soft, clean clothes, redolent of warmth, cinnamon, and spice. We carry this image in our minds as we carry our babies in utero. We do get that "ideal" baby about six months after birth, for as much as a few hours a day (and they're totally worth all the rest), except for the clean clothes. Unsullied clothes don't often happen, for the baby or for us. Nor does vomit-free hair, and even clean bodies.

Twenty-four hours a day, seven days a week, for eighteen years, can seem like a long time on a job—mundane details nobody tells you when patting your belly and wishing you luck. *Ask parents about the bad parts of having children, too.* Find out how junior has affected their relationship and how they feel about the choices they've made. Whether because of selective amnesia or misplaced good intentions (aside from labor and delivery nightmares), people usually don't impart negative information to expecting couples.

In a fit of insanity, my friend Kerry performed the nicest act anyone did for me when I was pregnant (not counting the many glorious people who brought me food). Our due dates three months apart, Kerry and I had bonded as pregnant women do, frittering away hours discussing our weight gain, names for our babies, and other such pleasantries. On her first day back to work, when Nathan was two months old, Kerry rushed into my office, slammed the door, and exploded:

> It's not the way they all said it was. I'm here to tell you what it's like to not have a shower all day, to have cracked, bleeding nipples, to never have time to take care of yourself, or even go to the bathroom, to hate your husband for leaving in the morning, and to want to kill to go out that door, alone.

Postpartum depression, I concluded. Also, she'd come back too early. I planned to take six months, I reassured myself. I would have a world of time to adjust. *Quite unfair of Kerry to tell me all of this during my thirty-eighth week,* I thought.

A month later, I often thought back to what she'd said. If I felt I had little skill as a mother, at least I always had a shower by noon. No matter how awful I looked, how much the baby ate or cried or spat up on me, or how exhausted I was, I would not go showerless as Kerry had. I knew exactly how she had felt and I loved her for telling me. Nobody else, and it seemed as if I had talked to thousands of women, had spoken the unvarnished truth.

Before you decide to get pregnant, talk to the real experts: parents. It goes without saying that you will love your baby more than anything on this earth. You will steal into your little one's room and stare at the peaceful beauty of her asleep, forever. You will sing more and act sillier than you could ever imagine, tell poo-poo jokes because she likes them, and know that being a mother is the best, most fun, and most important thing you will ever do.

But there's more to it than that. Think about sleep deprivation. All parents experience it, even those with healthy, happy, well-tended children.

LOOK INTO CHILD CARE BEFORE GETTING PREGNANT

Another seemingly obvious piece of advice usually unheeded: Research your child-care preferences and options before you get pregnant. Remember Janey and Ira Berk, who just assumed day care was the only possibility for them and then hated their pressured lifestyle? Many women, and even more men, give little thought to what they'll do with their hypothetical offspring during their pre-kindergarten years. Instead, they figure they'll look into it some time in the future.

The resources women consult lead them into a false sense that everything hinges on a wheat germ diet and keeping an open mind about whether to have an epidural. In *What to Expect When You're Expecting,* the bible for pregnant women, Arlene Eisenberg, Heidi Murkoff, and Sandee E. Hathaway make no mention of nannies or day care. In *What to Expect the First Year,* their best-selling sequel, the authors counsel pregnant mothers not to decide whether career or family will take priority until after the baby arrives. On page twelve they state, "but while it seems as though this is a choice you should make now, it really isn't." They then refer the overanxious reader to page 587 for advice about "how to make the decision once baby appears on the scene."

Large error. Better advice would be to look into child-care options first, and then create a financial and work situation that allows both parents to be flexible and committed to the family. At my mothers' group, many women explained how they unexpectedly ended up at home:

- "I wasn't comfortable with any of the nannies I interviewed."
- "I cried every time I walked into a day-care center."
- "I just couldn't leave my child in day care anymore. He wasn't getting enough attention and he was always sick. He needs to go outside more."
- "I went back to work and I loved my nanny, but then she quit. After I found another good one, she also quit. Finally, I quit because I couldn't find anybody else in the time I had and it's not good to have so many caregivers."
- "It was harder than I thought it would be. People who knew me before my daughter was born would never have guessed that I would take two years off. I didn't have any anticipation that it would be hard for me to leave my child with a caregiver but it was."

Do not assume you will like the arrangements others have found acceptable, or that good caregivers never leave. That's one well-worn path into the Mommy Trap.

Forty-five percent of mothers with babies younger than one year old come home to tend their families.[1] For the first time since 1976, the percent of new mothers in the workforce declined in 2000 from a record high of 59 percent in 1998.[2] The large numbers of mothers (and increasingly fathers) at home, many of them highly educated, come as a surprise to those who step out of the work world. I was shocked when I started talking to stay-at-home mothers, whom I'd previously dismissed as not like me, not career-oriented, or just incredibly domestic.

Undertake some examination before deciding how you will raise your children. Also, inquire about how satisfied women are with respect to division of new responsibilities. Remember, the most inaccurate expectations of pregnant women are how much their husbands will share child care.[3] Informed couples can guard against automatically falling into parental roles by designing the lives they want, in advance.

Before Getting Pregnant:

- Read the studies about child care (see Resources section in back of this book for how to obtain them).
- Talk to your friends who have children. Get their story — the whole story.
- Check out their caregivers, day-care providers, and their children.
- See how you feel about a caregiver hugging, kissing, diapering, and taking your baby into the bathroom with him or her.
- Ask yourself whether, or for how many hours a week, you would want that adorable baby in a day-care setting or with these caregivers.
- Go to a park to see what you think about kids and their interactions with baby-sitters and mothers.
- Do you notice any difference between children who attend day care, have nannies, or stay mainly with their parents?
- Talk to parents with varying arrangements. Find out how they like their life. Ask about their division of parental- and house-related responsibilities.
- Ask yourself what you would want, ideally.
- Understand you may not be able to find or afford the limited amount of quality substitute care.
- Devise Plan B in case you find you do not like or want to use a lot of, or cannot locate, substitute care. Include your husband in Plan B, unless you are extremely traditional *and* extremely wealthy.
- Talk to stay-at-home mothers and fathers and parents with nontraditional arrangements, and get their perspectives.
- *Do all of the above with your husband. Involve him in all pre-baby decisions and investigation. Make parenting a joint undertaking from the beginning.*

SPEND THE DAY AND NIGHT WITH A REAL LIVE BABY
And Don't Give the Crying Baby Back to His or Her Parents

Twenty-four-hour stints with newborns should form part of your fact-finding mission. Also, try a two-year-old, and why not visit with an elementary-school student and teenager as well? Consider these sojourns a test run to see how you do under simulated conditions, and to get a glimpse at where you're heading.

Lynne Swanson would not agree to try to get pregnant unless her husband, Guy, took on the role of primary on-call parent, because she knew what baby care involved. She had seen her sister struggle with a husband who didn't help much. Lynne and Guy had baby-sat for her sister's two children, then two months and three years old, when her sister's father-in-law died unexpectedly. As a result of this brief experience, Lynne and Guy divided their post-baby duties down to the last diaper, including rest periods. She states:

> I was so spooked that for years afterward I wouldn't entertain the idea of having more than one child. When Guy said he would take on the major responsibility for our kids, he knew what he was in for. It's been so much better than we thought, because we expected the worst. As long as you get a break, you can enjoy every little moment. But when you have to do it all yourself, it is overwhelming and your personal life is the first to go.

If you tailed a first-time mother for twenty-four hours, you would find that:

- Newborns eat ten to twelve times a day, around the clock.
- Newborns rarely sleep for more than two hours at a time.
- A feeding session can last an hour or longer.
- Newborns dirty their diapers up to ten times a day.
- Newborns vomit or "spit up" on their parents.
- Even well-tended babies cry. From the age of six weeks to three months, most babies cry consistently for a one- to two-hour period a day, usually around dinnertime (commonly known as "the arsenic hours").
- New mothers sweat and bleed for months.

Clearly, you can make a more knowledgeable choice about when and how to have a baby after getting a sense of what parenting and child care entail. *You will certainly enlist more help.* You will not assume mothers just "know" how to nurture or want to do it all themselves. Many women end up seeking more assistance from their husbands than they anticipate.[4] As we know, they have a better chance of succeeding when they ask for a lot of involvement from their husbands before their bargaining power takes a nosedive.

Babies are not just sweet smelling powder balls who sleep and act cute. *Know that before you take one home.* Not having had much experience with infants, the work, frustration, crying, repetition, and isolation that come with them surprise many new mothers. People who have realistic expectations about parenthood become happier parents than those with unrealistic expectations, and those who share their new responsibilities are happiest and most together of all.[5]

RESEARCH YOUR EMPLOYERS'
FAMILY POLICIES AND YOUR RIGHTS

Again, I seem to be stating the obvious. But many men don't find out what paternity leave they're entitled to, and certainly don't use it. Ditto with sick leave. Two weeks from her due date, a doctor who expects to share childrearing equally with her husband says:

> I don't know what his paternity leave is. He's toying around with taking the first week off. But that's not paternity leave. That's just him messing around with his vacation time. It's his decision. I think he thinks that he'll have more fun taking time off when the baby is a little older.

Some people always seem to know what policies exist and how to use them. Make yourself one of them, and encourage your husband to do the same, once you plan to become parents.

Understand that it is perfectly fine to assert your need for family time, rather than giving in to employers' possibly short-sighted desires. (And believe me, they can be short-sighted. For more on this issue, see chapters 12 and 13.) The old rule mandated that workers put in all the time, travel, and relocations the workplace required of them, without allowing home responsibilities to interfere.

The new rule: *Think about what your family requires and do what you can to provide it.* In today's world, work and home spill into each other, even for the best employees.

Nancy Kane, a work-life counselor at Catalyst Inc., has helped many Fortune 100 companies formulate cutting-edge employment policies. She explains why the work-life field has grown so much the past twenty years:

> Women make up about half of the labor force and forty-six percent of management positions. So that very fact, I think, brought the issues of work-life balance to the forefront. Because so many employees were bringing that to the table. You don't leave your personal life at the door. Most of these women do not have a stay-at-home husband, which was the old Ozzie and Harriet model. But that model really has declined and most families are dual-career couples. So more than half of the workforce is addressing this issue. And younger employees are demanding more flexibility.

In chapters 12 and 13, we'll discuss the time pressure the workplace exerts on employees. For the moment, inhale the freedom of recognizing that personal lives do intrude on work, and the best employers help to accommodate this fact.

KNOW YOUR PRIORITIES PRIOR TO PARTURITION

One of the first things to do is to consider your consumption targets. Rebecca Powell and Darrell Smith have one newer car and one old car. They have no debt other than the mortgage on their pleasant but small house. Rebecca explains their thinking:

> We are both "techies." We could have maximized our incomes but we chose family time instead. Everything I read showed me that the early years are the most important. We could have a bigger house without a band playing next door every Sunday morning.

Ann King says almost the same thing:

> I could have made a lot more money. But I don't know if I would be sane then. I need my time with my daughter. I can't

quantify the emotional value of the time with her. Or, I guess I can, and it's worth it.

A less acquisitive but by no means deprived lifestyle works for Rebecca and Darrell and the Kings. Others would find it constraining. Couples need to assess the amount of material goods they want, and their priorities, before the baby comes along.

SECURE TWO FLEXIBLE WORK
SITUATIONS BEFORE BABY ARRIVES

Almost nobody does this. The Kings expended a great deal of time and effort to achieve flexibility before trying to have a baby. The Smith-Powells put two reduced-hour positions in place before the birth of their child. My friend Kerry Beard and her husband, Antoine, also adjusted their full-time schedules. An attorney, she works from home all but two days a week. Antoine, a police officer, takes Wednesdays off and works one night. They chose flexible employers and positions because they knew they would want some extra time when they became parents, and didn't believe either income would support their family well.

As a result of shifting their hours around, the Beards use a family day-care provider for just twenty hours a week, enabling them to honor their preference for less rather than more substitute care. Having worked out the arrangements beforehand, the Kings, Smith-Powells, and Beards did not argue about how to divide their efforts, or whose job and time was more important. Instead, they set up mechanisms for accommodating their families and each other.

Creating two flexible positions is essential. Otherwise, dual-income couples may argue or become single-earner families with a reluctant stay-at-home parent (probably Mom). Couples cannot share their new responsibilities if one has rigid job requirements (the man) and one makes a flexible arrangement (the woman). That's the norm—and the transitional gender ideology at work. But the norm leads to inequity and unhappiness, a lose-lose-lose situation for mother, child, and father.

Dust off that negotiation theory. Before that twinkle in your eye becomes an adorable seven- or eight-pound reality, make clear the family will survive and flourish best if both you and your husband commit to making time for it.

THE BEAUTY OF COMPOUND INTEREST

As soon as we start earning income, we can begin to prepare our nest to receive children—even if we don't have a spouse, and even if having children is years away. J. P. Morgan called compound interest "the eighth wonder of the world."

My friend John would agree. He took a year off from work, traveling cross-country to Los Angeles to write the great American novel. He never seemed to get around to writing because he made a lot of friends and went out with them each night. He frequented movie festivals, nightclubs, cool bars, dive bars, everywhere.

John was quite generous, a heart of gold. When his money started to run low, he took crowds of people to Musso and Frank's and other expensive eateries, and *charged the meals.* He kept getting further in the hole. Ultimately, he left California, returning to his job and huge credit card bills, compounding interest daily. It took John years putting in overtime in the hot sun as a construction worker to erase his debt. Now that he has married and wants to have children, he wishes he had kept out of debt.

Fred Barbash, a financial expert and former *Washington Post* columnist, was able to quit his job to take care of his son in part because of long-term investments. He advises:

> You have to start early. Even if you think you cannot afford it, you must. If you start putting away even tiny amounts in a conservative way, barring catastrophic circumstances, you will have many more options and choices, and much more freedom, ten, fifteen, twenty years down the road. You will not be dependent on a job and therefore have to stay with it. You will have more choices for your children. If the public schools are not good, you can pay for parochial or private school. The secret is just getting started early, because of the compounding factor.

All of the parents we've met who set up nontraditional arrangements saved up their money so they could give their families their time. Allow yourself flexibility to deal with whatever complications may arise. Get that compound interest working for you rather than against you. That way, when the time comes, you can afford to devise alternative work schedules, or bring a parent home, if you want or have to.

GET A MORTGAGE ONE SALARY CAN CARRY

The mania to buy a house or apartment usually strikes somewhere between the desire for a pet and the yen for a baby. Part of the American dream envisions a house with a fence and a lawn. This dream can turn into a nightmare, as it did for my friend Susan. She and her husband bought a new house that depreciated substantially the day they moved in. A year later, they had a baby. Susan's mother took care of their son, William, for free, until she developed heart trouble.

They couldn't afford a nanny or a good day-care center because they had to make a hefty mortgage payment each month. As a result, the Thompsons took William to an inexpensive local family day-care home. They kept him there for two years, even though they did not think he got the appropriate developmental experience and had legitimate concerns about the home's safety and hygiene. Susan became consumed with hatred for William's caregiver, a nice person with no training looking for a way to stay home with her own daughter. At the time, Susan explained:

> We have no choice. We would lose so much money if we sold our house now. They're still building new houses two blocks over. And William is used to a big house and yard. He needs space to run around in. I would love to be home, but we both need to work or the bank will foreclose on our loan.

This family fell into another large section of the Mommy Trap. They made an unwise personal financial decision, even though Susan has a master's degree in business administration! Every member of the household suffered.

Another family had a better time when the unexpected struck. Deanna and Paul Donatello have four daughters, ages eight, seven, five, and one. When I first met Deanna, she worked full time as a scientist for a federal agency. Her husband, a computer hardware salesman who was laid off in a dot-com downturn, had taken care of their three daughters for a year. He landed a terrific job a month before their fourth daughter's birth.

Deanna planned to work part time but ended up at home. At ten months, baby Nancy refused to take a bottle. Deanna had used all of her maternity leave, and had switched to a twenty-hour work-week. Nancy's pediatrician recommended that Deanna continue nursing for two months longer, until Nancy turned one. Deanna requested two months of leave, relying on her doctor's opinion.

Management agreed but then flip-flopped, waiting until Deanna returned from vacation to tell her one Friday afternoon that they would begin termination proceedings if she did not come into work that Monday. Deanna could not secure alternate child-care arrangements so quickly. Seeing no other option, she quit. At home two weeks later, Deanna told me:

> I'm really upset about what happened. But I know we'll be okay, because we did it on one salary before. We didn't buy the biggest house we could afford. We made sure we'll never need two incomes to get by.

Things happen, suddenly. *Be prepared for any eventuality.* Couples who factor possible setbacks into their plans have more and better choices. Look before you leap, and expect a long and possibly hard as well as exhilarating fall. Most importantly, hold on to each other as you jump.

Men Must Get Involved Early: Rethinking Maternity and Paternity Leave 8

We always split the time, even when I was breastfeeding.
I actually got a full night's sleep when my second son was
born. Because we were both home, I never became
"the expert." I was afraid that if that happened,
that would be my role forever after.

— Rebecca Powell

THE EARLY BIRD SPECIAL

Here's the secret. *The best way to ensure Dad's participation is to provide him time alone with his infant, as often and as early as possible.* One employer I've heard about, a workaholic father of five, instinctively understands this particular fact of life. When an employee asked for three months of paternity leave, he took the father-to-be aside and whispered, "Don't do this. If you show competence early, you're ruined forever."

Fathers who spend time with their newborns want to continue, and their wives and children will rely on them to do so. If they hold their infants, dads develop protective feelings for and *crave* physical contact with them. Touching and smelling babies affects human beings like a drug. The release of oxytocin, the "hormone of harmony and attachment," stimulates an urge in both mothers and fathers to love, touch, kiss, and care for their child.[1] Another hormone—vasopressin—also leads men to fatherly behavior, nurturing, and cuddling.[2] And rather than ruining him, becoming close to his children completes a man in a way that will later seem natural and desirable.

Rebecca Powell's theory that she had to get her husband involved in the beginning is correct, from both a biological and a societal perspective. *Very often, the first three months determine the relationship a father will have with his child.*[3] Once women develop increased ability and attachment, men rarely catch up.

Also, children and fathers benefit from more contact specifically during those early months. Most of that good stuff about how well children do when fathers take an active role happens in the beginning. For example, children tended by their dads during the first six months become more socially responsive, deal better with stress, and achieve greater intellectual and motor development.[4] Think of the millions of dollars people spend on Baby Genius videotapes, Bach and Mozart recordings for in-the-womb stimulation, Gymboree classes, and the like. If they really wanted smarter, popular, more capable babies, they would simply arrange for Dad to spend more time at home.

ALL WE ARE SAYING IS, GIVE HIM A CHANCE

Usually, American fathers take a week or less off from work during and after the birth of a baby and American mothers at least six weeks.[5] At this point, the responsibility for childrearing (and most of the great parenting payoffs) devolves to women, often permanently. In *Kidding Ourselves: Breadwinning, Babies, and Bargaining Power,* Rhona Mahony notes:

> [T]he typical mother has a head start in developing strong feelings toward her newborn baby. She has been consciously taking care of it for six months. He [her husband] has just begun to hold it in his hands. In a sense, she is six months ahead of him.[6]

By the time a mother who takes a three-month maternity leave returns to work, she may be up to nine months ahead of her husband in knowledge of and involvement with their child. This difference will probably make Dad less inclined to share child care regardless of whether Mom returns to work or stays home. In turn, she may even discourage or belittle him each time he tries to "help," because she will read the baby's cues much faster.

This disparate expertise will look like biology, and it will result in part from her biological head start, but only in part. The remainder comes from the choices the couple made *not* to counteract female biology with male biology. As part of their study of the transition to parenthood, Phillip and Carolyn Pape Cowan set up support groups for couples during pregnancy that continued through the early months of the babies' lives. There, Carolyn Cowan and her staff observed the interaction of first-time mothers and fathers with each other and their babies:

> You could just catch it when it was happening. She just couldn't keep herself from telling him how to do it. It wasn't horrible, but it did interfere with giving him some space to figure out how he's going to do it.
>
> Now, if we could point it out, gently, especially with some humor and warmth, which we tried to do—most women said things like, "Oh, my gosh, I didn't even realize it, but that's really true." And they would really try. And then the guys would get braver, and just pick up the baby whether they knew what to do or not. They didn't necessarily feel comfortable at it in the beginning.

Fathers gain experience and interest in their children when they take on responsibility for and spend time with them, alone. Mothers gain competence and attachment the same way. Women don't realize that when they plan their maternity leave they map out their parenting roles forever after. They also don't recognize that they push their husbands away from their children when they could instead welcome them in and provide dads with the opportunities they need to learn to parent.

THE OFFICIAL MESSAGE IS WRONG

Why don't expectant mothers appreciate the repercussions of their maternity-leave decisions? For starters, most believe their husbands will partner rather than just lend a hand here and there. After all, today's men participate in labor and delivery, cut umbilical cords, and help push out and catch babies. They also attend classes that teach "natural childbirth," preparing them for what to do on that special day.

But after the first few days, many fathers distance themselves from or are marginalized at home. As a result of having soaked up the culture, peer group behavior, and tradition:

- Many women think they should take as much time as they can professionally and financially afford to be with their babies.
- Many men think they should go back to work as soon as possible and provide for their families.

Mothers gain expertise at home during the most intense, physical period of parenting. Fathers return to the world. *New parents cannot divide their new duties close to equally if they choose the usual way to structure maternity and paternity leaves.* Any person who tries to share a job with somebody who works somewhere else full time will end up with the lion's share of the position's responsibilities.

In addition to spelling disaster for sharing child care, the standard division of new parents' efforts harms children, mothers, and fathers. Children do not reap the benefits of early fathering (which translates into lifetime involvement). Though any doctor will excuse a new mother from work for six to eight weeks after giving birth, the normal deployment of resources forces women to go through the most exhausting and draining experience they will likely ever have, mostly alone.

Separating men from home during the early days as a family doesn't make them happy either. Every male expert I consulted emphasized that the birth of the first child represents the nadir of marriage for men. Dr. Robert Wohlfort, psychologist and father, explains:

> Oftentimes, the husband feels excluded. A third party comes in and takes a lot of the mother's time, so he may well be feeling on the outs. Which he is. It's not just that he feels that way. He is. There's more energy going in there.

In studying the transition to parenthood, Carolyn Cowan observed many new fathers having a hard time: "Everybody was finding it difficult. The men are really wanting more time. They don't want to miss anything with the baby, many of them."

Two thirds of first-time fathers become depressed during their baby's first three months, called "the fourth trimester" of pregnancy.[7] The best treatment for the dads' depression is more contact with their baby. But the statistics about leisure time and fathers' participation with children discussed in chapter 1 show that most men don't get more contact with their baby. Instead, they channel their efforts outside the family. Societal and familial beliefs about gender roles can take over, leaving an interested dad with nothing to do *other* than provide.

When my friend Jim became a father, he confided:

> It's hard on me to be at work all day. I want to know what's going on at home. I want to get to know my son. This is the most amazing thing that's ever happened to me and here I am pushing paper. I'm distracted all the time and my mind isn't on my clients.

By the time their second child was born, Jim wanted only for his wife, Tammy, and new baby to sleep in another room so he could return to work rested. A year later, he complained that she slept with the children and not with him. Where Jim and Tammy both worked and had careers before the birth of their first child, he had now become the primary breadwinner, and viewed his role as father mainly as provider and weekend playmate.

Jay Belsky performed the other definitive study on the transition to parenthood, in addition to the Cowans' study. He warns that fathers who don't make the time early on have difficulty developing closeness with their children:

> When I used to watch fathers, they'd come home and they'd pick up the paper and they'd go read it and they'd be behind this paper. And I thought, "This kid's going to be four years old and now they're going to want to go out and play ball." But then they won't have a relationship base.

That's the old, 1950s way we've supposedly discarded. The new family paradigm of parenting partners has distinct advantages for dads. They can create lifetime happiness by putting more time in at home in the beginning.

HOW IT HAPPENS

Most of the references women rely on during pregnancy do not warn of the pitfalls ahead. For example, the best-selling *What to Expect When You're Expecting* devotes only 9 of its 428 pages to fathers, in a chapter called "Fathers Are Expectant, Too." The authors assume mothers will choose whether to work or stay home, and fathers will have to try hard not to be left out. In a section headed "Can I Afford a Larger Family?" the authors wheedle and cajole the breadwinning man:

> If the new mother is planning not to go back to her job right away and this concerns you from a financial standpoint, recognize that weighed against the costs of quality child care, a business wardrobe, and commuting, the amount of income lost may really be minimal.[8]

Hello? What century are we in? Note the presumptions: Mom wants to be home, Dad doesn't want to be home and doesn't want her home because he's losing money, and the needs of the child are the mother's concern alone. In the next section, titled "Will I Be a Good Father?" after stating that few mothers instinctively know what to do but learn through on-the-job training, the authors counsel:

> But if you feel you'll be more comfortable with the tasks at hand if you're formally prepared, by all means take a parenting class—if one is available in your area—to learn how to diaper, bathe, feed, hold, dress, and play with your baby. If a class isn't available, or if you have an unquenchable thirst for such preparation, dive into a pile of childcare books.[9]

In effect, the authors say, "Dad, you're sweet to think you can do something here, but it's really not your job." To be involved, a father will need to do a lot more than follow up on this halfhearted advice. Even if he proves a real go-getter and reads all of those books, (a) he won't have a clue and (b) he won't get a clue because he'll be at work.

"A pile of child-care books" didn't show me what to do. Nor did instinct, my female predilection to nurture, or the fact that my body was exploding with mother's milk. I learned what to do with my first child because *I had no choice.* Trial and error, no more and no less. Do not take the advice in those books unless you want a traditional division of childcare, as in 90/10.

WHAT TO EXPECT WHEN YOU LEAVE IT TILL LATER

George and Lauren Martling got into unequal situations in the first week of their newborn's life. Lauren took no graphic design work for four months, tending Dan the entire time. George stayed home for three days, and went back to his job, full time, same schedule, including about six weeks in travel overseas every year. Looking back, Lauren says:

> Ever since George went back to work on day four, Dan has been my responsibility. George never learned how to do anything except play with Dan. I found Pilar, and I coordinate my schedule with hers. I didn't realize what had happened until he said his life hadn't changed. Then I saw that we had actually grown apart. I thought having kids would be more of a bonding experience.

Lauren signed up for the on-the-job training course, and her husband did not. Here's what the book *What to Expect the First Year* has to say about the possibility of "Dad Taking Time Off" during the early months:

> While changing diapers and doing laundry might not seem like much of a vacation, to some fathers enjoying those first days as a family can offer more fun than a Mardi Gras, more awe and inspiration than a view of the Grand Canyon, and more memories to cherish than a round-the-world cruise. If your husband feels this way, by all means make the time following baby's arrival vacation time. Be sure, however, that he is fully acquainted in advance with basic household mechanics: laundry, simple cooking, vacuuming, and so on.[10]

Having read these passages, it's no wonder women think they'll take care of everything themselves, and somehow share the ups and downs of their new life. In essence, the "experts" and the way most others arrange their lives give prospective parents the message that:

- Men's involvement stops at the hospital.
- Fathers don't significantly contribute to parenting (except as providers).

Carolyn Cowan observed parents in conflict over their roles during the first few years, and noticed they felt they had no control over how things evolved.

We asked them in our study how they expected it to be, and asked them later how it really was at a number of different points after having the baby. The couples tended to describe the who-does-what of life as if it had happened to them, as if they didn't have very much to do with it.

That's because they followed the old rules of the road, which will usually take parents to a mother-dominant, father-distanced arrangement. The new rules for men:

- Participation starts well before labor and delivery.
- Fathering involves significant amounts of time and effort, including regular time alone with a child beginning in the first moments of life.

How much parenting a father does depends in large part on the mother.[11] Here, women hold the cards. They can make changes so fathers don't get separated from children.

PATERNITY LEAVE: THE NEW FRONTIER
Given the importance of men's early involvement, paternity leave is a critical issue. Women must change their aspiration levels; they must ask their husbands to take the same amount of time they do, and to do baby care alone. That's if you want an equal effort. If you want 90/10, do it the regular way. If you want 60/40, try for a 60/40 split of paternity and maternity leave. Keep your aspiration levels as high as you can reasonably justify.

Back to BATNA (Best Alternative to a Negotiated Agreement): When you push that baby bomb out, your BATNA level will plummet to its lowest ever. If your husband expects before you marry and before you decide to have children that he will take time off, he will make himself available. If you do not understand that Dad must stay home for a while, alone, you may well find yourself in the Mommy Trap.

Rhona Mahony advises women who want to share childrearing do the following *before* getting pregnant:

> Have a conscious, open discussion. Count how much leave you can take. Negotiate hard for him to take time, too, in the months. Do not plan for the woman to do it all.

What would be the right amount of time for a man to take off for paternity leave? Months. Years. As much as the family can afford. *Do not assume the man's job is primary or more important, or that a father cannot trade income for family time.*

If economics, work policies, or personalities don't allow for months or years, then what? He needs, at least, to take more time off than that first couple of days. Perhaps a regular arrangement, like every Friday for three months, or an understanding that if a particular day looks grim, Dad will stop work and rush home— whatever makes life easier, and gets men more involved right from the start. No matter what, plan for:

- Dad's time alone with the baby with minimal and preferably no instruction.
- Dad to stay home for some period of time by himself.

These suggestions apply to stay-at-home mothers as well. Certainly, a full-time mother can and should go off the clock on weekends, holidays, and evenings, and every now and then enjoy a coffee break or long lunch hour.

THE BOOBS DON'T HAVE TO GET IN THE WAY

Sometimes people say breastfeeding causes the inequality of effort between parents. Yet more than 70 percent of American babies drink infant formula by the age of three months.[12] In 1995, little more than half of American new mothers left the hospital breast-feeding, exclusively or in combination with formula.[13] Clearly, women's ability to lactate does not fully explain why mothers take on more childrearing responsibilities.

Society gives such credence to this message that even Rebecca Powell initially assumed nursing and sharing couldn't work. After researching breast pumping technology and alternate work schedules, she changed her mind:

> It seemed less realistic that I would ever be able to be less involved when I nursed. But Darrell was leaving a job and I realized that with two flexible options we could put together a package instead of doing it serially. I do pump when I work, and with the second child, the doctors advised starting earlier. Who knew you didn't have to be up every two hours?

Parents can share baby-care responsibilities even during the nursing period, if they plan properly. When their first child was born, Darrell Smith had just started working from home. Rebecca took two months of maternity leave. During that time, Darrell worked whenever he could, making child care and errands his first priority. They split all the new duties, except for nursing. After the baby ate, Darrell often burped and held him. At six weeks, Rebecca began to express milk with a breast pump and Darrell took on feeding responsibilities, too. Though she was ahead of Darrell in expertise, she didn't get that far ahead, and they arranged for him to catch up.

When Rebecca returned to work three days a week, Darrell took over completely on those days, feeding expressed bottles of milk. On Rebecca's days at home, Darrell worked, went to meetings, and did the networking he couldn't do the rest of the time.

I visited the Smith-Powells six weeks after the premature birth of their second son. While we talked, Darrell held baby Charlie and older son, Mac, played near us. When Charlie woke up and wanted to nurse, Darrell brought him to Rebecca. He reminded her she should drink something and brought her water. They had created a situation where both had significant responsibilities, even in the beginning. As a result, Rebecca's maternity leave was wonderful, despite concerns about potential problems with their preemie. I felt a sense of calm and serenity in their household at a time that can often seem frenetic and stressful.

Nursing prevents a father's participation only if you allow it to. Let those aspiration levels soar along with your weight—you'll need your husband more now than ever.

LEAVE HIM ALONE

The experience of my friend Allison Pearlman highlights the importance of men having their own time with their babies. When she was pregnant, Allison and her husband, Howard, planned to equally share their new chores. Howard set aside two months for paternity leave, and Allison took six months for maternity leave. She earns almost twice his salary. I visited the Pearlmans when their daughter, Rosamond, was six weeks old. Allison answered the door wearing sweatpants and holding the baby. Howard's eyes were red and bloodshot.

Baby stuff filled their previously spotless living room. The coffee table spilled over with takeout Chinese food containers, napkins, and a basket holding baby shampoo and powder. A changing table stood by the window.

"Look at the house," Allison laughed when I asked how things were going. "I'm starting to get used to the sleep deprivation. In the beginning it was hard for me, I guess a little harder than I thought. Howard's been amazing. He does everything but breastfeed."

A few times Allison expressed surprise that Howard was better at comforting the baby than she was. He said:

It's frustrating for Allison. It hurt her so much for the first three weeks she had to take care of her breasts after nursing. So I'm the one who walks with the baby and rocks her. I will do whatever it takes to make her happy.

The Pearlmans passed through the first six weeks absolutely together, equally in love with their daughter. Howard knew that when he returned to work, Allison would not sit on the couch all day eating bonbons. They talked about each working a four-day week when Allison's maternity leave ended, to reduce the amount of time they spent away from their daughter and limit baby-sitting to three days a week.

I checked in on Allison a month later. During Howard's first week back at work, Allison and Rosamond had visited Allison's parents. Howard didn't see the baby for six days, returning to his old life. Baby Rosamond got easier, and decided she liked the pacifier after all. Allison told me:

Howard's definitely out of baby mode. He's a little freaked out and doesn't know how to think of me now that I'm a mother. He tells me I need to go back to work.

I'm a lot more competent now. We got mobile. I learned how to put her in the car seat when I'm eating. I put her down now because I have to. I did the bath myself because I had to. When Howard comes home, he plays with her and I do what I need to do in the house. I realized it wasn't making the baby happy for Howard to carry her around all the time. She prefers to suck.

Of course, I don't want him throwing her around. I read up on it, and he'll give her a detached retina.

The other thing is, he wants to go out to dinner and leave the baby with our next-door neighbor. Howard says, "Don't worry, a fourteen-year-old can watch an infant." But I wasn't sure I could do it myself a couple of weeks ago.

Allison stopped nursing at four months because she couldn't produce enough milk. During the remaining two months of her maternity leave, the gulf between Howard and Allison, and their relative expertise with and attachment to Rosamond, widened. The Pearlmans adopted polarized points of view: about how much child care to hire and whether to keep Rosamond up late to see her dad. Howard never asked for a flexible schedule at work. He refused to alter the time he starts and ends his job, and left all the family's mental, and most of the physical, baby responsibilities to Mom when she returned to work. Allison switched to a four-day schedule and hired a full-time nanny, though she desperately wanted Rosamond to spend only three days a week without her parents.

Despite Howard's time at home:

- Allison became a gatekeeper, doling out access to the baby and critiquing her husband.
- Allison became more involved in the child than Howard did and the child became her responsibility. She became "the expert."
- As a result of her greater investment in the baby, Allison preferred less substitute care and a higher standard of care than Howard did.
- Howard retreated into work. He began to see Allison's attachment to Rosamond as an obstacle, rather than as something he shared.

This couple reverted to traditional roles, not because of any gender-based predisposition to nurture or provide but because of how they had predetermined their participation, and because Howard never got a chance to do anything alone. They had agreed to share in everything and did, until he went back to work. Suddenly, Howard found himself very much out of the picture and, he often said, depressed at not seeing his daughter during the week.

When Allison returned to work, she gave up her decade-old daily exercise routine, came home for lunch most days, and took over all the grocery shopping. She stopped into my office after she had been back at work for six weeks and asked, "I have the greatest nanny in the world. I'm working part time. My daughter is such a good baby. Why am I not happy?"

Had the Pearlmans used their eight months (combined) at home differently, every family member would have benefited. Howard could have cured his depression by spending time with his daughter. Allison could have carved out much-needed time and space for herself. Baby Rosamond would have gotten more of what she wants and needs, too.

STRATEGIES FOR SHARING
MATERNITY AND PATERNITY LEAVES

Dual-income families who want to share parenting ought to consider staggering maternity and paternity leaves. Michael Selmi has written extensively about family leave and the gender wage gap. He advises:

> Women and men should not share their time at home, they should stagger it. That's better for the child—that way the child can stay home with his or her parents for longer. Shared time will still be mother's time, for the most part.
>
> If both parents are home, my sense is—and research shows— that men will tend to do some work stuff. Some men will work in their shop, on their cars—they don't do actual kid focus. When they're home with a child, they don't really have any choice. They have to be more dedicated to the child.

Selmi, a George Washington University Law School professor, took a fourteen-month sabbatical, beginning when his daughter was four months old. He noticed an immediate difference in his ability when his wife went back to work.

> My wife wasn't bad about giving instruction, but I did feel like I was being watched. When I was on my own, I was freer to do what I wanted. I let my daughter do a lot of things her mother wouldn't let her do. Climbing on stuff. She never got hurt. When she thought it was dangerous, she would stop. I did stuff that wasn't by the book. We just did different things.

Staggering leaves also worked well for Lynne and Guy Swanson. After the birth of their first child, Guy took a couple of days off.

Lynne stayed home for seven weeks, and then went back to work two days a week for a month. On her workdays, Guy used paternity leave and took care of their daughter. When Lynn returned to a full-time schedule, he took two more weeks off. Guy says:

> I'm pretty proud and happy that I did that, took the time to be with my first-born child for a while. You only get the opportunity once. My wife was upset because the baby always seemed to sleep more for me. I'd give her a bottle, play with her for an hour, and then put her in her swing, and she would sleep for four hours.
>
> It was actually a great break for me from my job, which was very stressful. Of course, they weren't thrilled about my taking the leave, but it was available and other people started taking it after I did.

Stagger paternity leave so that the husband gets a booster course of on-the-job training *after* the mother goes back to work. That way, he won't fall too far behind and will learn how to do whatever has to get done. Ideally, the father should also stay home during the initial siege when the reality of twenty-four-hour care of a tiny human being sets in. He will better appreciate what child care entails. Even if Dad does not have access to long or paid paternity leave, strategically staking out some time for him at the end of Mom's maternity leave, or on weekends, will yield great results.

Alternating leaves prevents that "inevitable" inequality from occurring. By putting in time at the right point, Guy Swanson developed the same level of expertise with his child as his wife did. Provide the time for father and baby to be together, and the bond between them will do the rest.

WHAT HE CAN DO
There's nothing a dad can't do, except lactate. Even here he can come close by feeding a bottle of expressed milk, or formula if the baby does not nurse. Men can and should, if at all possible (and it's possible if you want it to be), do the following:

- participate in choosing a pediatrician;
- attend prenatal sonograms;
- learn how to perform physical baby care and feeding;

- research paternity and parental leave options;
- take whatever leave is available, even if it is unpaid;
- attend the birth;
- diaper the baby before leaving the hospital;
- hold and touch the baby as much as possible;
- regularly spend time alone with the baby; and
- do everything the baby needs done.

In a 2000 Oxygen/Markle Pulse poll, American men reported that the most significant barrier to taking paternity leave is not that they don't value their roles as fathers or that workplace issues prevent them, but that they don't want to lose income.[14] Informed families, led by prepared mothers-to-be, can plan to forego the father's salary for a discrete period of time, just as they've been doing with the mother's. It will be a worthwhile investment. Providing the time and opportunity for dads to get involved in the early months will do more to change the division of labor, and conflict and stress levels, at home than any other strategy women might employ.

Divide and Conquer
Your New Roles   9 ▓▓▓▓

We're constantly sitting down with each other and tinkering
with the schedule of who is going to do what in a
given time period. It's an ongoing process.

—Mike King

SHE WHO HESITATES GETS TOO MUCH TO DO

Prospective mothers who don't want to do it all themselves must divvy up household and baby responsibilities *before* the baby arrives. Otherwise, they will likely join the more than two thirds of new parents in conflict over their roles.[1] Dr. Pamela Jordan, author of *Becoming Parents: How to Strengthen Your Marriage As Your Family Grows,* recommends that pregnant couples discuss their vision of parenting roles.

> Couples will likely find that their expectations, which emerge from their underlying values and beliefs, differ significantly. The couple then needs to sit down and negotiate how they want things to be in their family and their lives and develop strategies to make it so.
>
> It takes a couple working as a team. But the effort is so well worth it! It results in greater satisfaction with life and with the couple relationship, and, usually, two more happy and healthy people (mentally and physically) who can be more effective parents and workers.

The mothers I interviewed who created more equal arrangements gave similar counsel:

Rebecca Powell: "Discuss what you both want in a relationship and in parenthood. Down to the details of who will change the diapers when."

Lynne Swanson: "Don't get pregnant until you both are agreed, specifically, as to what you will do."

Dierdre Davis: "Work it out ahead of time. Talk about your expectations before you have the baby."

Ann King: "Plan to get men involved early. If I had to do it over again, I would divide the care of the baby more from the beginning."

Janey Berk: "If you're doing the traditional parenting, or doing the nontraditional, it's really important to figure out together what your roles and expectations are going to be."

Identify, reconcile, and plot out your desired roles before becoming parents. You won't be able to use your leverage for a long time, and it may never rise to pre-baby levels again. You'll have to stay put for a little while if not forever, so make sure you've set up the home you want.

TAKING CARE OF THE BAGGAGE

Perhaps you think you and your mate are so compatible, or egalitarian, that all this conflict over who does what at home and out in the world won't happen to you.[2] In Berkeley psychology professors Carolyn Pape Cowan and Philip Cowan's study of the transition to parenthood, a majority of couples predicted they would share the care of their baby much more equally than they shared their housework and family tasks before they became parents.[3] But when the couples had babies, even those who previously split household responsibilities experienced a marked disparity in male and female efforts at home. Mothers became upset, and conflict erupted, the Cowans concluded, not only because of uneven roles, but also as a result of the discrepancy between reality and the expectations both spouses held before having children.[4]

Forewarned is forearmed: Protect yourself in advance. The difference between those who get stuck in the Mommy Trap and those who go around it: Those who avoid the Mommy Trap set up flexible, personalized roles, and don't fall into traditional stereotypes.

Put some mechanisms in place so you don't come through the transition disappointed.

To avoid the default into the past:

- Make yourself aware of the tendency to revert to how your own family, culture, and most others divide parenting.
- Confront and reconcile your mutual expectations, taking into account your current career situations and personal ambitions.
- Make a pact that having a baby will not unbalance the equilibrium you have achieved so far, and that you will both make adjustments to your arrangement, if necessary.

Work actively against the distancing of fathers from children and home. If you do not, standard employment arrangements, society, and even trusted relatives will push you into outdated choices.

THE TIME OF YOUR LIFE

Remember from chapter 8 the importance of how you decide to divide your efforts during the early months. Second, and also crucial, come career, family, housework, and leisure time after parental leave ends. Make no assumptions that the way everybody else sets up their life will work for you—it's not working for most of them!

Talk to seasoned parents to see what new tasks both of you will need to take on. Figure out, together, how you will allocate these jobs, taking into account current responsibilities and respective strengths and weaknesses. Plot out a typical workday and weekend day with baby, considering everything the baby, house, and parents need done. Make sure to create a twenty-four-hour schedule, with a provisional agreement about waking up at night to feed, comfort, and change the baby, and getting up early in the morning.

If you cringe at the thought of making a list of all possible chores (as I do), including all the boring details about laundry, cooking, shopping, bill paying, and the like, there is a way out. Couples succeed best in apportioning responsibilities more equally when they allot men periods of time in charge at home, alone. Then, dads learn to keep the household going and the child content without maternal assistance or supervision.

Mom doesn't leave instructions or telephone to give guidance about junior. Dad has to deal with the situation on his own. If you do it any other way, the man becomes the helper or subcontractor, and guess who gets promoted to management, with the ultimate responsibility for seeing or doing anything that needs to get done?

Stay-at-home mothers can also make use of this method. In chapter 4, we met Jennifer and Joe, who had agreed to put in an equal effort at home in the first difficult months, even though he worked and she stayed home. She did most of the baby care, and he did most else in the beginning. He didn't retreat into work but instead took on much of the managerial, shopping, and household responsibilities that come with new babies. Because they plotted out the time and effort their new chores would require, Jennifer and Joe had a positive experience, together. They marveled at the joy and wonder of their son, Alex, both feeling lucky and appreciated.

THE GOOD, THE BAD, AND THE MESSY

A helpful hint when dividing and conquering: With child care comes house care! Whoever spends more time with the baby ends up doing more housework. As new tasks originate, the parent at home will likely take them on.

In addition to the satisfaction of watching their infants blossom, often women on maternity leave gain the dissatisfaction of seeing their domestic responsibilities balloon. (Remember, from chapter 8, Allison Pearlman's maternity-leave experience.) Consider the area of laundry. Say a couple has always split their laundry: Whoever can do it, does it. Then they have a baby. Mom spends three months at home. While doing baby's (voluminous) wash, a new task she has just taken on without thinking about it, she throws in the rest of the laundry, too. One evening, Dad tries to wash the baby's clothes, but instead of choosing Dreft or Ivory, he uses the stuff for mere mortals. She barks, and he doesn't try again, giving up his prior laundry responsibilities as well.

Perhaps this couple also used to share grocery shopping. The family needs some new diapers. Monitoring the Pampers became Mom's job since she's more intimately acquainted with them. While at the supermarket, she buys the food for the week, too.

Maybe they always shared cooking, or went out (not always a good idea, now). Since she's home, Mom has started to cook the

> ### ∎ Bring in
> ### a Third Party
>
> In addition to splitting the pie, reduce it. Whenever possible,
> pay someone to do the tasks neither of you likes to do,
> particularly during the early months. Outsourcing will result
> in money well spent and arguments well missed.

dinners. It makes more sense that way, and she's often very hungry. Her husband might even "baby-sit" while she makes the dinner, to give her a break.

Look at all the extra chores and mental responsibilities the mother has taken on without thinking. Further, because of her greater investment in the child, when she goes back to work, if she does, she may well cut back on her schedule or make whatever extra time she can for the baby.

What I just outlined happens every day. But not to Ann King, Rebecca Powell, or Lynne Swanson, because they planned to pool their resources from the start.

WHO SAYS YOU'RE THE ONE WHO HAS TO COOK?
Women fall into the Mommy Trap when they make assumptions about what each sex does. Let go of these stereotypes. Instead, ask who has the time, inclination, or talent to perform a particular task. A mother should not do all the cooking because she thinks only females prepare meals, especially if her husband wants to cook and can produce edible fare. Say good-bye to those ideals that create unnecessary dichotomies and extra female work, and say hello to practical solutions.

Cindy, a scientist whose husband stays home with their two teenagers, does 30 percent of the parenting and household work while her husband does 70 percent. They arrived at this arrangement by taking into account their abilities, interests, and schedules. Cindy explains:

There are certain things that he prefers that I do, like overseeing homework, or a school project, going over something
special. He thinks I'm better at it than he is, and that's probably true. I am more detail oriented. I still do the grocery shopping. I have been unable to give that up, much as I'd like to.
He'll come home with just anything, if something specific is
not there. Either one of us will do the laundry. He does most of
the cooking.

I haven't done a whole lot of housework in a while, and I
don't mind. I do the bills. It's not his thing. It's more mine.
Things have just worked their way out.

This mother describes herself as very satisfied with the division
of responsibility in her household. So did everybody interviewed
who created roles based on talent, desires, practicality, and fairness.

PUT A CONTRACT ON YOUR LIFE

Some parents have gone so far as to record their responsibilities in
a document. Creating and resorting to "the contract" formed a key
part of the Berk family's departure from the Mommy Trap. As you'll
see in chapter 12, they decided that Ira would cut back at work and
spend most of the week at home. Ira remembers:

We sat down with the contract and put down what my responsibilities would be and what my wife expected from me.
And also what I expected from my wife, being that she was
going to be out in the real world every day and I was going to
be home every day. And what our roles and expectations were
going to be.

We both signed it. In the first six months, we did go back to
it every once in a while and we looked at, "Yeah, you're supposed to do that" type of thing. It helped a lot to have everything written down.

The Berks gave Ira the title of "household manager" and put in
a section that said he would get "a break every once in a while."
When it didn't happen at first, Ira pulled out the contract and Janey
agreed that he was entitled to time away from the family, and arranged for him to have it. By anticipating the potential problems
attendant to devoting himself to the kids and house exclusively, Ira
made sure they didn't occur.

Janey says:

> I know a lot of stay-at-home mothers who are resentful because it wasn't a choice. It didn't just happen to us. It was what we both decided would be a good thing to do. It's worked because the whole thing was a choice. We asked how much time should I be working, how much time he would need off. We both made a good arrangement that was fair. Just the act of talking everything through helped: not just trying it, writing it down. There was no assumption of what either of us would do.

The Berks' contract may seem like an extreme measure. But talking about and writing down expectations can start the process of creating customized roles. And having a record of the conversation can preempt discussion later on about what either spouse said or intended.

VALUE YOURSELF

Do not presume that only mothers can make an accommodation for children. You must certainly consider income, but don't let it become the excuse for a lopsided division that makes everyone miserable. Women's fulfillment, and even recreation, should count for something, too. If you do not assign Mom's personal satisfaction a value in the beginning, later on it will become an issue. Dr. Robert Wohlfort, psychologist, pastor, and couples' workshop leader, has seen it happen over and over again.

> There's only so much time, there's only so many years with the kids, and some hard decisions do need to be made. What's going to happen is if someone gives up something important, it's going to come back and bite. I worry that people make compromises too soon sometimes, without really thinking things through.

While domesticity might seem romantic when envisioning a life away from the rat race, statistics show stay-at-home mothers more vulnerable to depression than mothers who do paid work. Although working mothers feel (and are) overstretched, a National Institutes of Health study found women who work for pay or otherwise combine life roles happier and healthier than those who don't.[5] Be careful before throwing career or personal aspirations away.

Here's an example of how a more personalized strategy worked for me and my family: When my daughter Elizabeth was seventeen months old, my mother became unable to baby-sit for even the sixteen-hours-a-week schedule to which I had cut back. She had recovered from an earlier operation, and then seven months later had a hysterectomy and needed time to recuperate.

Before getting pregnant, I had made a deal with my husband that his career would take precedence for three years. He had accepted a prestigious but hours-inflexible fellowship in reliance on our agreement. While I wanted to put our daughter first, I knew I needed my own identity apart from the house and family. I wanted time to work on a writing project I'd started (which became this book). Our experience of each of us taking care of Elizabeth alone, and then deciding not to use a substantial amount of paid child care, told us that raising our daughter was more important and harder than working for pay.

When my mother had to stop baby-sitting, I offered the following: I would quit my job as long as my husband didn't think he was getting a traditional housewife. I couldn't be that. I said I would cook dinner two or three times a week. And when he was home at night and on the weekends, I asked that he take charge of Elizabeth, so I could have time for myself.

A year and a half after giving birth, I had learned to divide the responsibilities before agreeing to anything. I thought about the type of job description that would work for my needs, as well as those of our family. Then I told my husband what I envisioned. Grateful to me for taking care of our daughter, he had no objection to the "work conditions" I suggested. Ed did say he would like a weeknight for himself, to go to happy hour, run, or do nothing, to which I readily agreed. I stayed home for three years and gave our daughter the very best I had to give.

I will always treasure the days the two of us had looking for fun wherever we could find it—Tuesday story hour, the lobster tank at the supermarket, or just walking down the street—and growing and developing so much along the way. Ed's involvement at home allowed me the space I needed for adult pursuits and "psychological relief." He became a working dad with a complete life, and created a super close relationship with his daughter.

In our discussions before I quit my job, I also laid the groundwork for returning to my profession. My husband promised that when Elizabeth turned three, he would start to work flexibly or stay home. Because I had a high aspiration level, Ed agreed to participate more in the family than most of the other dads we knew. As nice as he is, I have no doubt that had I not valued my time, our life would have looked very different.

AREAS TO WATCH FOR
Certain tasks seem to elude fathers. These barriers result from old assumptions about the sanctity of men's role as providers, and "traditional" functions of mothers. Very early on, make clear (to yourself and to him) that Dad can participate in every aspect of parenting.

Waking Up at Night to Feed Baby
Devise a plan for *both* parents to get some sleep during the first few months when the baby wakes up at night. *Dads can feed an expressed bottle of breast milk or formula, burp, change or walk with a baby in the middle of the night.* Often, parents offer the following rationale for a father's not doing so: "He has to get up for work tomorrow. He can't be tired."

Look at the respective responsibilities here. One has a twenty-four-hour-a-day, physically and emotionally grueling job (vital to the survival of the species) and just went through severe physical trauma, if not an operation. The other has, at most, a twelve- to fifteen-hour shift, which may or may not have any social importance. Need I say more?

Arranging for Baby-Sitting or Day Care
Beware of this area. Once a mother becomes responsible for setting up time without baby, the rest of the baby's time falls into her lap as well. During maternity leave, arranging for child care often devolves to Mom, who has to find a replacement for herself when and if she returns to work.[6] Make sure this does not happen. Dad can telephone references, check out child-care centers, and interview baby-sitters. He can also do some research about the benefits and disadvantages of child care and what makes for good care.

Even Rebecca Powell and Darrell Smith ("the quiz parents") skirmished over this issue. He wanted a back-up in case a meeting came up when Rebecca was at work. She did not have a work need for it, and had concluded that most emergency child care is of poor quality. When he told her that they really needed emergency day care, Rebecca said, "Well, if you find a good situation, that's fine."

Darrell looked around, and didn't locate a place he felt comfortable putting their son at the last moment. When he thought concretely rather than in the abstract about the problem, and took responsibility for handing over his offspring, he reacted the same way Rebecca did.

Staggering paternity and maternity leaves provides men a great opportunity to get involved in the management and emotion attendant to using substitute care, giving them a stake and interest in the issue. Because Guy Swanson was home during the time their son started day care, *he* checked the situation out.

> The "probation" monitoring became my responsibility by virtue of the timing. Lynne took her leave first, then me. I watched for signs of laziness and bad temper. I also popped in unannounced several times. I didn't see any red flags and the arrangement has lasted for four years now.

Men can do all these tasks as well as women do, as long as they get the chance.

Doctor's Appointments

In the first few months, taking baby to the doctor provides much needed social interaction and a report card on how you and he or she are doing. After the newborn appointment, Dad usually goes back to work and Mom takes on this responsibility forever after. Even if Dad goes to more than one appointment, he may never go alone. If the mother returns to work, she will probably be the one who carves out time from her personal life or misses work for regular and sick appointments. As a result, her productivity, advancement, and enjoyment at work may suffer.

In many families where mothers take on the role of primary breadwinner, or parents share child care, both parents go to their children's checkups. They make it a family affair. And as long as Dad gets his time in charge, he will gladly take a child to the doctor if he or she gets sick. Either Ann or Mike King brings Maggie to the doctor when she has to go, depending on their schedules.

Dads can take their children to the doctors, same as they take themselves. Worried that he'll forget something? He might. Let him correct it, and he'll remember next time.

Sick Days

Generally, women take time off when their children get sick and men do not.[7] Having to take time off unexpectedly at work poses a large problem for parents whose children attend day care, where they get sick more often than when placed in other arrangements.

I watched this issue dampen the career aspirations of my friend Susan. After she had used all her sick time taking care of their son, William, her husband, Bob, had to stay home with him when he got sick at day care. Bob's employer provides unlimited sick days, which employees may use to care for ill children, but Bob was too embarrassed to admit he stayed home with a sick child, and too honest to say he was sick himself. As a result, Susan explained:

> Our family didn't get to go on vacation last year because my husband used all of his vacation days to take care of our son, who had a terrible winter. First he got whooping cough, and then a whole bunch of ear infections, and finally the tube operation. Even after that, he still kept catching colds.
>
> We really needed a break. Now I do part-time consulting projects for a temporary executive agency. If someone gets sick, I can call in at the last minute. Of course, I don't get paid if I don't go in. It's worth it to have the flexibility. On my day off, I do all the errands and housework I used to do on the weekends. It's just a tradeoff I had to make. But sometimes it makes me so mad I had to give up my career just because Bob didn't feel he could ask for what he's entitled to.

Using old gender stereotypes for a new family situation pushed Susan into the Mommy Trap, engendering resentment along the way. Set out a fair policy before you have children that deals with what happens when and if they fall ill, and stick with it.

Household Administrator

Mothers seem to vent most often about the mental overload of managing everybody's schedules and the household. Even when dads share child care, women can still get stuck with more house and child management than they would like. But if couples consider natural talents, and provide time for men in charge, more equal arrangements result. Now that his sabbatical is over, for example, law professor Mike Selmi does 30 to 40 percent of the child care, but 60 to 70 percent of the household work. He does the cooking and shopping, takes the kids to day care, and generally runs the household.

The child social secretary function also usually becomes Mom's responsibility, a daily, thankless job. A few tricks:

- Set up a family calendar.
- Don't remind your husband of anything on the calendar.
- Parcel out responsibilities in advance, including scheduling.
- Do not step in if Dad fails to do what he is supposed to do.
- Let him identify the problem and remedy it himself.

You might consider linking up Palm Pilots or other hand-held-computer scheduling devices, as one couple I interviewed does. An Internet mogul with an involved husband explains her methods:

> I have to try to not do everything. It's keeping my mouth shut and trying to just decide, "Okay, I'm going to be helpful, I'm going to be clear, but not take this on."
>
> I've been trying to do that with my husband in scheduling kinds of things. I say, "You do it, just tell me what happens, of course, but you do it, and I can't redo it if you do it the way I don't like it.

In chapters 10 and 11, we'll get into more strategies for letting go. Moms need lots of practice in giving their husbands full rein, even to make mistakes!

Play Dates

Women often end up arranging for and overseeing their children's social lives. Here, again, Dad's time in charge helps. Catherine, a little girl in our neighborhood, rides around on her bicycle, ringing doorbells until she finds a kid available to play. When she rang ours, and Ed opened the door, he started arranging times with her mother for her to come by. Presto.

Buying Child-Related Items and Presents; Taking Kids to and Planning Parties

Most women retain all of these functions, unless Dad stays home or has regular time slots in charge. Don't assume fathers can't get involved in these areas. They can perform all these tasks. You may even benefit from having a male perspective. Having been a boy himself, Mike King selects presents a mother would not choose, which young boys reportedly love.

IF AT FIRST YOU DON'T SUCCEED

While dividing chores or time rigidly can work as an overall approach, maintain a bit of flexibility, too. It's best to do this procedurally.

- Set in place a regular mechanism for reevaluating your situation, and to deal with issues and problems as they arise.
- Make mutual promises that you will take the necessary steps to rebalance any disequilibrium or discontent that occurs.

When Ann King was pregnant with Maggie, she and Mike spent hours at the kitchen table planning what they thought they would have to do when the baby was born. At six weeks postpartum, they realized they hadn't understood the workload involved, or how penned in Ann would feel. They had decided that because Ann would breastfeed, she would do the baby care and Mike would work on projects for the house.

Tired all the time, Ann needed a change of scenery, and time away from the baby. They sat down and renegotiated time for Mike with Maggie, which he craved, and for Ann to exercise. Ann remembers:

> It wasn't so great in the beginning. I was with the baby all the time and he worked on the house. We had agreed we'd see how things work out and what needed to be changed. We have a weekly meeting where we discuss what's going on in the

family and at work, how everything is going. He was wanting to spend time with her but he didn't want to interfere with the nursing. So I joined a gym and it saved my life. Literally. I've got to work out or I go insane.

Always give yourself an out, an ability to reconsider. Hammering out a built-in review process during a higher BATNA period (remember—that's before baby comes) insures mothers don't become too disadvantaged during a low BATNA period. It also levels out men's BATNA, by preventing an uneven attachment between the sexes and their offspring. And, taking the long view, it will put men in better health, closer parent-child relationships, and happier marriages.

BUILD ADAPTABILITY INTO THE PLAN

In chapters 6 and 7, I emphasized the importance of securing two flexible jobs before baby comes along. Remember, in today's happy marriages, both partners make adjustments for the family. Flexibility at work and home enables couples to adapt to changing circumstances, whether they result from physical or economic need, career opportunities, burnout, changed desires, or time passing. This elasticity requires new skills, which your own parents probably didn't have to develop. Communication, a key element of any collaborative effort (and particularly marriage), becomes even more important.

In the Cowans' support groups for expectant parents, they emphasize the need to understand that things may and probably will change. The Cowans help parents adopt the expectation that they will have to make adjustments to suit their particular family needs as they go along. Carolyn Cowan says:

It doesn't mean even if you worked something out together that this solution or arrangement that you decided on will work all the time. And so, you have to be prepared to go back to the drawing board, so to speak. Or at least have some kind of arrangement so that you have a forum to talk about it when you have a really bad week, or month, or period where you're wondering whether what you're doing still makes sense. We call it taking an experimental attitude.

The one sure thing about kids is that they change every day. Whether because of unrealistic expectations of life as parents, rigid career demands, or gender stereotypes, remaining fixed in thinking or action often leads to the Mommy Trap. Modern couples who create happy unions take on different roles at different times, each adapting their efforts when necessary for the collective good.

IF YOU ALREADY
HAVE KIDS

Getting Unstuck **10**

> I sat down with my husband and told him I was not happy
> doing so much for the family and the house, and nothing for
> me. We made a list of our responsibilities and I was doing or
> overseeing eighty-five percent of them. Seeing it on paper
> made it real to him. So did my matter-of-fact tone. When I
> stopped yelling and complaining, he finally started to get it.
>
> —Rachel, a fifty-two-year-old Fortune 100 marketing
> specialist and mother of two teenagers

THE FIRST DAY OF THE REST OF YOUR LIFE

Didn't plan ahead? Don't worry. Although it may seem that you'll
never leave your current rut of resentment, overextension, or lack
of fulfillment, you can. To get out of the Mommy Trap, you must
first identify the areas you would like to change.

Make an assessment of your life as it stands now. Include personal and professional fulfillment, marital and parent-child relationships, and satisfaction with any and all care and educational
arrangements. Write down your concerns about your children, marriage, division of household labor, and personal situation.

Is your life the way you expected? Is your child's life the best you
and your husband could make it? Who comes first in your house?
Who or what should take priority? How has your marriage changed
since you've had children? What could improve?

Look at the decisions you made about when and how to get
married and have children. Analyze the points where you made

▌ Mommy Trap
Diagnosis

You are in the Mommy Trap if:

- You have an ongoing argument with your partner about who does what in the house, out in the world, or with your children.
- You have little or no personal time.
- You resent your husband for not making the same accommodations you have made, or for not doing as much, for the family.
- Your life seems to be all work and no fun.
- You would prefer another caregiver or care arrangement.
- You think your children would do better with more time at home or with the family.
- Your job, or your husband's, takes up too much time and or causes too much stress, preventing your family from getting the attention you think it needs.
- Every so often you flare up at your husband over a trivial incident, and complain about all you do.
- When your husband tries to help, you critique him or take over when he doesn't do it right.
- You have a hard time thinking of any child- or house-related task you could relinquish.

---

unconscious assumptions about what mothers and fathers, or women and men, should do. See whether you agree with those presumptions in the light of day.

Assume that no time or money constraints exist. Think about how you would like your life to be, and what would make it better. Then figure out how you can make the most critical of those changes happen. Always remember that high aspirations translate into success and low goals lead to failure.

BUSTING OUT

To make changes, you will have to stop doing what everybody else does, no longer accepting resignation and complaint as the only means of dealing with the Mommy Trap. Follow the lead of any acquaintances who have forged different arrangements, rather than commiserating with those who are also stuck. Take such couples as Ann and Mike King, Rebecca Smith and Darrell Powell, and Lynne and Guy Swanson as the new parenting role models.

Refer back to chapters 4 through 9 to see where you may have gone wrong. Do whatever legwork you can now to set up a better parenting structure, starting with figuring out your gender ideologies. Talk with your husband, calmly, about his expectations, desires, and satisfaction with the situation, as well as your own. Consider this phase a fact-finding and consensus-building exercise. You don't need to solve anything right away.

Validate your husband's experience and reality. By now, I'm sure you understand that it's not his fault you took on everything you did. You both made choices that led you to the Mommy Trap. Showing that you have heard your husband will increase your ability to persuade him of your point of view.[1] In addition, listening to your partner constitutes the cheapest, and often the most effective, concession you can make in negotiation.[2] Sometimes people just want to know that they've been heard, and sometimes they want something different than you think they do.

Where your gender ideology, experience, and desires differ, try to reconcile them, nicely. Mary Clayton found a conversation about parenting roles invaluable in starting the process to reclaim her professional and personal identity.

The day things started to change was the day Mark and I talked about our families growing up. His mother was so traditional, some part of him deep down inside thought women should stay home, and be happy about it. When I suggested he should have married someone like his mother, he said he didn't want that, he wanted an equal. I told him the price for having a wife with a career was that he couldn't just dictate how things would be, that he wasn't the head of the family like his father was. He took some time over this, but he agreed in theory. After a while, he put theory into practice.

If you can't even begin to talk about your expectations and desires without arguing, solicit outside help. Try couples' therapy, a relationship workshop, or the Enrich marital inventory-based program for married couples (see Resources section in the back of this book for more information). Get a baby-sitter and go. One way or the other, you must short-circuit the repetitive arguments and conversation you've been having.

You must change the tenor of the conversation from "me versus you" or "men versus women" to *us*, and how *we* can approach and solve the problem of our family going forward together. To that end, pick up some active-listening skills wherever you can. Dr. Robert Wohlfort counsels couples "not just to listen, but rather take your spouse in. Be him or her. See it from their point of view. As long as someone doesn't hear you, you never get to any sort of problem solving."

Better communication will facilitate the resolution of issues and put an end to any destructive relational patterns that have probably crept in by now. If you didn't put in all the preparation that can smooth the transition to parenthood before you started a family, do as much as you can now.

CHANGE YOUR BENCHMARK

Couples who get out of the complaint mode discard inherited stereotypes of the male provider and female nurturer. *Change your benchmark from standards set by your parents or other parents; create your own standards when figuring out how to provide what your family needs, striking a balance that satisfies both partners.*

Getting rid of the constraints of rigid gender roles opens up a world of possible alternatives. Ultimately, women's altered perspectives affect men's ideas, too. However, mothers must acknowledge their husbands' positions that today's men do a lot because they participate so much more than their own fathers did. Dr. Jay Belsky, who has studied the interaction of parents for years, explains:

> Fathers and mothers have different points of comparison. She's comparing him to her. He is comparing himself to other men. I think she has to appreciate that worldview difference if she wants it to become more like she wants it. Because if the message is "you do so much more I'm sure than your father ever did" as opposed to "you're not doing anything," that will encourage him. Rewards work better than punishment.

Appreciating men's points of view doesn't mean you agree. But validating your husband's experience is a necessary step toward creating a joint problem-solving process. To that end, Rhona Mahony, author of *Kidding Ourselves: Breadwinning, Babies, and Bargaining Power,* recommends that women doing more than their share emulate Rachel, who is quoted at the beginning of this chapter. Together, draw up a list of who does what family work. In different colors, highlight the contribution of the mother, father, and any paid or unpaid help. In a non-accusatory fashion, she suggests:

- Tell your husband how miserable or tired you are.
- Choose vivid words and phrases.
- Describe the division of labor in your household.
- Talk about issues of fairness and partnership.
- Remind him of your stated goals of marriage and life before you had children.[3]

Assuming a basically loving, not completely traditional husband, he may just hear you for the first time. Rachel's husband did, but only after she stopped flaring up when she felt overwhelmed. Timing is important. Arrange a mutually convenient time to discuss the issue, rather than forcing it down his throat during an argument (see "One Small Step for Mankind," below).

Comparing mothers' and fathers' efforts can facilitate a fairer allocation of household and child responsibilities for at-home parents, as Mary Clayton learned. She frequently argued to her husband, Mark, that he ought to compare his parenting contribution to hers, and not to his father's or other fathers'. While he worked full time and she stayed home, she reasoned, he could never spend as much time with their son as she did. Mary asked Mark to switch to a compressed four-day work schedule and to telecommute one day a week so she could have two weekdays to spend at the campus, teaching and attending meetings.

Mark refused, but offered to be "on-duty" whenever he was home (the good old "door-in-the-face theory" from chapter 4 at work). When their son, Jeffrey, stopped nursing at six months, Mark started getting up with him in the morning, changing his diaper and feeding him breakfast before leaving for work. When he returned in the evening, Mark took over for Mary and gave Jeffrey a bath. She went out running, did things for herself, or spent time with Jeffrey and Mark, if she felt like it. When I asked whether he resented the time spent with Jeffrey, when he might otherwise be blowing off steam, Mark said, "No, it's the opposite. I won't let anyone encroach on my time with Jeffrey, not even my wife. We do guy things together. He's a very fun kid."

Contrary to what others might expect, and Mark initially expected, he does not bristle at the arrangement. Instead, he took to his child like any parent who has the opportunity will—with the greatest pleasure in the world.

ONE SMALL STEP FOR MANKIND

The way the Claytons resolved the issue provides an example of the big, macro, door-in-the-face approach. You may also need to use the foot-in-the-door method (see chapter 4) to slowly chip away at the established order of Mom doing too much. Couples with older children who have a long-standing history of lopsided efforts at home find this step essential. Start by asking a father who resists the idea of taking on major parenting responsibilities to do discrete tasks.

Set up a time to talk, with nobody around and nothing to do. Sit down together, literally on the same side of a table. Create an atmosphere of cohesion rather than divisiveness.

Do not complain or say anything about the global order of your lives. Instead, initiate a calm conversation about a single item you would like your husband to take on. Think of what would make your life easier: where you could most use some help and where Dad might easily provide it. Ask your husband to take on a task or time period, and nothing more. Cede *one* block of time, activity, or chore with your children or household.

Even dads who work long hours can find the time, as long as a specific, reasonable request is made, rather than a lament or an attack. One law firm partner takes his eighteen-month-old daughter to music class every Saturday. She beams from ear to ear for the entire class. Another father gets up with his son every morning at six-thirty and takes him to the local Starbucks where he gulps some much-needed caffeine and the baby smiles at the other regulars. Rachel's husband, a physician, began proudly helping their teenage son with his math and biology homework every weekend once she asked him to take over that task.

Your husband will be relieved (and surprised) to hear that you would like him to do just one tiny thing to help out. Let him know that research shows he can make a tremendous difference to his children. Dad will quickly warm to the idea that he can make his own unique, valuable contribution. Make him feel good by referring to something he does well with the kids, that you do not do as well.

At this point in time, you have to give him permission to take on the tasks not traditionally associated with males, especially now since you've run so many laps past him already. Encourage him, nicely. Otherwise, nothing will change.

While it may seem like more work for Dad, stress that actually he will have more fun, your marriage will improve, and that you will appreciate him more. He will feel more important at home, and closer to his children and to you. As long as you stay rational and start small, you're sure to succeed.

A word of caution: Do not give up on larger-scale change just because you got your foot in the door. This is only the beginning. Continue, as Mary Clayton did, to ask for the moon and the stars. It's the only way you'll get it.

LETTING GO IS HARD TO DO
Okay, so now he's ready to take on one new chore, perhaps the nightly bath. Watch out here! Often mothers become their own worst enemies in achieving paternal participation. Have you ever known a micromanager at work who has problems delegating responsibility? Many in the Mommy Trap will have such issues at the outset.

What might happen now? George Martling describes an early effort to get involved:

> One day I came home and tried to give Dan a bath. Lauren had to show me how. As if I haven't been having baths for the past forty years. The next night she let me do it myself. She stayed close to the bathroom, listening to my every move. Dan got shampoo in his eyes and cried. She ran in and pushed me out of the way and started wiping his eyes. She said I couldn't

do the baths because I always get shampoo in his eyes. That's fine with me. I watch TV instead.

In their study of the transition to parenthood, discussed in chapters 8 and 9, Carolyn Pape Cowan and Philip Cowan found that it takes very little implied criticism before fathers hand their baby back to "the expert."[4] Nobody likes to feel incompetent, especially men! In a Catch-22 situation, fathers can take on child- and home-care responsibilities only if they develop competence. Yet mothers often prevent expertise from developing.

Some realities: For men to take on more work at home, women will have to give up some. Sounds good? Realize that you may even have to relinquish some of the things you like best. In exchange for getting rid of the chores you like least, you have to share some of the profits, too.

Consider your husband a full partner, entitled to the same autonomy and perks you get. He's not going to be your clone. If you don't want a subcontractor, you can't treat a man like one.

Perhaps your husband will even show you that you've been using the wrong spoon, fastening the diaper too tightly, or getting into unnecessary struggles over homework or curfew. You must be open to the possibility that he knows something you don't or could know something you don't and can do better than you do in some areas. Remember: You want to *share* the mental responsibility and stress of childrearing, and that includes competence.

To prepare yourself for the new order, cast off those gender stereotypes that caused so much trouble in the first place. Otherwise, giving up anything related to the family will prove difficult. No matter how much you want it, the disparity between mothers' and fathers' experiences, and inherited ideas about who ought to do what, will interfere with the changing of the guard.

Wave good-bye once and for all to the notions that:

- mothers have a unique capability and obligation to nurture children;
- fathers are inept, distant, unemotional, unresponsive, and inferior caregivers;
- mothers should always stay home, cooking, cleaning, and taking care of others instead of themselves;

- mothers have to feel guilty whatever they choose to do; and
- mothers are justified in critiquing and belittling fathers' efforts.

Pressing on with the project will yield progressively better results. Slowly, each parent will realize that women can enjoy themselves while their husbands have fun with home, hearth, and kids. We'll get more into specific strategies in chapter 11. For now, take a taste of the following imperatives that pop up as a result of throwing away those old ideas.

Get out of Dodge: Moms find it excruciating to watch men bumble along, especially when they know precisely what ill is about to occur. So, don't look. Remove yourself from the fray. He'll learn how to take care of the children and the house. Incidentally, the kids will lap up (and benefit from) Dad's more relaxed style.

No gatekeepers allowed: Accept, encourage, and praise all efforts to help from your husband. Stop the practice of gatekeeping, in which mothers mete out times and events when fathers can interact with their children, replete with instruction. Unless a father is a drunkard, drug addict, or abuser, gatekeeping is not appropriate. The only way to get rid of all that mental overload is to release it.

PUTTING IT ALL TOGETHER

Mary Clayton, the professor who, back in chapter 1, turned away from her husband's kiss, gradually reclaimed her selfhood and marriage. First, she began to testify as an expert witness in court cases, which brought her back into the workforce and provided income, credibility, and motivation. When Jeffrey turned one, she located a gym with a great nursery and started exercising regularly.

At her request, Mark Clayton put half of the family's assets into Mary's name, which made her feel more equal and less dependent. All of these moves improved her life and status within and outside the marriage. She increased her bargaining power by making her BATNA more favorable.

Next, she and Mark learned some conflict-resolution skills at couples' therapy. Sunday nights, after Jeffrey went to bed, became family discussion nights, where they used the intentional dialogue they had practiced in counseling. They also slotted four hours a week alone together, hiring Lauren Martling's nanny, Pilar, on Saturday nights, and started to have fun together again.

With the help of their psychologist/marriage counselor, they worked out an arrangement that enabled Mary to return to work without disrupting Mark's career trajectory. Mark switched to a compressed four-day workweek, working flexible hours from home on one of those four days. He now takes care of Jeffrey when Mary teaches and Jeffrey is not in preschool. It took them three years to achieve a better balance. Both report great satisfaction in their new arrangement.

To accomplish all of this, Mary Clayton:

- performed research before formulating and articulating her position;
- explored and talked with her mate about his and her ideas of gender roles;
- knew she could negotiate her life roles;
- had a high aspiration level;
- used the foot-in-the-door and door-in-the-face approaches;
- resorted to a third party to help resolve differences;
- learned marriage communication skills;
- enabled her husband to have solo time with their son;
- set up a weekly time to review the relationship and make necessary changes;
- set up a weekly date with her husband;
- valued her time; and
- cast off inherited assumptions about what each sex does.

Why did Mary Clayton succeed when many others don't? The largest factor seems to be sheer will to make her life different. Often, mothers who conclude, as Mary did, that they don't like substitute care for very young children, give up the rest of their ambitions. They feel as if, in selecting family over work and having a personal life, they've made "The Choice" for the remainder of time. Perhaps because of her academic training and belief in theory, Mary Clayton would not accept the options the world had foisted on her. She says:

> People always tell me I'm so lucky Mark does so much. Luck had nothing to do with it. I worked to get the situation the way I wanted it. And I watched the Kings. Nothing seemed that hard for them, and I didn't see any reason we couldn't be like that, too.

The best thing I did was to get more intentional about my life choices. And you should see how well Jeffrey is doing. Mark adds something I can't. I think I'm a good mother, but there's a spirit of fun, maybe even a "guy thing," that they share. I am so happy to be able to be with my son and to be out in the world again.

Why did Mark finally consent? Partly because of Mary's persistence. But lots of women complain. It was more than that, he says.

I agreed to ask for a flexible schedule because it's not fair to her that she has to give up everything. And she wouldn't tolerate it if I didn't. She kept telling me she would stop complaining if I would do this one thing. We weren't having sex. She said men who do more housework and more with their kids have more sex. The idea that she would stop talking about how unfair everything was had a big appeal to me. To be honest, so did the promise of sex.

After a while, I could see that she was right. My son is more important than what some guy at work who never sees his family thinks. I never felt like my father really understood me. It will never be like that for Jeffrey and me. We're really tight.

Fortunately for the Claytons, they readjusted and found the equilibrium lacking since the first months of Jeffrey's life. It is possible to redistribute responsibilities, with lots of persistence, patience, and BATNA.

HOUSEHOLD HELP

Mary Clayton had one advantage that many do not. Her husband already did a lot of the housework. Many of the tactics she used will work for redistributing household chores, too. Rhona Mahony offers these suggestions for reallocating the cooking, cleaning, and management of the house and children:

- Think of three tasks where you can out-wait your husband and stop doing them.
- Ask who has the time or talent to do a particular chore.
- Ask whether you can farm out a chore to a paid helper.
- Exchange like for like (I will stay home with the kids so you can go out if I can then go out another time).

- Lower your standards of cleanliness.
- Eliminate some chores or activities, for example, ironing.
- Carpool to ballet or soccer practice.[5]

All of these tactics can help change the workload. For some of these strategies, you don't need to say a single word. Everybody will appreciate that.

DEALING WITH DIRTY POOL

What if no matter what you do, your husband will not negotiate or recognize your point of view? He might make personal attacks, stonewall, or ignore whatever you say. First and always, try to raise your BATNA. Harvard Negotiation Project experts William Ury and Roger Fisher also recommend the following approach for dealing with "tricky tactics," such as refusing to sit down to talk, reneging, or voicing threats:

1. Recognize the tactic.
2. Raise it explicitly and discuss it.
3. Question the tactic's legitimacy and desirability.
4. Negotiate over the tactic.[6]

For example, my husband promised to take a four-month leave of absence from his job so that I could complete this book. When he inquired at work, his employer offered a two-month leave of absence during the summer, and to allow him to work part time for two months once our daughters' school began again in September. I wanted to draft a schedule to see how it would look before I consented. Ed never said how many hours he might work or when. At the same time, he kept asking me to decide quickly.

I told him I couldn't agree to something if I didn't know what it was, and that I didn't think it was fair for him to ask me to do so. After that, we sat down and determined that if he worked a twenty-hour week spread over four days, it wouldn't affect me adversely. Although I had asked him to take four months off, I made a concession when I saw no reason other than stubbornness to adhere to my original request. Talking about Ed's pressure tactic allowed us to go forward and solve the problem before us, together. Deal with the specific strategy first and then move on to the issue at hand.

YOU CATCH MORE FLIES WITH HONEY

Certain tactics will not work. Name-calling. Personal attacks. Storming out. Throwing sharp or heavy objects. Things like that. Vanessa Robbins, whose husband stays home with their daughter, explains her approach:

> I do try to hold my tongue. And to think about what I say before I say it. I try to remember to say "thank you," too. I was given a tip by a working mom whose husband stays home with three small children. She said, "Never say, 'You're doing that wrong!' " So I have tried not to say that.

Be nice to your spouse. You used to be in love with him, remember? Talking quietly about the difficulties you've encountered helps. Compliments work wonders. Encourage your husband to feel comfortable as a parent. You'll get more help this way. Resentment only goes so far.

DOES IT REALLY MATTER?

Part of letting go of the old ways of thinking may entail letting go of some of the lovely aspects of your day, like dressing your child in gorgeous (or matching) clothes. Many moms complain about their husbands not doing various tasks such as dressing, cooking, or packing, and then make fun of the way their husbands dress, cook, or pack when given the chance. Ask yourself, "Does it really matter?"

Kathleen Merrigan, an agricultural policy professor married to law professor Michael Selmi, remembers:

> Mike was really big on letting Fiona pick out her own clothes—unbelievable outfits between the two of them. But in the scheme of life, so what if the clothes don't match? If she's happy and everything else is working, why stress out over that? I probably have said a few things like, "What kind of outfit is that?" And Mike would feel hurt and say, "Well, you know, I'm doing all this stuff." And he was right. And so there's a little bit of my mother in me that's a bit of a perfectionist and you have to just sort of pull back.

Ridiculing a man for doing what you've asked him to do won't make him feel appreciated or encourage him to comply with what you request in the future. A word of comfort: Sometimes the more absurd the outfit, the cuter the child looks, anyway. And you can always make sure your child looks extra special when *you* get the opportunity.

Here are a few more tips:

Rome wasn't built in a day: Change is hard, particularly when convention, the workplace, society, and extended family may oppose it. More than likely, a little bit of patience will be required. Look for a gradual change over time rather than a thunderbolt moment. Don't be unreasonable—*you* as well as your husband will not and cannot alter everything tomorrow.

No helpful suggestions, please: The tendency to yell just one more hint as your husband and child walk out the door overwhelms even the most avowed egalitarians among us. Unless you see your baby in a walker at the top of ungated stairs, or a teenager who doesn't know how to drive with car keys in hand, refrain.

Let Dad figure it out for himself. He'll never learn to pack a diaper bag, open the stroller, help with homework, or make dinner if you always make it easier or do it for him—which means you'll never be able to get away from that particular responsibility.

Communication: When two parents share childrearing substantially, they must communicate with each other more than parents used to. All job-sharing arrangements work best when the coworkers talk about what happened during their shift, what they're planning for the future, and what to look out for in the days ahead. Otherwise, gaps may occur, and something important may fall through the cracks.

Do it better with the next one: Knowing what you know now, you can make real changes before you have the next child. At least learn from your mistakes. So you didn't know any better with the first one? Now you do. Refer to chapters 4 through 9 before you start pinpointing that ovulation time.

Strategies That Work: More on Mommy Letting Go

11

When Maggie was four months old, Mike was throwing her down the slide. She couldn't even sit up. All of the other mothers came up to me and said, "Do you know what Mike is doing?" And I said, "Do me a favor, don't tell me."

—Ann King

THE WILL-IT-KILL-THEM TEST

Most successful strategies for redividing family and home responsibilities involve two components:

- The mother must let go of a responsibility or chore or period of time.
- Unless she can think of something positive, she must say nothing about how Dad performs (other than "Thank you").

Remember that old adage, "If you don't have anything nice to say, don't say anything at all"? You might even have passed on such a concept to your children. Take it to heart and embrace it. In tandem with providing men time alone with their kids, the approach of saying nothing or even giving compliments is crucial to effecting change.

Ann King explains:

The best advice I got when I was pregnant was from an ecumenical group of women at my baby shower. They said, "Whatever he does, if it doesn't put your child in mortal danger, keep your mouth shut."

That's how you get lots of help. My husband can be there in lots of ways I can't because he's physically stronger. I tell everybody, "If you have a problem, talk to him about it. If I'm not there and I don't see it, I don't want to know." If I was thinking only from my own framework, I would have attacked him many times.

Ann King does not look over Mike's shoulder. She might ask him what Maggie ate or what they did, so she doesn't repeat his efforts. However, she never checks up on him or gives instructions about what to do with Maggie. Instead, she trusts Mike, even when he undertakes activities she would never consider.

Almost unique among mothers, Ann does not engage in the practice of complaining about her husband. She will not say a word against him, even when offered the opportunity. Ann and Mike King seem like a team in the way that they refer to each other, evincing mutual respect. Take what Ann has told us here as precepts to live by:

- Ask "Will it kill our child?" If the answer is no, do not get involved.
- Recognize that all individuals have different interests, strengths, and talents.
- Understand that mothers and fathers have equal rights, ability, and say in determining how to rear their children.
- Refuse to gatekeep or bad-mouth your husband.
- Treat your husband as a trusted and valued partner.

Use this approach as a guide for a new type of mothering. When Mary Clayton began to emulate Ann King, she got herself out of the Mommy Trap.

WATCH OUT FOR THE AUTOMATIC RESPONSE

Remember those problem areas where dads tend to avoid involvement? Mothers who want to do less at home can run into hurdles in those spheres, which include household administration, child's social scheduling, staying home with sick kids, play dates, doctor's appointments, birthday parties, and purchasing house- and child-related goods and services.

It goes like this. An expectant mother says, and thinks, she wants an equal partner. Later on, she finds that she cannot bring herself to release 80 percent of the work created by her child and home. She may love doing some of it. *She may also believe "that's what mothers do" and that whatever it is must be done the way mothers do it.* This processing goes on internally without the mother's awareness that her *own* beliefs and actions undermine her husband's ability to share the mental and physical load.

Psychologist Jay Belsky says women must consciously work against inherited beliefs of what is appropriate:

> I like to set the example of the father who dresses his toddler in the morning. He puts on the same shirt as he put on the kid yesterday, with a chocolate stain on it, and the mother says, "You can't wear that" as opposed to "Thank God, I don't have to dress the darn kid."
>
> Sure, that's changeable, but the mother has to be self-aware that what she's taking as some fundamental, basic value of childrearing is really just her own standard. And that he may not share it. And then the issue becomes, "What's more important? Him sort of tacking to my direction or my having a partner?"

This is gender ideology at work. Fortunately, we *can* change our gender ideology. Once a mother recognizes her predetermination about which sex should perform a particular function, or how to execute it, she may decide whether to retain or discard the preconception. Even women who believe in equality, or near equality, of the sexes must address their ideas about specific situations as they arise.

For example, while I was writing the last chapter—the section about letting go, no less—a crisis developed in my house. Our younger daughter, Annie, had come to the dreaded moment where she constantly vaulted out of her crib, but did not yet have her own bed. The period when our older daughter, Elizabeth, moved to a bed ranks as one of the hardest in my life, as it coincided with a move to a different neighborhood and the birth of Annie (a beautiful but colicky baby). At the same time that I wanted a smoother transition into a "big-girl-bed" for Annie, I had scheduled a lot of interviews and had a submission deadline coming up.

As the home-decorating czar, I remarked to my husband that we should purchase a bed for Annie as soon as possible. An involved dad with two kids to entertain and nothing to do that day, he offered to go to the store where we have bought all the girls' furniture and pick out a bed for Annie. What did I do? Automatic choke. I said, "No, I can't go today, I have too much to do. It'll have to wait until I have some more time."

Did you catch the assumption that only I can select a bed for our daughter to match the furniture already in her room, bought from the same source? By this time, Ed had read all the chapters in this book more than once (poor guy). He said, "I can take them and pick it out myself."

My instinct? To say no, he'd have to wait, and the urgent problem should sit until Supermom could get to the store and shop. I started to laugh, when I thought of the chapter I was writing. I realized that somewhere in my mind I thought only women take the lead in choosing furniture.

I ran it through my checklist:

- Identified gender stereotype: Women decorate kids' bedrooms.
- Could it kill them if he did it wrong? No.
- Fear: Unlikely, but Dad may buy something that doesn't match.
- Can I live with it? Yes.
- Okay, now I don't believe only I can shop for the house.

He went. I stayed home and worked. The girls jumped on beds and picked out a beautiful one. Not only didn't it kill them; I benefited by not taking the time from my work for something my husband had the interest and ability to do, and he and our daughters benefited by finding an activity and solution to our sleeping problem when they needed one.

My experience demonstrates the strength of the default to tradition. I have read up on, written about, and ranted against it and still cannot prevent myself from reacting according to script. Sometimes, though, I can control what I do after I notice my response.

At first it feels unfamiliar to let go of dominion over the household and children. Things seem too easy—only in the beginning. After a while, a new reversion to whoever has the time and talent for a particular task replaces the old default. Then family life can function much better than it did before.

A GREAT LEAP FORWARD

At some point, women in the Mommy Trap must take a leap of faith that fathers can parent, cook, clean, or do whatever needs to get done, and nothing terrible will happen. Due to her husband's more advanced age, Cindy switched from staying home with her then eight- and ten-year old children to working full time. When her husband became a full-time dad, she had to give up many functions she had always thought were the mother's, and had always performed.

> It was hard to let go of the control of the household at first. That probably still is an issue for me in some ways. I'm so picky about certain things. I still nag about certain things.
>
> The first time he had to take my daughter to the doctor for a sore throat, I was worried, "Is he going to tell the doctor everything he needs to know." But then, it just worked out and got taken care of.

As I did with the bedroom furniture, ask yourself, "Am I stepping in here because I want to be involved or because I think I should? Can he do this? What's the worst thing that can happen if he does it wrong? Can I live with the consequences?"

Most of the time, analyzing transactions with the above mind-set leads to the conclusion that the interest in getting a task done outweighs any potential harm. As long as it's already met the "will-it-kill-them" threshold, many chores can fall by the wayside. Undoubtedly, women feel a moment of terror the first time they let go. Those who have pressed ahead anyway report that after the initial release, casting off all of those "shoulds" benefits everybody in the family.

Once mothers shed some control of their children and house, the momentum changes. Doing less gets easier for several reasons, Dr. Belsky explains:

> The first day I leave him with the baby, I'm anxious. The thirty-first day I leave him with the baby, it's like water off a duck's back.
>
> What you're really talking about is how do you prime the pump. How do you get the skill-development process going? It's like if you start a dance with your partner and you're standing with your partner before the music starts, it's easier to learn to

dance than if all of a sudden, she is dancing and you have to jump in.

Working through the default to traditional gender stereotypes enables men to catch up. Clearly, it would have been easier had you not gotten so much better at the dance. But fathers can still learn, as long as they get some practice. They may even show you some great new steps.

LEAVE THE HOUSE OR ARRANGE FOR THEM TO LEAVE THE HOUSE

The hardest step in letting go is actually to let go or let them go the first time. Many of my friends have given up on their husbands doing X, Y, or Z after seeing how their husbands do X, Y, or Z. But if Dad never gets time alone with his children, he will never share mental or physical responsibility with his wife.

Moms find not watching or knowing what goes on when Dad takes control essential. Midori goes out or encourages her husband, J.D., to leave the house when he spends time with their daughter. At first, he kept calling on his cell phone to ask Midori questions. She stopped answering the phone.

Create a "commitment mechanism" that forces the issue. Make dates with friends or other appointments that cannot be broken easily. Sign up for a class. Pay money in advance so you have an

---

▌ **Getting Dad Involved**

Jay Belsky's suggestions for how mothers can encourage fathers to become more involved:

1. Realize that you're going to have more of a partner and less of a helper. And you're going to lose some of the control you might think you need (although you probably don't need it).
2. Enable the father to exercise his latent abilities so that they will become regularly manifest.

incentive to follow through with your plan, and not cancel at the last minute. Necessity can light the way around the Mommy Trap. Mothers such as Cindy, who have to go to work and rely on their husbands to parent, find they do just fine.

Studies and empirical evidence demonstrate that men best learn to parent without their wives present. According to Dr. Kyle Pruett, because society has discouraged men from nurturing, they can find their latent caring ability only by allowing it to come forward when taking care of and just hanging out with their children, alone.[1]

Recall that the fathers in Pruett's study became competent when their wives left for work, and not before. Previously, they served as subcontractors and the mothers as the brains of the operation. After they'd done child care for a while, the mothers asked them for advice. The mothers did not know how to handle problems with which they'd had no experience. In my interviews of nontraditional couples, I heard many such reports: The more experienced parent (whatever the sex) displays more knowledge, patience, and skill with children. It's all a matter of opportunity.

NO APRON STRINGS ATTACHED

Mothers who share childrearing with their husbands emphasize the importance of recognizing the value of fathers' abilities. *Women must let go of control over the mode of performance.* Delegating a task and directing how to do it doesn't count. It also doesn't work. Deirdre Davis reports that the following approach helped her to give up dominance at home: "Understanding that men make wonderful parents. They are great at raising kids. They just do it differently, and that's okay."

It becomes a question of accepting another style of parenting. Remember that women tend to keep children closer and fathers to give them wider rein, to encourage exploration and mastery of skills without interference. To get out of the Mommy Trap, mothers must acknowledge that fathers' mode of interacting with children has validity, too. Cindy accepts that her husband doesn't watch their teenage son as closely as she does, recognizing that though they have a different approach, both are appropriate.

> I'll come home and ask my husband, "Where's Paul?" He'll say, "Oh, he's down the street." I would ask my son where he

was going. They're always right in the neighborhood and he wouldn't go anywhere without telling us, but I would know up-front where he was going whereas my husband's more, "He's just down the street." That's fine. And Paul likes the fact that his dad respects his judgment. Right now, he seems to need a little more rope than I would give him.

Mothers have to relax their rigid requirements that fathers do everything the way they would. *The goal is for him to do more, not to do it exactly as you would.* As long as mothers retain the goal that fathers should act like mothers, men will not do much more than they do already.

Understanding this fact can work wonders, almost instantly. Fathers feel better and participate more when they make their own choices about how to be with their children. Mothers feel better when they release some of that mental load. Moms can create personal time once they understand they may let go of their way of doing things.

Some books and experts recommend that women lower their standards. Instead, think of *suspending* your standards, not worrying about how things are done when you're not around, or on duty. Here's a liberating exercise. When your husband asks what he should do during your time off—what to feed your child, how to conduct a play date, or what movie to rent—say, "I don't know. Whatever you want."

Do not try to dictate what will happen in your absence. Otherwise, you'll still carry the mental load of household and child administrator around. Also, your husband will not respond the way you would like. Men enjoy freedom to make their own rules, same as women do. My brother-in-law, a pretty traditional guy, loves to take care of his sons whenever my sister-in-law goes away for a day or two. He describes his pleasure in spending time alone with the boys:

> It's the only time when I can do things my way, when I think they should be done, or the boys want to, not when she wants to. It's much easier because I don't have to worry about whether I'm doing it the way she does it or even if she can see what we're doing.

All dads say this. Listen to them. Don't breathe down your husband's neck. It's counterproductive, unrelaxing, and causes strife. Marital therapist Mary Ray explains:

> The other day, a mother told me she'd come home and her husband hadn't changed the baby's diaper. The older child hadn't eaten. Their middle son was eating clay. So I asked her, "If you give him hell, will he do it again?" She thought for a moment and said, "No."
>
> "That's right," I told her. "It doesn't have to be perfect. It doesn't have to be your way. That's the beauty of two different relationships and two parents."
>
> Often, a mother will come in and say, "What's going on?" Don't shame your partner in front of the kids. That undermines him, the kids are not going to listen to him then, and he won't want to get involved again either.

Ray describes classic Mommy Trap behavior. We all do it from time to time. That's the old model. Look to Ann King instead, and show appreciation for your husband's efforts.

DEALING WITH THE PANG

Once you get beyond the feeling that you ought to do everything yourself, you may run into the next hurdle, "The Pang." Sometimes, a mother who shares childrearing with her husband feels a clear moment of angst after she has given up responsibility. A doctor's appointment, a milestone, or some other "traditional" function of mothers will pass by her nose, accompanied by a sense of loss, fear, or an urge to get that task back, at once.

For example, Rebecca Powell says:

> There have not been that many times where I felt bad not to be there, but I did feel that the first time Mac rolled over and Darrell called me at work to tell me. It's not hugely strong because we both do everything with him. I got over it. There have been times when he prefers his dad in some way, but it seems to be balanced by other times when he preferred me or different situations occurred.

One mom, a financial executive whose husband quit his job to stay home when their daughter was two, recalls:

I had always bought more of the clothes than Jeff did. And one day, when he came home with all these clothes, I had this feeling like, "Hey, wait. I want to pick them out, too." But then he said, "If you want to return some, we can." And I realized, "Well, it's not that important, and I can go out and buy her a dress."

Usually only the initial moment of payoff associated with a particular event brings the Pang. The Pang results from internalized beliefs about what a mother *should* do, as well as giving up something you may like (or liked one time out of a hundred). Once you get to the Pang, pat yourself on the back. You've come a long way. The Pang is a loss, but it is also a gain.

The mothers I interviewed, and those in Pruett's study of primary parenting fathers, derived pleasure from sharing responsibilities with their husbands rather than reigning as queens of nurture.[2] The women also found that splitting parenting duties makes them less onerous and eases dissatisfaction with work as well.[3] Think of the Pang as a necessary step when discarding the notion that moms should do everything and always be there for their children. And remember, you can always participate in the event next time— maybe even all together.

USE CHANGE AS AN OPPORTUNITY

What if you work full time, and feel so guilty, anxious, or regretful about the time away from your children that you can't imagine giving up a single moment or chore on your plate? Or, what if you have achieved so much skill and the disparity between you and your husband is so great that you can't bear the thought of him performing any child- or house-related functions? *When a new job arises, don't gain the expertise or habit of doing it.* Instead, allow Dad to take on, plan for, and execute whatever it is.

Lauren Martling used this tactic to get out of the Mommy Trap. When her son, Dan, entered kindergarten, his nanny, Pilar, left for another job. Where Lauren used to have until four o'clock to do her work, she now had to stop at two-forty-five. She and her husband, George, had decided they wanted to spend more time with Dan.

Lauren had become friendly with Ann King, who doesn't pros-
elytize, but whose example seems to spur her acquaintances to
change. Together, Lauren and George determined how they could fill
the gap caused by Pilar's departure. Lauren says:

> I asked George if he would make Dan's lunch. Before that,
> Pilar had always taken care of lunch. I said, and this was true,
> "You're so much better at making sandwiches than I am."
>
> I also asked George to take Dan to soccer on the weekend,
> and make sure he got signed up for it each time. That was a new
> activity and George is more into sports than I am. I didn't want
> to have to pick Dan up from school and spend every afternoon
> not working either, so I asked George to do it twice a week when
> he is not traveling. I knew I didn't want all of the new jobs to
> land in my lap.

Take any moment of transition as an opportunity to change the
distribution of labor. It might be a new job, baby, school, or child-
care arrangement. Even if you didn't sit down before to divide and
conquer, make use of whatever comes your way and redistribute the
family work.

FREAKY FRIDAY

A little role reversal can cause a sea change, for both mothers and
fathers. When couples become polarized, it often seems that neither spouse can entertain the other's reality, for even a second. My
friend Jim, whose wife quit her job to take care of their three children, has made the following statement to me many times:

> My wife forgot what it's like to make money. All she sees is
> what somebody else has and she wants it, too. If she knew how
> many hours I had to work to get all that stuff, she'd be singing
> a different tune. She hasn't worked outside of the house in years.
> She doesn't remember what it's like.

He makes a good point. When I cashed my first paycheck after
three years at home, I immediately thought of what Jim had said. I
related my lawyerly efforts to health club dues, an expensive dinner,
or a Saturday night baby-sitter payment. Though I hadn't believed

Jim's assertions, I discovered then that I *had* forgotten the correlation between work and money. Everything seemed to cost more than I had realized.

Jim's wife has a valid point to make, too: He doesn't appreciate the difficulty of staying home alone with the children, because he has never done it. He says:

> Many dads have an unspoken hunch that they could do a better of job of raising children than their wives. Why does she lose her composure and become so frazzled, a luxury we don't have in the workplace? No doubt raising children is one of the most difficult and all-consuming occupations, but can it be that much harder than running a law practice? Is putting a meal together while juggling the kids that much more difficult than sifting through briefs and motions while fielding nonstop phone calls from clients and lawyers?

Two older at-home dads in second marriages, whose first wives stayed home with their now grown children, quickly realized that, in their first marriage, they had not understood the amount or difficulty of the work involved for full-time parents and homemakers. A former senior official in a Cabinet department who takes care of his five-year-old daughter explains the difference between his experiences as primary provider the first time around, and primary nurturer the second.

> I loved them, and was very involved, but I had no idea. We had three in diapers, three years apart. I would go away for weeks at a time. I had no idea what mothering was like, for ten, twelve, twenty-four hours a day, with no relief—because there were no nannies in those days. You better believe I get upset if my wife comes home late because of traffic, because I've been looking forward to a break.

Jack Mahon, a former television reporter who quit his job to take care of his eight-year-old daughter, was also surprised by the amount of work and efficiency home and child care require.

> Only now do I realize since I have to do it myself how incredibly time consuming it all is. And how organized you have to be. It's a little business, a house.

The time goes by so fast. You think you have all this time—
my daughter is in camp from eight-fifteen to three o'clock—
then you realize that as the day goes on all of a sudden it's two-
thirty and I've started all sorts of projects that I can't complete,
and I've really gotten almost nothing done. You start on something that requires you to find something that takes an hour and
you look at the clock and the time is gone.

Swap roles for at least a day. Include waking up time to bedtime,
and staying in and tidying up the house after bedtime. One at-home
mom flew from Washington to New York to visit a friend on a Saturday, saw a play, and came home the same night. Her husband got
a glimpse of what goes on in his absence, and the planning, skill,
and patience required.

If you both work for pay, arrange for your husband to take on
your daily routine on a work or weekend day. Let him spend the
evening at home while you dine with an old friend, find a movie
buddy, take a class, work out, whatever. When you return, your
husband will better appreciate your complaints. Don't rub it in,
though.

OUT IN THE WORLD

Signing up Dad and child for a class or activity can start the process
of more-engaged fathering. Men learn to take care of babies or children by themselves, packing whatever they need, and going out as
father and child. This can create a powerful experience that leads
to warmth, intimacy, and more male responsibility. Law professor
Mike Selmi recalls the early days of his sabbatical:

> Probably the best thing I did, which was kind of hard for me
> to do, was when we went to Gymboree. Because it broke down
> a barrier where I was more willing to go do stuff like that, to go
> out. My daughter had a great time. I hesitated in doing that.
> The singing and stuff was different from what I was used to,
> but it was fun.

After that, he can sign up for a new class if he likes, or do something else with your child or children during that time slot. By then,
Dad will want to keep that interlude, as long as you don't make the
experience unpleasant for him.

ACT LIKE A MAN

When fathers take on primary parenting, they stake out their territory in a way mothers rarely do. Every breadwinner mother I interviewed takes over for her husband when she gets home. Having done it themselves, moms appreciate the difficulty of full-time child care. Working moms also take steps to prevent burnout for the full-time parent.

Jason Marx describes his recreation during the year he stayed home and wrote freelance articles:

> I have more leisure time than Theresa. I try to stay in shape by playing hoops. Reading. Goofing off with my friends, which I do more than she does. I'm out more than she is; I have more things going on.

Aspiration level, again. Fathers expect breaks and leisure activities and so they get them. All of the full-time dads I met negotiated their desired roles *before* taking on primary parenting. For example, former television reporter Jack Mahon remembers:

> We discussed our worries about the situation. I said, "My worry is that you're going to treat me like an employee. You can't leave lists for me. I can't have that. You are not entitled to critique my work in the way you would critique an employee." We had a very straightforward talk about this because this is potentially a marriage wrecker if you do it wrong.

Full-time mothers can protect their status and interests in the same way. Jack Mahon identified potential issues with his new job and addressed them before he agreed to stay home, as did Ira Berk, who drafted a contract spelling out his responsibilities and ensuring some free time. Figure out what you fear might happen and what you need and want, and brainstorm together about it how you can get it.

Many at-home dads work or participate in an activity unrelated to kids, house, or religion. Every full-time dad I've spoken to does something else or has some child-care relief so he can have personal space. Fred Barbash spent a month getting used to his new routine, then began to take on occasional writing assignments for the *Washington Post* and to volunteer for a civil liberties organization.

In addition to serving as president of a support group for stay-at-home dads, Ira Berk works ten to twelve hours a week as a social worker for a crisis line. He uses after-school day care for his children for an afternoon a week.

At-home dad Gary Mancini uses twelve to fifteen hours a week of baby-sitting so he can get to the gym and do errands. His wife, Meryl, who owns a wellness center, works flexible hours four days a week, and occasionally works from home on the fifth. Gary recalls how their arrangement evolved:

> The first sixty to ninety days, I was trying to figure things out: what my roles were and how I was going to be a responsible parent. How I was going to be able to have a house that wasn't chaotic. And also at the same time, to be able to go to the gym a couple of days a week, and not feel as if I've sacrificed all my time and I don't have any time to myself. I'm really fortunate that my wife acknowledges my needs and allows me to try to get to do my stuff, where I feel like I'm well physically.

Upon noticing that Gary had no energy and needed an outlet, he and his wife determined they needed a part-time caregiver. They hired a bonded nanny they had known for years to come three days a week during their daughter's naptime.

Mothers would do well to emulate these involved dads in setting up their own lives (and working dads would do well to emulate these working moms). Researcher Amy Olson explains:

> Women are amazing caregivers, but often the last person to benefit from this is the woman herself. We need to realize that asking for what we want for ourselves does benefit and trickle down to our loved ones. It's really hard for us to think that way. But there are so many benefits to being assertive—physical and emotional. In general, women need to be very clear and specific about what they want.

That's why they had the women's movement in the first place: so women could have a comfortable existence outside the house and family. We can now complete the circle, looking to our new examples of how to achieve personalized work and parenting roles, and satisfied, supported, and supportive families.

Sharing the Career 12
Accommodation

We evaluated our schedules and careers and came up with a
compromise, working with what was available to us. We
realized that we would both need to make sacrifices in the
early years and were ready to do so. The bottom line for me
is that if it will benefit my girls, I will do it. It can be hard
but the benefit to our daughters is significant. If things
really get out of hand, he can vary his schedule and
I can take some vacation time.

—Charlie Watson, adoptive father of two daughters
whose partner equally shares in their care

FAMILY BALANCE

In addition to chipping away at the ideal of Mother as nurture czar,
we must now discard the belief in Father as sole provider for the
family, and nothing more. The old job description for men doesn't
automatically apply anymore, if at all. Almost 25 percent of American women who work for pay earn more than their husbands do.[1]
In 55 percent of households with children under the age of one, the
mother works outside the home.[2] In the past decade, the number of
two-parent households with an at-home dad increased by 70 percent, from 1 million in 1990 to 1.7 million in 2000.[3] And as we have
seen, even stay-at-home moms with traditional values expect men to
nurture a little bit.

Yet when push comes to shove, the transitional belief system
under which most of us operate still slots the domains of the house-

hold and children to women and of providing to men. With one full-
time parent at home and one full-time wage earner, families can
achieve a functional balance if they behave according to these ideals
(so long as the parent at home values domesticity and gets a break
now and then). But anyone who wants or tries a different arrangement without first casting off the old roles will have a hard time.[4] As
a result, in countless polls, dual-income couples say they desperately
need more time for their families and for themselves and cannot
achieve a comfortable equilibrium.[5]

Retaining gender stereotypes from the past makes the old roles
seem the most desirable. One can perform most child-care and
household duties only when one is not working at another job. Ad-
herence to the "do-whatever-it-takes-to-get-ahead" male provider
model prevents men from pursuing alternate work arrangements
and women from asking their husbands to do so. Fathers cannot
then easily take on much responsibility at home.

Adhering to the old "ideal, full-time worker" standard makes it
seem as if the most functional situation is to have one parent at
home (the mother) and one at work (the father). For example, a nationwide *Los Angeles Times* poll found that, in 2000, 76 percent of
men and 71 percent of women agreed with this statement: "It is better for the children if one person works outside the home while the
other stays home with the children."[6] The pollsters later asked
whether stay-at-home mothers or working-but-fulfilled women make
better mothers, but not the same questions about fathers.

Like many prospective parents, the *LA Times* poll didn't consider
a dad staying home, two parents reducing their workforce participation, or how children and marriage might fare in those arrangements. Eliminating such a circumscribed perspective leads to all
sorts of other possibilities. We get infinitely more solutions once
we recognize that men can nurture and make career accommodations, too.

Pamela Jordan designed the Becoming Parents Program to help
people think about all their options. She observes:

> There's much more support for women to try to balance
> work and family responsibilities than there is for men to do the
> same. We need to move away from that so there aren't those

kinds of preset sex roles and stereotypical expectations. So that we have instead the expectation that people have the whole smorgasbord to choose from, and they'll choose whatever they like, whatever is best for them.

Sharing couples demonstrate that we have a larger menu than most of us realize from which to choose our family options.

BREAK ON THROUGH TO THE OTHER SIDE

Assume fathers as well as mothers can make accommodations for children. All our new role models did. The concept of balancing work and family changes from a baby-juggling female trying to perform two full-time functions on a high wire, to a supported, grounded family effort. Higher aspiration levels and altered expectations expose opportunities people never knew existed.

Just as women have to work through their default to traditional roles, fathers must confront the expectation that they must work full time, at all costs. The Berk family's exit from the Mommy Trap demonstrates the tools needed to eliminate the default to a man's provider role.

Janey Berk earns a good living as a health-care policy consultant for hospitals and cities. For the past two and a half years, Ira Berk has stayed home with their five- and seven-year-old children, fitting part-time hours as a crisis counselor around the kids' schedules. Before that, the Berks each averaged more than fifty hours a week at their jobs, and kept their son and daughter in day care for even longer. The Berks all had a terrible quality of life. Ira remembers:

> It was a very stressed household. We tried to relax on Sunday, but Monday though Friday, the main goal was getting ourselves ready for work and waking the kids up and getting them ready for day care. We'd rush through breakfast so we could drop them off and go to our jobs. And then the same thing occurred at night. We'd come home and we had to get dinner on the table. By the time we ate dinner, it was time for the kids to be bathed and to go to bed. Saturday was for errands and shopping.
>
> There was a year before I stayed home when getting them to bed was a nightmare. They stayed up until ten or so at night, and we had to do a lot of coaxing them into bed. They con-

stantly got out. Now we think they were just trying to get our attention. That just stressed us out more because that left us maybe a half an hour just to ourselves. We were fighting with each other every night, because we were so tired.

Ira did not volunteer to stay home, despite the fact that he earned half his wife's salary, and his life was unmanageable. When he looked for a new job after completing his graduate work, Janey Berk suggested, half in jest, that he stay home with the kids instead. Ira did not feel that he could do that. He recalls:

> And I sort of laughed at the idea, and I said, "No, I need to work full time." I think I had the stereotypical male idea, and I wasn't ready for her to be the main income person in the family. It goes to what society tells us, that I'm male and she's female. I felt I needed to contribute to the family's income.

Ira took a new job farther from home, which added more strain on the Berk household. Then, one day, a truck carrying explosives turned over on I-95 just south of Washington, D.C., creating a huge traffic jam. After many cell phone calls, Ira arrived at his son's day care three hours late.

> He was two at the time, but he said in a very clear manner, "Daddy, I thought you were never coming to pick me up." It hit me then that something needed to change in our life. That we can't do this anymore. And that's when my wife and I started to sit down and seriously talk about the fact that something had to change. The one thing that we decided was that the best change for the whole family was for me to leave work full time.

The Berks did not allow the male provider and female nurturer norms to constrain their vision of the possible. Janey first offered to reduce her work hours or stay home. Then, as she and Ira began to talk about *Ira* making a career accommodation, Janey worked through her own gender beliefs. She says:

> I had mixed emotions about not being the one to cut back. I had never really pictured this kind of arrangement. But I don't feel forced into it. If I came home and said, "Work is over, I've had it," we'd find a way to make it work.

When a crisis occurred, rather than denying the problem or arguing without resolution, the Berks:

1. sat down together and talked calmly, seeking a solution both parents agreed was fair and effective;
2. focused on their shared interests in their children, family life, marriage, and each other's contentment;
3. considered all possibilities, even Dad taking on a primary nurturing role and Mom a primary provider role, and a hybrid arrangement with Dad working part time;
4. created personalized roles that both parents thought were fair and wanted to take on; and
5. knew that each spouse would make a change and go back to the drawing board if their new arrangement did not work.

Only then could the best use of time and talents win out. Now the Berks are both "extremely satisfied." Their children have responded positively to more parental attention, more time at home, and living according to their own schedules. *This five-step approach exemplifies the type of communication and flexibility adopted by every satisfied couple I interviewed.* Whether in one- or two-income households, and whether the dad, the mom, or both made a career accommodation, couples that were dissatisfied with their division of efforts had bypassed some or all of these steps.

THE WORK-LIFE BUFFET

When we understand that men can also provide some time, strategies for balancing work and family become obvious. Sharing couples come in all shapes and sizes. All approach important decisions together, considering everybody's needs, interests, and desires. Any number of solutions exist.

Spreading work accommodations can help families keep two careers going *and* honor childrearing preferences. Two four-day-a-week jobs enable children to spend more time with their parents than without them, a desirable goal in light of child-care research. Kerry and Antoine Beard both work four compressed-hour days, using a shared nanny arrangement for twenty hours a week. Kerry goes into work early on two of her workdays; Antoine stays home later on those mornings. They have sacrificed nothing in the way of promotion opportunity or salary. As a result of both parents' flexi-bility, the Beards have significantly reduced the amount of substi-tute care they use and greatly increased family time.

Charlie and Derek, male partners who adopted two young girls from Russia, both made career accommodations, because they be-lieve that the best way to cement the bond with adoptive kids is for parents to spend as much time as they can with them during the first few years. Charlie shifted his full-time hours as an attorney and works from five in the morning to two in the afternoon, all but two of the days from home. A child and adolescent psychiatrist, Derek works outside the home from three in the afternoon until nine in the evening, and takes care of paperwork and some phone calls from home. He gave up a lucrative position as director of a day psychi-atric clinic so that he could shorten his hours.

Just changing expectations regarding the second shift can make a world of difference. When Lynne Swanson was pregnant, Guy switched to a flexible position, reducing his travel commitments. He served as on-call parent for two years. Lynne took care of the shopping, cooking, and household management. When their second child was born, Lynne switched to a part-time schedule and took on the role of on-call parent. Guy put more effort into work but continued to work flexibly and remained an involved partner rather than helper. The stress level in their house has remained low and everything runs smoothly.

Combining two part-time jobs presents an intriguing possibility for those who prefer parental care. Using a baby-sitter only for their weekly date, Mike and Ann King each work two-thirds time from home. Ann works from eight to one, and Mike from one to six, Mon-day to Friday, and each works every other Saturday. They like to mix work and child care most days because they find a whole day doing either can be too much. Since Maggie started preschool at age two and a half, Mike has worked more than Ann, but has the role of on-call parent if Maggie falls ill, school gets canceled because of snow, or something else unexpected happens. On a recent visit, they seemed triumphant, happy they had given their daughter their all and eager to reenergize their careers.

Donna and Pete Diederle took another road. Pete, an international trade attorney, stayed home for three years. When he went back to work, Donna, a Foreign Service officer, stayed home for two years. She returned to work half time, after negotiating the first job-share at her level in the State Department. Each year, Paul negotiates with his employer for more vacation time instead of a raise because he wants to spend more time with their kids.

Stacie, one of the most satisfied stay-at-home mothers I've seen, runs marathons, takes graduate classes, and sometimes works as a Russian language translator. Her husband accommodates Stacie's requests for help because they both value her time and satisfaction as much as his.

Deirdre Davis and her husband, John Wang, share the same job as public defenders, earning one salary and a complete benefits package. They got the idea from doctor friends who shared a practice. Though they have unique situations, many others job-share with individuals who are not their spouses, an arrangement that allows employers to retain valued employees, and gain extra job coverage and perspective.

Once we begin to think creatively, we can follow families like the Berks out of the Mommy Trap. We may not be able to, or want to, achieve equal sharing. We may want to eliminate or limit substitute care, or we might just want a break now and then. Regardless, these couples provide a new standard, a hybrid of the mother/nurturer and father/provider ideals. They show us that both parents can participate in the family and enjoy personal or professional lives at the same time.

SIDE DISHES
In creating flexible options, employers and employees have most often used flextime, compressed work schedules, time shifting, telecommuting, work-at-home, and part-time initiatives.

Flextime
Under flexible working hours or flextime, an employee may start work early or late, freeing up different parts of the day than the standard nine-to-five job allows. Many of the couples you've met in this book have two flexible-hour positions, some even on the weekend.

Compressed Work Schedules

Couples can combine compressed work schedules to reduce time in substitute care. Under compressed schedules, workers may work a full workweek in fewer than five days by working more hours each day that they do work. Compressed work schedules give employees extra days to spend with their families. They make for long parental absences on workdays, unless both parents also use flexible hours that allow one to start work early and one late.

Compensatory Time

Compensatory time, or time shifting, allows an employee to work an extra hour and take that hour off another time. An employee can accumulate a week off and take a week's vacation without using any vacation time, or take two hours off if a child is sick or has a piano recital or the employee has something else to do that day.

Telecommuting or Work from Home

The Information Revolution offers the opportunity to bring parents and children back together and alleviate pressure in households. With e-mail and the Internet, the virtual office is a reality. Often, people can do work more productively at home, with fewer distractions or with preferred distractions. Working from home eliminates commuting time, and enables parents to monitor child care, take a snack or lunch break with a child, breastfeed, go to a doctor's appointment, run errands, or shift work to nap or bedtime, if desired.

Flextime, compressed-work schedules, compensatory time, and work from home can help families juggle their responsibilities without radically changing work commitments. But they do not make a significant difference to family balance in two-earner families unless *both* parents make use of them (remember the exhaustion of Lauren Martling, who worked from home and couldn't find a respite anywhere).

ENTREES

Part-time employment constitutes one of the best options for giving families time together. Unlike other policies, it reduces time working. However, women make up more than 90 percent of American parents who work part time.[7] If fathers begin to use them as well, part-time work arrangements during the early years cut a clear path to a balanced family. Work-life specialist Nancy Kane believes that if men worked through socialized gender roles to ask for part-time positions, they would find them available. She says she has found more men willing to do so, "particularly with the effects of the September 11 attacks. We're seeing even more interest and attention paid to flexible work arrangements. Because people have taken stock of their lives and reevaluated where work fits in. That's true for both men and women."

Part-time work can enable *both* parents to continue their careers, without making huge sacrifices with their children or family life. Parents get a new choice with some definite advantages: to raise their children themselves without losing all adult satisfactions, and to work in a more relaxed way during a stressful time period.

If part-time work is so great, why can't women continue to scale back while men work hard and get ahead? Right now, taking part-time work is a shortcut to the Mommy Trap. Mom may have too much to do, and may resent having to make all the accommodations. *And women will never be equal to men anywhere as long as they drop out or scale back and men don't.* As a group, they will not gain the ability to persuade their husbands to do more at home.

Think of it as BATNA leapfrog. As the part-time flexible superwoman kneels down to wipe her child's nose, her husband, or somebody else, vaults over her down the path of worldly success, regardless of whether he (or she) has more intelligence or ability than the mother does. She'll have a hard time catching up, particularly if she stoops for more than one child.

As long as only women utilize part-time policies, cutting back at work will remain mostly a second-tier "Mommy Track." Once men also begin to scale back, part time will lose some of its stigma and become more of an attractive option with more benefits and promotion potential.

Employers have already started to see the value of good part-time work, because it increases retention, efficiency, and profit. Catalyst Inc.'s study, titled "Flexible Work Arrangements III: A Ten-Year Retrospective of Part-Time Arrangements for Managers and Professionals," followed the part-time arrangements of twenty-four senior level female employees over ten years. Study manager Nancy Kane reports:

> These women have been able to come up with a holistic approach for work-life balance. Their companies have supported them in doing that. Not one of their paths is similar. It really varied in terms of their arrangements, their hours, their days, their schedules. That's really an important message. Anything can go.
>
> These women were pioneers. When they first started their flexible work arrangements, for the most part, they were the first ones doing them, and for the most part doing them before their companies had policies that sanctioned it. They had progressive managers who didn't want to lose them. They created these arrangements to keep them, and it worked.

The majority of American families with young children don't need two salaries; most could (and do) get by on one, or one and a half, instead. The old rules say that the primary salary has to be the father's, or that the one-and-a-half salary has to consist of a male full-time salary and a female part-time salary. *Change your analysis to include other options, including what you can earn if both work part time.*

IF YOU DON'T ASK, THE ANSWER IS NO

Asking for something new or unusual can make the difference between finding a solution and staying stuck. After crying during visits to day-care centers and homes, Jackie, a woman in my mothers' group, decided she couldn't put her three-month-old daughter into day care. She had expected to return to work full time after having her baby. Her employer, a small public relations firm, had no policies in place for part-time workers.

A few weeks before she was due back at work, Jackie asked if she could work part time. Her employer agreed immediately, seeking Jackie's input in creating a formal policy. Her husband happened to work for a flexible employer. He asked for and received permission to work part time. Jackie and her husband each tend their baby when the other is working. Jackie takes pride in her flexible arrangement, and how easily she achieved it.

True, workers may have legitimate fears about asking for a flexible arrangement. But if a good employee makes a reasonable

What You Don't Ask for You Don't Get

Work-life expert Nancy Kane's step-by step-guide for requesting a flexible arrangement:

1. *Do your homework.* Research your company policies: what you have, what you don't, and what best-in-class or competitive companies offer, so you understand the ramifications to your benefits, time off, and so on. Put your feelers out for success stories and best practices. Find out who's doing what, how they made it work, and try to learn from that.

2. *Draft a proposal.* Include the impact of your desired flexible work arrangement on your job, manager, and workgroup. Present the challenges and propose solutions to them. Even if you don't have solutions for all of the challenges, you're much more likely to be met receptively from a manager when you've thought it all through.

3. *Pilot your flexible work arrangement.* Managers are much more comfortable with the idea of a temporary arrangement. In three to six months, review with your manager how the flexible work arrangement is going. Collect feedback from anybody on whom the new schedule might have an impact: people who report to you, peers, colleagues, customers, clients, and so on.

4. *If they say no.* If there's no good reason to deny your request, then like any other business challenge, you come up with Plan B. You might say, "I'm going to come back to you in three or six months after I've done X, Y, and Z, and I might ask you again." You might need another manager or peer of the person who said "No" to go to bat for you, or blow your horn and give you a little bit of recognition to show how valuable you are. Be very careful about going above your manager to the next level. You might ask the human resources department, if you have one. If the answer is just a flat no, you've given it your best shot, and you've tried more than once to make it happen, then maybe it's time to think about an employer that does want to meet your needs.

request, many employers will attempt to accommodate him or her. If a worker who never makes a request quits because work and family can't coexist, everybody loses. If a worker never asks for an accommodation, he or she may continue to run the treadmill unnecessarily. If you never ask, you'll never know.

In my own quest for more help, I've been amazed at how easily my husband has secured alternative schedules, a long paternity leave, and even a sabbatical from his supposedly inflexible employer. When his Aunt Kiki came to visit and saw Ed home with the girls, she said, "Oh, well, they let him do that."

But his employer did not volunteer to allow him do anything, other than work long hours and travel overseas for weeks at a time. Ed asked his office to accommodate his desire and need to participate at home.

Once men start to carve out time, others will follow suit. There is strength in numbers. Many of today's employees need or want time away from long hours at work, temporarily. Nancy Kane reports that in Catalyst's study of dual-income families:

> Seventy percent of male and female employees who participated in that study are looking for ways to customize their career path. And that means taking lateral moves. That means stepping off the fast track for a period of time; turning down a relocation, being able to be asked again; and using flexible work arrangements. Because roughly fifty-five percent of the workforce is dual career, what they're telling us is that cushion of incomes gives them an increased sense of freedom to take risks with their jobs.

Just as sharing responsibility at home has become a prerequisite for a happy marriage, women's advancement has made career flexibility an essential tool for employers and relationships. Men can—and are beginning to—reduce stress, strife, and inequality by making use of available policies and creating them when they're not already in place.

THE BUSINESS CASE FOR BEING FRIENDLY

The benefits of implementing flexible policies far outweigh the costs. Creative employees and employers, in this country and abroad, have already solved the problems of creating a work-life balance. The workplace has all the necessary tools and incentives.

Flexible employers have reduced turnover and recruiting and retraining expenses. They enjoy increased morale and productivity, and enhanced public images.[8] Studies have uniformly found an increase rather than a reduction in efficiency for part-time workers.[9] In a 1999 survey, 100 percent of managers said flexible employees were "the same as or more experienced, focused, and motivated when compared to other workers."[10] Each year, American employers lose millions of dollars and productivity when well-trained, experienced workers leave as a result of having no flexible or part-time options.[11]

Nancy Kane observes:

> It's become a competitive advantage for companies to address this issue. And younger employees are demanding it. It's a recruiting advantage to be able to say, for example, that you have the ability to telecommute. The employees now know to look for it and ask for it and to expect it.

Employers committed to their employees, who understand that it makes good economic sense to be flexible, succeed. And employees who ask for what they need often get it.

BROADEN THE TIME FRAME

Many perceive stay-at-home mothers as more privileged than their work-for-pay counterparts, spending their days at the country club sipping iced tea. However, most families with mothers at home are not wealthy. According to Census Bureau statistics, a father with an unemployed wife earns roughly the same income ($37,116) as a father whose wife works for pay ($35,713).

In my interviews of full-time parents and families where two parents work part time, I saw little evidence and heard little talk of what they had to give up. Most owned their own homes and two cars. Some parents bought toys and clothing from flea market sales. Many pointed to flaws in their decorating or living schemes, but everybody was safe, warm, and had lots of things.

Ira and Janey Berk have saved more money since Ira has worked part time than they would have had he remained in a full-time position. Having a parent at home and reducing day-care use to one afternoon a week, they report, has improved life for everybody in the family. Ira says:

> It's much more relaxed now. When it is time for them to go to bed, they usually stay in bed. They go to bed earlier than they used to. They're getting much more sleep now and so are we. We've reduced the stress level in our house. It really was a one-eighty.
>
> We sent them to a Montessori preschool because we felt strongly that they should get a good education. The other piece is that afterward, they would have gone to the day care at the school. When they were both in day care, they weren't able to do any activities. But when I started to stay at home, my kids were allowed to have friends over and to go to friends' houses. Now they have more of a social life.

Recognizing that families can thrive for a few years on one middle- or upper-middle-class salary opens up vast possibilities for redistributing the workload at home. In return for stepping off the merry-go-round, families find tangible benefits in their home life, including decreased stress, children who are easier to deal with and less tired, reduced conflict in their marriages, more quality and quantity family time, and the opportunity to spend time with aging relatives.

The experience of the Kings, Smith-Powells, and Berks show that sometimes it is okay to fall behind the Joneses for a small window of time—and you may well be happier as a result. While workplace pressures seem constant and immediate, careers can and do take turns, go on hiatus, and burn more brightly at one time or another. Others parents, such as Ted Koppel, Sandra Day O'Connor, and Eleanor Roosevelt, have achieved great success in their careers, despite making the time for their young children.

Ted Koppel quit his job at a top-rated ABC news show and worked part time while his wife attended graduate school so he could help tend their daughters. Sandra Day O'Connor took five years off from her legal career to stay home with her children and still became a state senator and Supreme Court justice. Despite giving birth to six children in eleven years and raising five of them (one died) under the domination of her disapproving mother-in-law, Eleanor Roosevelt did countless good works and became one of the leading figures of the twentieth century. Slowing down for three or even eleven years will not end parents' lifetime accomplishments outside the family.

ALL ABOARD

Are you thinking, "Yes, that's all true, but . . ."? Don't focus on the reasons you can't create a better situation. If you give in to the Mommy Trap, you might fail at something very important. Children's development correlates with marital and parental satisfaction.[12] In turn, parents' happiness and fathers' involvement bears a direct relationship to marital satisfaction.[13] Our society loses out each time talented women leave the workplace, children don't get what they need, mothers become miserable under the weight of too many responsibilities, or a marriage becomes a battleground. The best interests of families, society, and children all militate in favor of finding a better solution to the dilemma modern parents face.

Today, couples can share the responsibilities of providing for and taking care of the family. Dr. Pamela Jordan, author of *Becoming Parents: How to Strengthen Your Marriage As Your Family Grows*, advises:

> People need to sit down thoughtfully and reflect on what is important to them and, sometimes, to orchestrate their lives in a way that really reflects what their core values are. It might mean that you don't live in the biggest house, that you can't have two expensive cars. You really have to think about how you're living your life and whether it reflects what you value in your heart.

If you want to give your children more time, you will probably have to give up something to do so, at least temporarily. Figure out what that might be, together, and how high it ranks as a priority in the overall scheme of life. You might end up with a family day on Tuesday. Or, you could work on Saturday while your husband takes care of the children. We *can* have it all at the same time and like what we have, as long as the "we" includes both parents.

HAVE CONVICTION IN YOUR CONVICTIONS

It is difficult to swim against the tide. Sometimes fathers who make different choices encounter initial disapproval. People don't like arrangements that challenge the norm. Focus on your children, their smiles and warmth and hope. Eventually, more balanced relationships and more active fathering will become accepted, and will no longer be something to comment on. We are making progress, and we will all be better off as a result.

13

Laws That Can Help ▬▬▬

> One day, people will look back on what we had
> to go through and be shocked.
>
> —Janice, a mother of two who quit a prestigious
> movie studio executive position because she
> could not do her job and be home when her first son
> woke up or was ready to be tucked in at night

IS IT REALLY SO GREAT IN SWEDEN?

Among industrialized countries, the United States ranks second to last in terms of national maternity, paternity, and parental leave, and child-care policies.[1] Only South Africa does worse. The combination of federal inaction, old expectations, poor quality of available child care, and time demands at work give women a big shove into the Mommy Trap. We would do well to look to the models of other countries with higher standards of living in revamping the U.S. agenda.

All European Union countries provide *paid* maternity leave before and after birth, which generally lasts fourteen to eighteen weeks in all.[2] For example, in France paid maternity leave extends from six weeks before birth until ten weeks after delivery. During this time, French Social Security pays 90 percent of the mother's salary.[3]

Some European countries provide up to eleven weeks of paid maternity leave *before* the birth of a baby to "protect the mother and unborn child in the last months of pregnancy."[4] According to the European Union, "Maternity leave is a health measure to protect mothers and infants in late pregnancy and the early post-natal period."[5] And they're right: Providing paid maternity leaves greatly reduces the incidence of low-birth weight and deaths of infants and young children.[6]

In addition to paid maternity leave, most European countries also provide parental leave and "career breaks" that enable parents to spend time with and care for young children without jeopardizing their careers.[7] Parental leave allows fathers and mothers to stay home to care for their children after maternity leave has ended.[8] In Sweden, either parent may take one year of paid parental leave after the birth or adoption of a baby.[9] Parents may also use an additional three months of leave, at a lower pay rate, bringing the total parental leave time to fifteen months.[10] Sweden goes further than any other country in providing paid parental leave. Most other European nations do not offer paid parental leave, or provide only some minimal assistance.

The European Union views paternity leave as a male *right*. Because their governments encourage men to do so, European dads share parenting responsibilities more equally from the beginning, forging close bonds between father and child.[11]

The career break, another policy prevalent in Europe and relatively unknown in the United States, entitles employees to periods of time off from work, usually unpaid. Workers may return to jobs *at the same level they left,* without affecting promotion prospects. In France, either parent, if employed by a large employer (one hundred or more employees), is entitled to three years of guaranteed unpaid leave.[12]

Career breaks enable parents to spend time with their children without forfeiting whatever professional and economic status they have accumulated. I interviewed many full-time moms in the United States who would like to return to the workforce but believe that nobody would hire them at anything close to the level where they left. In contrast, Doug and Carole, two married Canadian journalists living in France, see a wide range of options and support for both parents. Carole reports:

> At my place of work, I was given twelve weeks maternity leave after the baby was born and six weeks at the end of the pregnancy. Coupled with vacation time, this meant that I was

able to take six months off to be with my son. Believe me, this was gold. I also got a few baby bonuses from the state to help cover the costs. I remember a colleague in Washington who took two months off after her baby was born and then was back at work, putting in ten-hour days. In hindsight, I don't know how she did it.

Here, the seven-hour day is the norm. The workplace is not as dynamic as in the U.S., but as far as juggling family and career, I think that France does give couples, in particular women, more breathing space.

Dad has also enjoyed some flexibility and involvement. Doug says:

When our son was born, I took the week of paternity leave to which I was entitled by law [now extended to two weeks]. To that week, I added two weeks of vacation time. So I spent a total of three weeks at home after the birth.

When my wife's leave ended, I took an additional seven weeks of vacation. I took Louis to Canada—just us boys—to meet his paternal grandparents, played househusband, and got to know my son. For all of that year, I was off eleven weeks— ten weeks of vacation and one week of paternity leave. By law, I get seven weeks vacation a year. In addition to that, I had banked a couple of extra weeks before Louis' birth by volunteering for overtime. Paternity leave was the beginning of a certain take-him-with-you attitude. Now, we cover a lot of ground together, me and the boy.

By law, I am not required to work more than thirty-five hours per week. And since Louis came along, I don't. So you see, we have plenty of family time. In my opinion, this is as good as it gets in a family where both parents have full-time jobs.

Another great provision is the *conge parental d'education*. This allows either mother or father to take up to three years of unpaid leave. Their job, salary, and seniority level are guaranteed. I might avail myself of this at some point. My wife's employer may eventually offer her a cushy job at some tropical bureau. When we get back to Paris, my job would be there waiting for me.

Is it just me, or did you get goose bumps reading those quotes? Unlike the United States, and most American employers, Europe does not treat pregnancy, labor, delivery, and infant care as illnesses, vacation, or personal (especially female) choices. The European Union has built into work and society the understanding that it is desirable and necessary for children to spend time with their parents (not only the mother). As a result, these countries fashioned national policies that foster the public interest in developing healthy, well-adjusted children and unstressed families.

THE AMERICAN WAY

Note that European policies include parental leave and career breaks, not just maternity leave. In the United States, the Family and Medical Leave Act (FMLA) represents the only national policy entitling parents to anything like parental leave. FMLA allows twelve weeks of job-protected, *unpaid* parental leave for new mothers and fathers who work for employers with fifty or more employees, to be used in the year after a baby's birth. Employers can require an employee to use all of his or her accumulated vacation or sick leave before taking FMLA.[13]

For example, in creating my six months of "maternity leave" under FMLA, I combined two months of accumulated sick leave, vacation time, and compensatory time, and then took four months of unpaid leave, with no entitlement to benefits during those four months. This policy tends to get women back to work sooner rather than later, without allowing them to feel competent at home, bond for long with their babies, or hold out for the best child-care arrangement. It also tends to force expectant mothers to work until the last minute, to the discomfort of very pregnant and anxious women, and those with the misfortune to be around them. I went out to lunch on the day Elizabeth was born and delivered nine hours later.

The health aspect of the European concept of maternity leave is radical here. Instead of preventing medical problems, U.S. policies add to the stress on mother and child during those last weeks of pregnancy and early months of life. We penalize women for getting pregnant. A mother must use all of her accumulated sick and vacation time simply because she functions as most female humans do.

Although they have the same entitlement as women under the law, few fathers make use of FMLA after the birth of their babies.[14] Because it is unpaid, taking advantage of FMLA would directly contradict the ethos that says males must provide for their families. In fact, most people, and many middle managers (those charged with implementing work–life policies), view FMLA's extension to fathers as a formal necessity to pass constitutional muster by making it theoretically available to men.[15]

FMLA covers just 55 percent of American workers.[16] And FMLA has an extremely low utilization rate—just 2 to 3.6 percent of employees entitled to benefits under FMLA make use of them.[17] Legal scholars, and others, have criticized FMLA for discriminating against low-wage earners who most need paid maternity and paternity leave but cannot afford to take unpaid leave, and for preventing fathers from becoming more involved.[18]

Law professor Michael Selmi, who has written extensively about FMLA, says:

> FMLA should be paid, for both mothers and fathers. Women need some replacement income for the initial time they take off. Everyone should be entitled to at least three months. Asking people to go back to work before three months is just not fair.
>
> The unpaid FMLA is almost worthless. It's better than nothing but only a little bit because if we had nothing there might be more of an impetus for paid leave.

Nineteen states have enacted family leave laws that offer more benefits—such as longer or paid leave, or extending to employers with fewer than fifty employees—than FMLA.[19] For example, Kansas, Maryland, Massachusetts, New Hampshire, Montana, California, and Puerto Rico require most employers to provide temporary disability leave for pregnant employees (usually six weeks). But most states provide no such guarantee. Even when they do, partial payment for leave is not always available.

FMLA frequently acts as a twelve-week maternity leave for those who can afford to go without pay for that long, leaving lower-income families with no real options. And because only 49 percent of American employers offer some form of paid maternity leave,[20] most American mothers and fathers don't move along the continuum to the parental leave or career breaks offered in Europe, or even realize that such options might exist.

Selmi observes:

> I don't know exactly why our policies are so bad in compar-
> ison to other countries and why it's so hard to change. I think
> we remain ambivalent about the role women should have.
> Politically, Republicans think women should still stay home for
> the most part, and that's what the policy should be. So they
> don't want to support women in the workplace even though
> they know that's just not going to be the reality anymore. I'm
> not sure why the Democrats haven't made it more of an issue.
> There is such a shortage of good day care.

Politicians will respond to the desires of their constituents if
the constituents demand it. The needs of families cut across party
lines. Once we address our ambivalence about the roles that parents should play, we can improve our family leave options. In light
of the importance of parents spending time with children, the need
to get fathers involved early, and the benefits to employers of flexible alternatives, short and nonsubsidized FMLA (and leaving it to
the states to decide whether to fill in the gaps) harms parents, the
workplace, and society.

IN YOUR FACE
Did you catch the thirty-five-hour-a-week limit for full-time work in
France? We don't have that here. For example, during my tenure at a
corporate law firm, I worked for Ted, an admittedly male chauvinist
partner. Ted opined about just about everything, making among others the following pronouncement: "Every weekend hour, or other
hour not worked by an attorney, is a billable hour lost forever."

This edict demonstrates a misguided workplace norm that makes
working mothers less successful in their careers than their male
counterparts. It depicts an American corporate culture that values
hours worked more than anything else, including productivity. In
a law firm where profits accrue in relation to hours billed, a parent
involved with his or her children becomes a liability. While law
firms may be the most extreme example of this phenomenon, a large
proportion of American businesses require more than a nine-to-five
commitment, promoting employees who put in the most hours or
"face time."

Our society doesn't have to make this choice, and we don't have to adhere to it, personally or collectively. Again, Europe and non-traditional families provide a different model. For example, in *The Overworked American,* Juliet Schor found that American manufacturing employees work the equivalent of two more months a year than their Western European counterparts.[21] She also found that the average modern American works the equivalent of an extra month a year compared to the average American worker in 1970.[22] Her research showed a rise in hours across all income categories, industries, occupations, and family patterns.[23]

Nancy Kane, work–life counselor for Catalyst Inc., reports:

> Face time, where you're judged based on presence not performance, is still an issue in today's workplace. That really has to do with management. More and more, [with] companies that are on "best lists," and companies that win the Catalyst Award in general, we see a lot of companies where face time isn't an issue. But it really comes down to the department and ultimately the manager. A lot of enlightened managers are using results to evaluate performance, not face time.

If you work in an environment where face time is important, you can raise the issue of changing to a performance-based evaluation, try to carve out some personal time, or leave. If your BATNA is good, your employer may well accede to your requests. If enough employees (both male and female) speak out against unnecessary time requirements or vote with their feet, employers will have to change their ways.

CHANGES WE CAN'T AFFORD NOT TO CONSIDER

We have a crisis on our hands that will certainly haunt us in the future if we do not address it now. Investment in our children and our future is just as important as, for example, plowing billions into the Russian economy so that capitalism can succeed in a country thousands of miles away from us. Other western countries have placed value on the family in formulating national policies, enabling parents to spend time with their young children. They are right to do so. We should not let this morass of ad hoc arrangements, which do not work, continue.

In our current system, many American parents do not feel as if they have a wide range of choices when it comes to family, work, and care arrangements. Though they may have more than they think, the system (or nonsystem) in this country needs an overhaul. Too often, it prevents mothers and fathers from making their best family effort. A number of laws would soften the choices for parents between educating, tending to, and providing for their children, and fulfilling themselves. Especially intriguing, we could push for legislation that provides incentives for men to make use of flexible policies.

Here are some reasonable suggestions that can make a big impact:

Tax Credits

A tax credit for part-time or stay-at-home parents of children ages three and younger, limited to those with upper-middle-class incomes and below, would help give time at home to those who can use it the most. Adding a tax credit and saving on child-care expenses will help part-time incomes go further, facilitating family time.

A double credit for men will encourage fathers to do more child care and less paid work. It can give men governmental and societal permission to parent, and an excuse for getting involved with their children. If they can help provide income for the family in the form of a tax break, men can honor the old provider model as well as their newfound nurturing role.

Right now, despite the desirability of two part-time jobs for parents and children, using such an arrangement carries great financial and professional costs. According to Jason Marx, who works part time as a professor and whose wife, Theresa, works part time as a nurse:

> Health insurance is a biggie for us now. There is no family friendly anything in this country. If we both got full-time jobs, the insurance would be redundant. But we'd have to pay half a salary to a stranger to watch the kids.

A tax credit for parents who stay home or work part time would help our society make the important investment of time in our children when they need it most. In addition, as we have seen, it is in the interest of this country to raise productive citizens.

Longer and Paid Maternity Leave

Most maternity leaves in this country are family-hostile. Workers should push for paid and longer maternity leaves, emphasizing the needs of the changed workforce, and the costs employers must absorb when they lose trained employees who cannot meet all of their responsibilities at home and at work.

Studies have shown that the cost of replacing workers who leave ranges from 1.2 to 2 times the salary of the replaced worker, and that it takes about a year for a new employee to achieve maximum efficiency. A Families and Work Institute study found that it costs far less to support a paid maternity leave and unpaid parental leave than to replace the employee permanently.[24] It costs 150 percent and 70 percent of annual salaries to replace managers and nonmanagers, respectively. But the average cost of supporting a maternity leave is just 32 percent of annual salary.[25]

We don't need to spend a public cent in creating paid maternity leaves. Either employers can foot the bill, actually a savings in the long-term, or we can buy temporary disability insurance plans for pregnancy and childbirth, as those in California, New York, New Jersey, Rhode Island, Hawaii, and Puerto Rico already do.

Forcing women to take sick and vacation leave for getting pregnant and having babies is wrong. Society benefits from and could not continue without women having babies. Society also benefits if parents do childrearing right and pays the costs if parents do childrearing badly. For starters, children whose parents lack paid leave or flexible hours are two to three times more likely to end up with reading, math, and behavioral problems.[26] Somewhere along the line, we will have to pay for someone else's kids in some way. Why not do it up front, in a way that will make our futures better?

The American College of Obstetrics recommends that new mothers refrain from working for four to six weeks to physically recover from labor and delivery, which is neither an illness nor a vacation. American employers should provide at least eight weeks of paid maternity leave, including two weeks of leave before a due date, to encourage maximum child and mother well-being during this critical time.

In addition to causing employees stress and health problems, many American employers' policies cost them money. Childbearing itself does not have a large impact on a woman's job performance.

However, the subsequent childrearing and homemaking responsi-bilities she takes on affect her job performance, and may lead her to leave the workforce altogether.[27] *It is not that women have babies and men do not that makes women less-committed workers, but the current allocation of family responsibilities once babies are born, com-bined with short-sighted employer policies.* Encouraging and provid-ing time during the early years for both dads and moms through proactive measures for men and paid maternity leave will benefit children, parents, marriage, society, and the workplace.

Longer and Paid Paternity Leave

We should push for ten days of *paid* paternity leave. Society bene-fits when fathers bond with their infants, participate in childrear-ing, and help their wives recover while temporarily disabled. *The federal government should provide incentives to employers whose em-ployees make use of paid paternity leave.* Even in Europe, men do not take paternity leave unless it is paid at a rate close to their earn-ings.[28] We might also consider the radical but practical suggestions of a 1998 Japanese government conference: Make one month of paid paternity leave mandatory and provide incentive bonuses to couples who stagger their child-care leave.[29]

Longer and Paid Parental Leave

Ultimately, the United States will institute some type of parental leave similar to those in France and Sweden. We need to raise this issue and start working toward it, educating the public about the benefits of parental care for small children, and the realities of sub-stitute care in this country. We can start by seeking unpaid parental leaves beyond the twelve weeks afforded by FMLA. Parents can (and many would like to) trade salary for time with their children. As unpaid parental leaves cost little, we may convince employers that providing unpaid parental leaves of up to a year would cost less than paying turnover costs.

Career Breaks

Either parent should be able to take two years off after the birth of a child, knowing that at the end of those two years he or she can return to his or her job, at the same level of pay and responsibility.

While it might seem onerous to keep jobs open, once the policy gets rolling, at any given time workers will be both coming back and leaving. The money saved by not having to hire new employees and provide job training offsets the costs of administering career breaks. Many employers have already agreed to informal career breaks, granting sabbaticals or leaves of absence.

It might seem undesirable for companies to keep jobs open for employees falling behind in their jobs. That's the "cannot" attitude. Career breaks have worked for European employers with "can do" attitudes. Dow Benelux, a Netherlands company, regularly informs people on career breaks about developments in their fields and about job openings. It also provides refresher courses on reentry to the company and the option of working for other employees during sickness or holidays.

National Westminster Bank, a United Kingdom employer, requires career breakers to work a minimum of two weeks a year. The bank allows career breakers with particularly good job performance reentry at the same grade, and offers those without such stellar records jobs from waiting lists. Providing two tiers of reentry gives National Westminster Bank the flexibility to tailor career breakers' returns to the Bank's needs at any given time. National Westminster Bank holds seminars on banking issues for career breakers each year, recognizing that they can become isolated and out of touch.

Employers can address their own needs at the same time they provide career breaks. Why do these companies want to? Because investing minimally in valued, already trained workers costs less than replacing them. As with other family-friendly policies, career breaks reduce turnover, increase morale, enhance public image, improve career opportunities for women, and improve management and staff relationships.[30] Along with men making more use of part-time work, career breaks prevent women from giving up on the workplace once they have children, and may encourage men to step out of the provider mode for a while.

Prorated Part-Time Benefits

I found the issue of benefits one of the largest stumbling blocks for couples who want to reduce their workforce participation. Many who wanted to couldn't go part time because they would lose too much in health insurance, life insurance, and other benefits (about 40 percent of a full-time salary).[31] Catalyst researcher Nancy Kane agrees:

> It's a very real issue. I would say that most of the best practice companies I see give benefits to employees who work twenty hours or more [a week]. Full benefits. We work with a lot of progressive Fortune 500 companies. I know not everyone has access to that. But, I think at its most basic level, these policies enable them to retain a talented workforce.

A federal law mandating prorated benefits for part-time workers working twenty or more hours a week would make the choice of part-time work more attractive for parents and others who have elder-care responsibilities or outside interests they want to pursue. This legislation would lead to enhanced productivity, retention of employees, more profits, and better-adjusted parents and children.

Tax Credit for Flexible Employers

The government should provide tax incentives to employers when employees *use* family-friendly policies such as part-time work, flextime, work-at-home, parental leave, career breaks, and time shifting. The tax code could award a double credit every time a man made use of part-time work and career breaks for the first ten years of the program. Then, employers would have economic incentives to get their middle managers (who can make or break flexible arrangements) to encourage flexible arrangements for men. Such a change would foster the public interest in parents spending time with children, and enhance marriage and kids' achievement.

We need to push for flexibility, for ourselves, for our fellow employees, and for all employees. Nonparents can also benefit from these policies, which will help change our workplace from a time-oriented to a results-based apparatus.

Breast Pumping Hour

Current medical opinion holds that a baby cannot properly digest cow's milk until he or she is a year old. Breast-fed babies have fewer illnesses and greater intelligence.[32] The most recent recommendation of the American Academy of Pediatrics, the most stringent ever, urges women to breastfeed for a year. While no mother should feel bad if she cannot or does not want to breastfeed, nursing stimulates and creates attachment between mother and baby, an outcome in everybody's best interest. Since breast-fed babies have fewer illnesses, breastfeeding also furthers the interests of employers: The fewer illnesses a baby has, the less time a parent needs to take off from work to care for a sick child.

Employers ought to make it easier for women to express milk at work. A policy allowing a breastfeeding hour for the first year would be relatively easy and not costly to implement. It would last only for a finite period of time, and benefit the company and its employees. Women would no longer have to skulk around, carting pumps and ice packs around, holing up in cubicles or restrooms, tense and afraid that someone will walk in at the wrong moment.

In an ideal world, employers would create a mother's room where employees could leave pumps. The nursing room could also contain a small refrigerator for the storage of expressed milk. We could require businesses to provide a nursing room by passing city and town ordinances mandating commercial developers to include them in their new buildings. Unions could also demand an accommodation for nursing.

Day-Care Quality Standards and On-Site Day Care

We must also address our child-care crisis. As noted in chapter 2, good substitute care is difficult to find, regardless of price. Good-quality day care in centers costs a lot to produce, but only about 10 percent more than poor-quality care. However, both high- and poor-quality day-care centers charge similar fees.[33] Because parents can have difficulty recognizing good care, they do not provide enough market incentives to force day-care providers to improve quality.

Parents need to have better information about what makes for good care, and to ask for quality services when they do not occur. Per the recommendations of the 1995 Cost, Quality & Child Outcomes Study Team, the government should disseminate information "to help parents identify high-quality child care programs and to inform the American public of the liability of poor-quality programs."[34]

Some of the other measures already suggested will reduce the demand for substitute child care by enabling more family time. But government intervention can enhance quality, safety, and accessibility of child care for those who want or need to use it, providing families with better outcomes and less worry. The nationwide registry of child-care workers and methods for checking backgrounds of workers from state to state that the Clinton administration proposed, and Congress did not act on, makes good sense.

Similarly, the government could provide tax incentives to employers to maintain on-site day-care and early-learning centers. Parents prefer knowing what type of care their children get, checking in on them, and participating in their day. With on-site care, children don't have to go nine, ten, or twelve hours without seeing a parent, and parents can better monitor the quality of care.

We should also promulgate and enforce quality standards for day-care centers and family day care. Rigorous accreditation procedures with periodic surprise inspections more than a few times a year can make quality programs the rule rather than the exception. Regulated and licensed day-care providers provide higher-quality care.[35] Accreditation, enforcement, and a reduced demand made possible by other family-friendly policies, a changed workplace, and better information for parents, can weed out the bad programs.

LET'S GET TOGETHER AND FEEL ALL RIGHT

Today, moms and dads have more life possibilities than ever before. Let us raise the collective voice and arms of soothing, supportive, and supported parents, children, and communities. We can create a world in which mothers and fathers find satisfaction inside and outside the home, and in each other. There, children can grow, play, and learn according to their own schedules, with those they love best and who love them best. Sound idealistic? Maybe, but I've seen that new place and it is ours to claim.

NOTES

Throughout this book I have quoted from unpublished interviews I conducted with parents who have a wide range of work and child-care arrangements. I formally interviewed thirty-five couples with nontraditional arrangements and five couples with a traditional parenting division of labor. I informally interviewed an additional forty sets of parents whose arrangements ran the gamut.

I used the same questionnaire with each couple so that I could glean a minimum, standard level of information for comparison's sake. The interviewees lived all over the United States, and one couple lived in France. The greatest concentration was from Washington, D.C., and its outlying suburbs. Some were on their second marriages and second set of children, but most were first marriages of parents in their mid-thirties to early forties. Though a few were college and graduate students, the majority of those interviewed were well established in their careers. While most held graduate degrees, a few had received no education beyond high school. Except where authorized to provide their real names and circumstances, I

have changed the names and some of the distinguishing characteristics of the families.

Chapter 1: THERE'S STILL A LONG WAY TO GO, BABY

1. Pamela L. Jordan, Scott M. Stanley, and Howard J. Markman, *Becoming Parents: How to Strengthen Your Marriage As Your Family Grows* (San Francisco: Jossey-Bass, 1999), p. xi.
2. Arlie Russell Hochschild, with Anne Machung, *The Second Shift* (New York: Avon Books, 1989), p. 3.
3. For example, Joseph Pleck found that between 1965 and 1988, the amount of time fathers spend with their children increased from 25 percent of the time mothers spend with them to 33 percent of the time ("Community Spotlight: The Changing Roles of Fathers," *Parent News for June 1998,* on-line at http://npin.org/pnews/1998/pnew698/pnew 698c.html). Averaging studies from the 1980s and 1990s showed fathers' proportional engagement was 43.5 percent of mothers'. Joseph H. Pleck, "Paternal Involvement: Levels, Sources, and Consequences," in *The Role of the Father in Child Development,* ed. Michael E. Lamb, 3rd ed. (New York: John Wiley & Sons, 1997), p. 71; Tamar Lewin, "Men Assuming Bigger Share at Home, New Survey Shows," *New York Times,* April 15, 1998, p. A18. (Despite the self-reported increases in men's participation, 70 percent of working parents said they did not have enough time to spend with their children, 56 percent of employed mothers said they wished the fathers would spend more time with their children, and 43 percent said they wished the men would do more household chores.)
4. Michael Bittman and Judy Wactman, "The Rush Hour: The Quality of Leisure Time and Gender Equity," Social Policy Research Centre Discussion Paper No. 97, February 1999.
5. *Two definitive studies:* Carolyn Pape Cowan and Philip A. Cowan, *The Landmark Ten-Year Study, When Partners Become Parents: The Big Life Change for Couples* (New York: BasicBooks, 1992), pp. 93, 97; Jay Belsky, Ph.D., and John Kelly, *The Transition to Parenthood: How a First Child Changes a Marriage: Why Some Couples Grow Closer and Others Apart* (New York: Delacorte Press, 1994), p. 227.
6. Many of the women Hochschild studied tried to convince their husbands to participate more equally, and then gave up. For example: "[T]he Holts tell us a great deal about the subtle ways a couple can encapsulate the tension caused by a struggle over the second shift without resolving the problem or divorcing. Like Nancy Holt, many women struggle to avoid, suppress, obscure, or mystify a frightening conflict over the second shift. . . . But beneath the happy image of the woman

with the flying hair are modern marriages like the Holts', reflecting in-
tricate webs of tension, and the huge, hidden emotional cost to women,
men, and children of having to 'manage' inequality" (Hochschild, *The
Second Shift*, pp. 56–58).

7. A National Institutes of Health study found that mothers who worked
   outside the home are "less depressed, less anxious and more zestful
   about their lives than homemakers." Rosalind C. Barnett and Caryl
   Rivers, *She Works He Works: How Two-Income Families Are Happy,
   Healthy, and Thriving* (Cambridge, Mass.: Harvard University Press,
   1996), pp. 28–32, 39.

8. See, for example, "EHarlequin.com Surveys 8,000 Women to Find Out
   What They Really Want," October 16, 2001, on-line at http://biz.yahoo
   .com/prnews/011016/nytufns1_1.html; Belsky and Kelly, *The Transition to Parenthood*, p. 140 (noting that most of the couples studied
   were transitional, between the traditional and the egalitarian gender
   ideology).

Chapter 2: WHY QUALITY SUBSTITUTE CARE IS NOT A COMPLETE ANSWER

1. Barnett and Rivers, *She Works He Works*, pp. 28–32, 39 (see chap. 1,
   n. 7).

2. Throughout this book I have included quotes from experts I interviewed about issues related to the Mommy Trap, including those who
   have researched and written about child development, substitute care,
   negotiation, marriage, the transition to parenthood, work–life issues,
   family leave, sex discrimination, and employment law. I also interviewed psychologists and psychiatrists, pediatricians, educators, baby-
   sitters, day-care workers, and financial experts. Unless a footnote
   accompanies a quote, I am quoting directly from an interview.

3. "Positive effects of high quality, center-based programs on children's
   cognitive and language skills have been demonstrated in experimental interventions for infants and children from low-income families
   (Burchinal et al., 2000; McLloyd, 1998; Ramsey et al., in press). It has
   not been established if there are similar beneficial effects for center-
   type experiences for children from affluent families or beneficial effects
   when the quality of care is not exemplary or when the care is used for
   brief periods of time." (Deborah Lowe Vandell, "Early Child Care and
   Children's Development Prior to School Entry: NICHD Early Child
   Care Research Network," presented at the April 2001 SCRD conference,
   pp. 4–5.) "[T]he negative relations of poverty to children's cognitive,
   social, and physical development also are well documented (McLloyd,

1998). Children from poor homes begin school at a disadvantage that has been judged to be large enough to warrant public expenditures for Head Start, Title I early education programs, and other services. Hence, parenting quality and family poverty are significant contexts with which to compare child care." (Vandell, "Early Child Care and Children's Development Prior to School Entry," pp. 6–7.)

4. Pleck, "Paternal Involvement: Levels, Sources, and Consequences," pp. 96–97 (see chap. 1, n. 3); Kyle Pruett, *The Nurturing Father: Journey Toward the Complete Man* (New York: Warner Books, 1987), pp. 35, 74–75, 200; N. Radin, "Primary Care-giving and Role-sharing Fathers," in *Nontraditional Families: Parenting and Child Development,* ed. M. E. Lamb (New York: Erlbaum Associates, 1982), pp. 173–204.

5. In addition to the demonstrated advantages of father care discussed in the text (*see* Pruett, *The Nurturing Father,* where 100 percent of children securely attached to fathers achieved superior development test scores), mothers report highest satisfaction with father care. "Sydney Family Development Project: Longitudinal Predictors of Children's Socio-emotional Development" (paper presented at the Australian Early Childhood Association National Biennial Conference, Darwin, 1999); Ellen Galinsky et al., *The Study of Children in Family Child Care and Relative Care: Highlights of Findings* (New York: Families and Work Institute, 1994), p. 87. In my interviews, every mother who was a breadwinner expressed great satisfaction with her husband's care of her children, and a belief that parental care was better than hired care as a reason for the family's arrangement; see also Kyle Pruett, *Father-need: Why Father Care Is As Essential As Mother Care for Your Child* (New York: Free Press, 2000): "The wives of the primary caregiver dads in my study also deeply appreciate that they do not have to worry about the quality, consistency or devotion of their child's caregiver" (p. 73).

6. "Conclusions: among nonpoverty and nondepressed mothers, higher qualities of mother-child interaction were observed at 36 months when mothers used no regular child care than when they used full-time care across the first three years" (Mother-Child Interaction and Cognitive Outcomes Associated with Early Child Care: Results of the NICHD Study, Nonmaternal Child Care and Qualities of Mother-Child Interaction: Findings); Belsky found substitute care of more than twenty hours a week in the first year of life a "risk factor" for future psychological and behavioral difficulties, associated with insecure attachment, heightened aggressiveness, and noncompliant behavior (J. Belsky, "The 'Effects' of Infant Day Care Reconsidered," *Early Childhood Research*

Quarterly [1988], pp. 3, 235–72); "We do not recommend full-time day care, 30 or more hours of care by nonparents, for infants and toddlers *if* the parents are able to provide high-quality care themselves and *if* the parents have reasonable options" (T. Berry Brazelton and Stanley I. Greenspan, *The Irreducible Needs of Children: What Every Child Must Have to Grow, Learn, and Flourish* [Cambridge, Mass.: Perseus Publishing, 2000], p. 48); Sara Blaffer Hrdy, *Mother Nature: A History of Mothers, Infants, and Natural Selection* (New York: Pantheon Books, 1999), pp. 506–7. The NICHD found that starting care later made for greater attachment, cognitive development and a better mother-child interaction (NICHD study, Conclusions: "Negative effects of hours in the first 6 months showed a persistent effect at 36 months on mother-child interaction").

7. "Children with more child care hours per week (quantity intercept) had more problem behaviors according to their caregivers than did children with fewer child care hours. . . . Large amounts of child care were associated with behavior problems, even after quality of care was controlled" (Vandell, "Early Child Care and Children's Development Prior to School Entry," pp. 16, 21); more time in care led to evaluations listing traits including "bragging/boasting, demands lots of attention, and argues a lot, as well as on items that reflected disobedience/defiance, such as talks out of turn, disobedient at school, and defiant, talking back to staff, but on items that were unambiguously aggressive in nature too, including gets into many fights, cruelty, bullying or meanness to others, physically attacks people, and explosive, showing unpredictable behavior" (NICHD Early Child Care Research Network, "Further Explorations of the Detected Effects of Quantity of Early Child Care on Socio-emotional Adjustment," presented at SCRD conference in April 2001). Belsky, "The 'Effects' of Infant Day Care Reconsidered," states "higher quantity of care or a history of more hours in child care was associated with . . . more reported problem behaviors when the children were two years old." Lower quality care (about 90 percent of care purchased) predicted "less harmonious mother-child relationships, a higher probability of insecure mother-child attachment of mothers who are already low in sensitivity to their children, and more problem behaviors, lower cognitive and language ability and lower school readiness scores" (NICHD Study, Nonmaternal Child Care and Qualities of Mother-Child Interaction: Findings).

8. "When not in care, children of low-risk (nondepressed and nonpoverty) mothers showed more positive engagement with mother at 36 months

than when in full-time care, regardless of its quality. . . . Among non-poverty and nondepressed mothers, higher qualities of mother-child interaction were observed at 36 months when mothers used no regular child care than when they used full-time care across the first three years" (NICHD Study, Nonmaternal Child Care and Qualities of Mother-Child Interaction: Findings).

9. "The decline (in childcare provider education and training) may well be related to the generally low wages in the child care field, which have not improved over the 1990s. Teachers average between $13,125 and $18,988 for full-week, full-year employment, assistant teachers only $6.00 [to] $7.00 an hour. It is not surprising that turnover is high, with 20 percent of centers losing half or more of their staff in the course of a year" ("Child Care Quality: Does It Matter and Does It Need to Be Improved? Executive Summary," Department of Health and Human Services, 2000, p. 2).

10. J. Campos, K. Barrett, M. Lamb, H. Goldsmith, and C. Stenberg, "Socioemotional Development," in *Handbook of Child Psychology*, ed. P. Mussen, vol. 2 (San Francisco, Calif.: Jossey-Bass, 1983); D. Coates and M. Lewis, "Early Mother-Infant Interaction and Infant Cognitive Status As Predictors of School Performance and Cognitive Behavior in Six-Year-Olds," in *Child Development* 55 (1984): 1219–30; Galinsky et al., *The Study of Children in Family Child Care*, p. 26.

11. *A child's brain develops most during the first three years:* Betty Hart and Todd R. Risley, *Meaningful Differences in the Everyday Experience of Young American Children* (Baltimore, Md.: Paul H. Brookes Publishing, 1995), p. 45; "Studies Show Talking with Infants Shapes Basis of Ability to Think," *New York Times*, April 17, 1997, p. D21. *The brain develops through hearing words:* Hart and Risley, *Meaningful Differences in the Everyday Experience of Young American Children*, pp. 10–11, 45; "Studies Show Talking with Infants Shapes Basis of Ability to Think," *New York Times*.

12. Hart & Risley, *Meaningful Differences in the Everyday Experience of Young American Children*, pp. 124, 145, 192; "On average, preschoolers perform better on standardized cognitive tests when their caregivers are better educated and trained—for example, if they have at least an associate arts degree in a child-related field. The children also have better language skills, are more persistent in completing tasks, and in general are more ready for school" ("Child Care Quality," HHS, p. 2); Hart and Risley found socio-economic status governed effect and frequency of negative versus positive interaction. Many researchers have noted that children of educated mothers receive the greatest disparity between

maternal and substitute care. See also Galinsky et al., *The Study of Children in Family Child Care and Relative Care*, p. 38 ("Providers with higher levels of education are more likely to be rated as offering good or adequate/custodial care").

13. Hart and Risley, *Meaningful Differences in the Everyday Experience of Young American Children*, pp. 145, 192; "Child Care Quality," HHS, p 2.

14. *91 percent of family day-care homes:* Only 9 percent of family day-care homes are of good quality; 35 percent are inadequate or growth harming; 56 percent provide adequate custodial care, neither helpful nor harmful to children's development. Galinsky et al., *The Study of Children in Family Child Care and Relative Care*, p. 4.

86 percent of day-care centers: A 1995 four-university study of day-care centers found only 14 percent meet children's needs for health, safety, warm relationships, and learning. Most day-care centers studied (74 percent) provide care rated as minimal, meeting basic health and sanitary needs but providing children with little attention or educational encouragement. Forty percent of infant and toddler care provided in day-care centers earned a poor quality rating of "less than minimal." Cost, Quality & Child Outcomes Study Team, *Cost, Quality, and Child Outcomes in Child Care Centers, Executive Summary*, 2nd edition (Denver: Economics Department, University of Colorado at Denver, 1995), p. 2. "This may represent a rather optimistic picture, for the sites that did not consent to the study seem likely to have offered lower-quality care" ("Child Care Quality," HHS, p. 2).

The turnover rate in the child-care field: (see chap. 2, n. 9).

Changing care arrangements can be disruptive: E. H. Cummings, "Caregiver Stability and Day Care," *Developmental Psychology* 16 (1980): 31–37; M. Whitebook, C. Howes, and D. Phillips, "Who Cares?: Child Care Teachers and the Quality of Care in America," Final Report, National Child Care Staffing Study (Oakland, Calif.: Child Care Employee Project, 1990); Brazelton and Greenspan, *The Irreducible Needs of Children*, pp. 27, 47, 49; "Instability of care, as measured by the number of entries into new care arrangements, was found to be associated with higher probability of insecure attachment in infancy if mothers were not providing sensitive and responsive care" ("The NICHD Study of Early Child Care" [NICHD Publications On-line (www.nichd.nih.gov/publications/pubs/early_child_care.htm), prepared by Robin Peth-Pierce], p. 16).

Infants in poor quality day-care centers: "Density and turnover rate important risk factors in day care infections: crowding, direct contact, the opportunity for indirect transmission and lack of toilet training can increase the spread of infection in a day care setting" (G. Sandler, "Infectious Diseases in Children," July 1996); "Higher-quality settings are likely to have better health and safety practices, resulting in fewer respiratory and other infections among the children, and have fewer playground injuries" ("Child Care Quality," HHS, p. 2).

15. Galinsky et al. *The Study of Children in Family Child Care and Relative Care,* pp. 83, 87. The mothers in the national family day-care study whose children received care rated as higher quality were not more satisfied than the mothers whose children received lower-quality rated care. See also Marybeth Shinn, Ellen Galinsky, and Leyla Gulcur, "The Role of Child Care Centers in the Lives of Parents" (New York: Family and Work Institute, 1991): "As in previous research, satisfaction with child care arrangements was quite high even though the National Child Care Staffing Study (Whitebook et al., 1989) found that the quality of care in the centers from which we drew parents was frequently quite low" (p. 21). "Ninety percent of parents rate programs as very good, while the ratings of trained observers indicate that most of these same programs are providing care that ranges from poor to mediocre. . . . The inability of parents to recognize good-quality care implies that they do not demand it. There is little difference in fees between poor-quality and high-quality centers, which lends credence to this hypothesis" (Cost, Quality & Child Outcomes Study Team, *Cost, Quality, and Child Outcomes in Child Care Centers, Executive Summary,* p. 9).

16. Cost, Quality & Child Outcomes Study Team, *Cost, Quality, and Child Outcomes in Child Care Centers, Executive Summary,* p. 9.

17. Burton L. White, *The First Three Years of Life: New and Revised Edition* (New York: Fireside, 1985), p. 271.

18. "We do not recommend full-time day care, 30 or more hours of care by nonparents, for infants and toddlers *if* the parents are able to provide high-quality care themselves and *if* the parents have reasonable options" (Brazelton and Greenspan, *The Irreducible Needs of Children,* p. 48).

19. Penelope Leach, *Children First: What Society Must Do—and Is Not Doing—for Children Today* (New York: Vintage Books, 1994), p. 78.

20. Patricia Edmunds, "Now the Word Is Balance," *USA Weekend,* October 23–25, 1998 (www.usaweekend.com/98_issues/981025/981025 millennium.html).

21. Joan K. Peters, *When Mothers Work: Loving Our Children without Sacrificing Ourselves* (Reading, Mass.: Addison-Wesley, 1997), pp. 110–11.

22. "The bedtime routine seems particularly difficult for parents who are away at work for much of the children's waking time. Because their

children must adhere to the parents' schedules all day, they try to avoid more conflict in the evening" (Cowan and Cowan, *The Landmark Ten-Year Study, When Partners Become Parents,* p. 78 [see chap. 1, n. 5]).

23. "The means of dealing with parents' time deficit at home—hurrying, segmenting, and organizing—forces parents to notice, understand, and cope with the emotional consequences of the compressed second shift. Children respond by protesting, having tantrums, dawdling, refusing to leave when it's time to go, and trying to leave when it's time to stay" (Arlie Russell Hochschild, *The Time Bind: When Work Becomes Home and Home Becomes Work* [New York: Metropolitan Books, 1997], pp. 51, 83, 214–18).

24. Stanley Greenspan, *The Four Thirds Solution: Solving the Childcare Crisis in America Today* (Boston: Perseus Publishing, 2001), p. 95.

25. The Bureau of Labor Statistics reported 440,000 male part-time workers and 3,102,000 female part-time workers in households of married people with children under six years old for 1995–96. Bureau of Labor Statistics, Table 5. "Employment status of persons by sex, marital status, and presence and age of own children under 18, annual averages 1995–96," last modified June 13, 1997.

Chapter 3: YES, MEN CAN, AND IT WILL BE GOOD FOR THEM, TOO

1. Pruett, *The Nurturing Father* (see chap. 2, n. 4), pp. 76–77.

2. Michael E. Lamb, "The Development of Father-Infant Relationships," in *The Role of the Father in Child Development,* ed. Michael E. Lamb, 3rd ed. (New York: John Wiley & Sons, 1997), p. 107.

3. Fathers respond to babies' distress signals such as sucking, pausing, and spitting up by stopping feeding, looking more closely, and feeding the baby again (Ross D. Parke and Armin A. Brott, *Throwaway Dads: The Myths and Barriers That Keep Men from Being the Fathers They Want to Be* [Boston: Houghton-Mifflin, 1999], p. 25); Lamb, "The Development of Father-Infant Relationships," p. 106; Pruett, *The Nurturing Father,* p. 32.

4. "We concluded that there were no biologically based sex differences in responsiveness to infants and that behavioral dimorphisms emerged in response to societal pressures and expectations" (Lamb, "The Development of Father-Infant Relationships," p. 105).

5. For example, infants more securely attached to both parents are more sociable. Those securely attached to both parents are more pleasant (Lamb, "The Development of Father-Infant Relationships," p. 116);

Children whose parents are both involved in their schools do best in school (U.S. Department of Education and U.S. Department of Health and Human Services, "A Call to Commitment: Fathers' Involvement in Children's Learning" [Washington, D.C.: U.S. Department of Education, 2000], p.5); Pruett, *The Nurturing Father,* p. 248.

6. Lamb, "The Development of Father-Infant Relationships," pp. 109–10.

7. "Increased paternal involvement thus does seem to strengthen infant-father attachment although as long as mothers assume primary responsibility for child care, they appear to be preferred attachment figures" (Lamb, "The Development of Father-Infant Relationships, p. 111).

8. "While primary caregiving fathers may be 'capable' of nurturing, the child preferred the working mother as often as the primary caregiving father when both were available" (Robert Frank, "Is the Male in Child Care Role Changing? Primary Caregiving Males Demonstrate the Changing Family Structure: Implication for Social Work Practice" [published at Slowlane.com], p. 9).

9. Sarah Stapleton-Gray, "Raising One's Children Is a Job Best Shared," *Washington Post,* November 15, 1999, p. C4.

10. See, for example, Kyle Pruett, "How Men and Children Affect Each Other's Development," *Zero to Three Bulletin* 18 (1997): 2; Parke and Brott, *Throwaway Dads,* p. 23.

11. James A. Levine and Todd L. Pittinsky, *Working Fathers: New Strategies for Balancing Work and Family* (New York: A Harvest Book, Harcourt Brace & Company, 1997), p. 41.

12. Levine and Pittinsky, *Working Fathers,* p. 41.

13. Kevin McDonald and Ross D. Parke, "Bridging the Gap: Parent–Child Play Interaction and Peer Interactive Competence," *Child Development* 55 (1984): 1265–77; John Snarey, *How Fathers Care for the Next Generation* (Cambridge, Mass.: Harvard University Press, 1993).

14. Richard Kuestner, Carol Franz, and Joel Weinberger, "The Family Origins of Empathy: A 26-Year Longitudinal Study," *Journal of Personality and Social Psychology* 58 (1990): 109–27.

15. See, for example, Pruett, *Fatherneed,* p. 73 (see chap. 2, n. 5), where parents in the study express satisfaction that they are showing their sons and daughters that they will have many options for raising their own kids; children living in counter-cultural communities are more flexible about appropriate occupations for girls and boys than those in more traditional families (Parke and Brott, *Throwaway Dads,* pp. 105, 114).

16. Pruett, *Fatherneed,* pp. 50–51; "Family Resource Coalition Report," *Fatherhood and Family Support,* vol. 15, no. 1 (Spring 1996): 3; *Kids*

Count Data Book (Baltimore, Md.: The Annie E. Casey Foundation, 1995), pp. 5–7; Carol W. Metzler et al., "The Social Context for Risky Sexual Behavior Among Adolescents," *Journal of Behavioral Medicine,* vol. 17, no. 4 (1994): 419–38; U.S. Department of Health and Human Services, *Survey on Child Health* (Washington, D.C.: National Center for Health Statistics, 1993).

17. Levine and Pittinsky, *Working Fathers,* p. 41; Pleck, "Paternal Involvement: Levels, Sources, and Consequences," pp. 96–98 (see chap. 1, n. 3); Pruett, "How Men and Children Affect Each Other's Development," pp. 4–11.
18. Pruett, "How Men and Children Affect Each Other's Development," p. 4. Mothers are more conservative once the child shows signs of frustration and move in sooner to help.
19. Pruett, "How Men and Children Affect Each Other's Development," p. 4; Pruett, *The Nurturing Father,* pp. 33–34.
20. "They could quiet and regulate themselves, but their appetite for engaging the outer world and brining it into their own was especially sharp" (Pruett, "How Men and Children Affect Each Other's Development," p. 7).
21. Pruett, "How Men and Children Affect Each Other's Development," p. 7.
22. "In the primary caregiving female family, the child most often turned to the mother for nurturing. The primary caregiving father did not participate in nurturing more than the primary caregiving female. However, he did show a greater amount of nurturing than the working father . . . the working mothers were providing an equal share of the nurturing in primary caregiving families" (Frank, "Is the Male in Child Care Role Changing?" p. 9).
23. Robert Frank, Ph.D., and Kathryn E. Livingston, *Parenting Partners: How to Encourage Dads to Participate in the Daily Lives of Their Children* (New York: St. Martin's Griffin, 1999), p. 51.
24. James A. Levine, "The 90's Father: Who Is He?" *Child* (March 1993): 96–99, 146.
25. Levine and Pittinsky, *Working Fathers,* pp. 17, 21–22.
26. "For the majority of American men, an internal shift in value has created what I call the invisible dilemma of *DaddyStress,* a largely unrecognized conflict between their double duties of work and family that they feel they should not expose" (Levine and Pittinsky, *Working Fathers,* p. 17). See also "Dealing with Daddy Stress: Corporate America wants them at work. Their families want them at home," *Forbes,* September 6, 1999.

27. "Babysider," *Santa Fe New Mexican,* July 21, 1996, Focus, p. E1.

28. See, for example, Levine and Pittinsky, *Working Fathers,* p. 21.

29. Pruett, *Fatherneed,* p. 72.

30. Pruett, *Fatherneed,* p. 72.

31. Parke and Brott, *Throwaway Dads,* p. 12, reporting on: Rosalind Barnett's NIH study that showed that men with the fewest worries about relationships with their children had few health problems and those with the most troubled relationships with their children had the worst health problems; and John Snarey's research from the 1940s to the present, which demonstrates that dads who provide high levels of socio-emotional support for their children from birth to age ten and high levels of intellectual, academic, social, and emotional support from eleven to twenty-one were more likely to be happily married at midlife. Snarey also found that fathers involved in childrearing have more successful careers.

32. Parke and Brott, *Throwaway Dads,* p. 12.

Chapter 4: NEGOTIATION 101

1. Chester L. Karras, *The Negotiating Game: How to Get What You Want* (New York: HarperBusiness, 1992), p. 18; "The best rule of thumb is to be optimistic—to let your reach exceed your grasp. Without wasting a lot of resources on hopeless causes, recognize that many things are worth trying for even if you may not succeed. The more you try for, the more you are likely to get. Studies of negotiation consistently show a strong correlation between aspiration and result. Within reason, it pays to think positively" (Roger Fisher and William Ury, *Getting to Yes: Negotiating Agreement without Giving In* [New York: Penguin USA, 1991], p. 179).

2. Betty Carter and Joan Peters, *Love, Honor & Negotiate: Making Your Marriage Work* (New York: Pocket Books, 1996), p. 2. Carter notes that many of couples' personal complaints result from social and economic pressures rather than their own shortcomings, and that the outdated traditional model of marriages makes those pressures worse. She says that most couples don't know they're in a traditional marriage or that its unspoken rules don't work anymore.

3. Karras, *The Negotiating Game,* p. 220.

4. See, for example, Fisher and Ury, *Getting to Yes,* p. 100; Rhona Mahony, *Kidding Ourselves: Breadwinning, Babies, and Bargaining Power* (New York: BasicBooks, 1995), p. 43; "Having a strong BATNA also protects the planner from entering into a contract with which he or she is uncomfortable. 'It protects you from accepting terms that are too un-

favorable,' add Fisher and Ury" (Kecia Jensen, "You Want a Deal?" *Successful Meetings* 44 [September 1995]: 51–52).

5. Fisher and Ury, *Getting to Yes,* pp. 102, 104.
6. Fisher and Ury, *Getting to Yes,* p. 106.
7. See Hochschild, *The Second Shift,* p. 57 (see chap. 1, n. 2) for a description of how BATNA and the possibility of divorce force women to accept unequal situations they don't want. "They do not struggle like this because they started off wanting to, or because such struggle is inevitable or because women inevitably lose, but because they are forced to choose between equality and marriage. And they choose marriage."

Chapter 5: THINK ABOUT WORK AND FAMILY ISSUES BEFORE ANGLING FOR THE RING

1. Mahony, *Kidding Ourselves,* pp. 73, 76 (see chap. 4, n. 4). The more-involved parent tends to favor more parental care. A mother's threat points are higher, meaning the level of bad behavior required to force her to leave must be quite high, as she and the baby need the father.
2. Mahony, *Kidding Ourselves,* pp. 76–77.
3. "The 'pure' traditional wants to identify with her activities at home (as a wife, as a mother, as a neighborhood mom), wants her husband to base his at work and wants less power than he. The traditional man wants the same. The 'pure' egalitarian, as the type emerges here, wants to identify with the same spheres her husband does and to have an equal amount of power in the marriage. . . . Between the traditional and the egalitarian is the transitional, any one of a variety of types of blending of the two. But in contrast to the traditional, a transitional woman wants to identify with her role at work as well as at home. Unlike the egalitarian, she believes her husband should base his identity more on work than she does. . . . A typical transitional man is all for his wife working but expects her to take the main responsibility at home too. Most men and women I talked to were 'transitional.' " (Hochschild, *The Second Shift,* pp. 15–16 [see chap. 1, n. 2].)
4. Hochschild, *The Second Shift,* pp. 15–16.
5. Hochschild, *The Second Shift,* p. 143.
6. Hochschild, *The Second Shift,* p. 143; Belsky and Kelly, *The Transition to Parenthood,* p. 141 (see chap. 1, n. 5).
7. Belsky and Kelly, *The Transition to Parenthood,* p. 7.
8. Belsky and Kelly, *The Transition to Parenthood,* p. 7.
9. Belsky and Kelly, *The Transition to Parenthood,* p. 128; Jordan, Stanley, and Markman, *Becoming Parents,* p. 79 (see chap. 1, n. 1).

10. Jordan, Stanley, and Markman, *Becoming Parents,* pp. 109–12
11. Jordan, Stanley, and Markman, *Becoming Parents,* p. 260.
12. Monica McGoldrick, *You Can Go Home Again: Reconnecting with Your Family* (New York: W. W. Norton & Co., 1995), pp. 38–39.
13. McGoldrick, *You Can Go Home Again,* p. 57. McGoldrick provides these questions and others to jostle an accurate rendition of family expectations. She notes:

> Gender is, of course, another major factor in establishing identity. You need to ask what the rules have been for men and women in your family and to what extent they conform to the society of the time. Cultural groups also differ in the specific rules defining gender arrangements. . . . The gender role constrictions on both men and women in families have played a powerful role over the centuries. . . . One of the most interesting things to look at is how members of your family responded to these constrictions. Did they sometimes break out of the stringent gender roles of their times? If so, how was this received by others inside and outside the family. . . . You will learn a lot about yourself and your family by exploring this dimension. (p. 53)

Chapter 6: MARITAL CALISTHENICS: BUILDING A MORE PERFECT UNION

1. Michael E. Cavanagh, *Before the Wedding: Look before You Leap* (Louisville, Ky.: Westminster John Knox Press, 1994), p. 1.
2. *Percentage of those who marry:* See, for example, Darrell E. Owens, "In Marriage, an Ounce of Prevention," *The Bergen County Record,* August 23, 1998, p. LO5.
3. David H. Olson and Amy K. Olson, *Empowering Couples: Building on Your Strengths,* 2nd ed. (Minneapolis: Life Innovations Inc., 2000), p. 5.
4. Scott M. Stanley and Howard J. Markman, "Acting on What We Know: The Hope of Prevention," based on a paper presented by Scott M. Stanley to the Family Impact Seminar, June 1997, Washington, D.C., p. 5. Other factors that increase the risk of marital dissolution: the wife's employment and income, premarital cohabitation, difficulties in the areas of leisure activities and sexual relations, parental divorce, communication positivity-negativity, communication withdrawal and invalidation, defensiveness and withdrawal, difficulties in communication and problem solving, having dissimilar attitudes, and others.
5. Stanley and Markman, "Acting on What We Know," p. 5.
6. Monthly Vital Statistics Report, vol. 43, no. 9(S) (National Center for Health Statistics, March 22, 1995).

7. Jordan, Stanley, and Markman, *Becoming Parents,* p. xii (see chap. 1, n. 1).
8. Ferdinand M. De Leon, "Rocking the Cradle—and a Marriage—after D-Day: Programs Help Couples Prepare for Parenthood," *Seattle Times,* October 24, 1999, p. L1.
9. Hochschild, *The Second Shift,* pp. 213–15 (see chap. 1, n. 2).
10. Hochschild, *The Second Shift,* pp. 260, 270.
11. Hochschild, *The Second Shift,* pp. 260, 270.
12. Cowan and Cowan, *The Landmark Ten-Year Study, When Partners Become Parents,* p. 102 (see chap. 1, n. 5).
13. Cowan and Cowan, *The Landmark Ten-Year Study, When Partners Become Parents,* p. 102.
14. Cowan and Cowan, *The Landmark Ten-Year Study, When Partners Become Parents,* p. 199.
15. Belsky and Kelly, *The Transition to Parenthood,* p. 124 (see chap. 1, n. 5) (reporting on a number of studies as well as that documented by the study that is the subject of the book).
16. Belsky and Kelly, *The Transition to Parenthood,* p. 124.
17. Andrea S. Larsen and David Olson, "Predicting Marital Satisfaction Using PREPARE: A Replication Study," *Journal of Marital and Family Therapy,* vol. 15, no. 3 (1989): 311–22. In previous studies, roles satisfaction did not predict marital satisfaction.
18. Olson and Olson, *Empowering Couples,* p. 70.
19. See, for example, E. Mark Cummings and Anne Watson O'Reilly, "Fathers in Family Context: Effects of Marital Quality on Child Adjustment," in *The Role of the Father in Child Development,* ed. Michael E. Lamb, 3rd ed. (New York: John Wiley & Sons, 1997), pp. 52–55. In harmonious marriages, mother-child and father-child relations are more positive and parents more likely to have shared and reciprocal roles within the family; poor marital quality has a negative effect on father-child relationships; gender-role differentiation between spouses typifies distressed marriages and may increase as marital relations worsen.
20. Center for Marriage and Family, *Marriage Preparation in the Catholic Church: Getting It Right* (Omaha, Neb.: Creighton University 1995).
21. P. Giblin, D. H. Sprenkle, and R. Sheehan, "Enrichment Outcome Research: A Meta-Analysis of Premarital, Marital, and Family Interventions," *Journal of Marital and Family Therapy,* vol. 11 (1985): 257–71.
22. Olson and Olson, *Empowering Couples,* p. 160; see also Normal D. Glenn and Sara McLanahan, "Children and Marital Happiness: A Further Specification of the Relationship," *Journal of Marriage and Family* 44 (February 1982): 63–72 (study of six national surveys and a review of research concluding that, more often than not, children have an

adverse effect on marital relations, without regard to sex, race, religion, education, or employment); Barbara Thornes and Jean Collard, *Who Divorces* (London: Routledge and Kegan Paul, 1979), p. 89 (finding that the birth of a first child often causes the most problems a marriage encounters, sometimes reaching crisis proportions).

23. Clint O'Connor, "No Kidding! Children Can Affect the Happiness of Your Marriage," *Plain Dealer,* August 16, 1997, p. 15.
24. Belsky and Kelly, *The Transition to Parenthood.*
25. Belsky and Kelly, *The Transition to Parenthood,* p. 179. "Constructive fighters" know how to use conflict to promote long-term happiness. Even in serious disagreement, each partner gets the chance to air his or her thoughts and ventilate frustrations and grievances. This prevents them from crossing the line in an argument into a "street fight whose only aim is to inflict punishment."

Chapter 7: LOOK BEFORE YOU THROW AWAY THE BIRTH CONTROL

1. Martin O'Connell, "Labor Force Participation for Mothers with Infants Declines for First Time, Census Bureau Reports" (CB01-170), Census Bureau Press Release, October 18, 2001.
2. O'Connell, "Labor Force Participation for Mothers with Infants Declines."
3. Belsky and Kelly, *The Transition to Parenthood,* p. 227 (see chap. 1, n. 5).
4. Belsky and Kelly, *The Transition to Parenthood,* p. 131.
5. Belsky and Kelly, *The Transition to Parenthood,* p. 226.

Chapter 8: MEN MUST GET INVOLVED EARLY

1. "Current evidence suggests that the chemistry of pregnancy facilitates the bond between a mother and her young but that there are many other ways to arrive at the Jerusalem of overwhelming love. Cuddling a newborn, holding it against your naked breast, stroking it at the soothing rate of 40 strokes per minute, smelling its fontanel—all these gestures appear to release in the brain the flow of peptides like oxytocin, the hormone of harmony and attachment. So it is that father love can be as powerful as mother love without the benefit of gestation, and adoptive parents can fall madly in love with a baby the moment they hold it in their arms. The human body is built to love, whether it owns a womb or borrows one. It is easy to love a baby, any baby . . ." (Natalie Angier, "Baby in a Box," *New York Times Sunday*

Magazine, May 16, 1999, sec. 6, p. 86, col. 1); Natalie Angier, "A Potent Peptide Prompts an Urge to Cuddle," *New York Times,* January 22, 1991, p. C1.

2. Pamela Warrick, "Right Chemistry: Biological Explanation Sought for Monogamous Tendencies," *Houston Chronicle,* December 20, 1993, Houston sec., p. 6; "The presence of vasopressin in men, and the similar-acting hormone oxytocin in women, explains why parents show a slave-like devotion to their young, cleaning, feeding, entertaining and responding to their demands 24-hours a day. The hormones act like drugs, encouraging this self-sacrificing behaviour in parents" (Kate Muir, "Cuddle up with a Hormone," *The Times,* November 11, 1993, Features).

3. Pruett, *The Nurturing Father,* p. 288 (see chap. 2, n. 4).

4. Pruett, *The Nurturing Father,* p. 35; Levine and Pittinsky, *Working Fathers,* p. 41. (see chap. 3, n. 11).

5. See, for example, 2000 Oxygen/Markle Pulse poll in which, on average, men report taking less than a week of paternity leave: "Oxygen/ Markle Pulse Poll: Two out of three Americans believe men should take more than two weeks paternity leave; Half of Americans would vote for a candidate who extends the Family and Medical Leave Act to include paid leave; American women are split over Cherie Blair's belief that her husband, British Prime Minister Tony Blair, should take paternity leave when their fourth child is born in May; Fewer women support paternity leave for an American president; On average, men take less than one week of paternity leave; Few Americans know anyone who has taken more than two weeks" (PR Newswire, April 5, 2000).

6. Mahony, *Kidding Ourselves,* p. 76 (see chap. 4, n. 4).

7. Pruett, "How Men and Children Affect Each Other's Development" (see chap. 3, n. 10).

8. Arlene Eisenberg, Heidi E. Murkoff, and Sandee E. Hathaway, *What to Expect When You're Expecting* (New York: Workman Publishing, 1996), p. 417.

9. Eisenberg, Murkoff, and Hathaway, *What to Expect,* p. 417.

10. Arlene Eisenberg, Heidi E. Murkoff, and Sandee E. Hathaway, *What to Expect the First Year* (New York: Workman Publishing, 1989), pp. 12–13.

11. Michael Lamb, "Introduction," in *The Role of the Father in Child Development,* ed. Michael E. Lamb, 3rd ed. (New York: John Wiley & Sons, 1997), p. 7; Pleck, "Paternal Involvement," pp. 89, 95 (see chap. 1, n. 3).

12. "Virginia Company Shakes Up $3.6 Billion Infant Formula Industry," *Business Wire,* July 26, 1999.

13. American Academy of Pediatrics, statistics; Fiona Phelan, "Continue Breastfeeding after Returning to Work . . . In Style," *Fairfield County Woman,* December 31, 2000, p. 22.
14. "Oxygen/Markle Pulse Poll."

Chapter 9: DIVIDE AND CONQUER YOUR NEW ROLES

1. Cowan and Cowan, *The Landmark Ten-Year Study* (see chap. 1, n. 5).
2. See, for example, Belsky and Kelly, *The Transition to Parenthood* (see chap. 1, n. 5); Cowan and Cowan, *The Landmark Ten-Year Study,* pp. 107, 227 (92 percent of men and women in the study who became parents described more conflict and disagreement after becoming parents); Dr. Theodore Greenstein, "Husbands' Participation in Domestic Work: Interactive Effects of Wives' and Husbands' Gender Ideologies," *Journal of Marriage and the Family,* 58 (August 1996): 585–95; Dr. Theodore Greenstein, "Gender Ideology and Perceptions of the Fairness of the Division of Household Labor: Effects on Marital Quality," *Social Forces,* 74 (1996): 1029–42.
3. Cowan and Cowan, *The Landmark Ten-Year Study,* p. 20.
4. Cowan and Cowan, *The Landmark Ten-Year Study,* p. 26.
5. Barnett and Rivers, *She Works He Works* (see chap. 1, n. 7).
6. "With a few notable exceptions, the mothers gathered all the information about childcare resources, made most of the visits, and spent hours worrying about the alternatives. Though most seemed to assume this is their job, many resent the responsibility, particularly because choices are so difficult, and seem to have such far-reaching consequences" (Cowan and Cowan, *The Landmark Ten-Year Study,* pp. 130–31); even when the husbands insist on going out, the wives have the responsibility of finding a baby-sitter.
7. See, for example, James T. Bond, Ellen Galinsky, and Jennifer E. Swanberg, *The 1997 Study of the Changing Workforce* (New York: Families and Work Institute, 1998), p. 7; 83 percent of mothers in dual-income families say they are more likely to take time off when a child is sick versus 22 percent of fathers.

Chapter 10: GETTING UNSTUCK

1. Fisher and Ury, *Getting to Yes,* p. 181 (see chap. 4, n. 1).
2. Fisher and Ury, *Getting to Yes,* p. 34.
3. "Negotiating an End to the Second Shift," personal notes used in talks, provided by Rhona Mahony.
4. Cowan and Cowan, *The Landmark Ten-Year Study,* p. 103 (see chap. 1, n. 5).

5. Cowan and Cowan, *The Landmark Ten-Year Study,* p. 103.
6. Fisher and Ury, *Getting to Yes,* pp. 130, 138.

Chapter 11: STRATEGIES THAT WORK: MORE ON MOMMY LETTING GO

1. Pruett, *The Nurturing Father,* p. 281 (see chap. 2, note 4).
2. Pruett, *The Nurturing Father,* p. 249.
3. Pruett, *The Nurturing Father,* p. 249.

Chapter 12: SHARING THE CAREER ACCOMMODATION

1. Robert Taylor, "A Friendly Touch: The Increase of Women in the U.S. Labour Market Has Spurred a Call for Family Oriented Employee Programs," *Financial Times,* June 29, 2000, p. 13; "Families without Kids" *The Economist,* November 27, 1999; U.S. Census Bureau, 1998.
2. U.S. Census Bureau, CB97-192; Employment Characteristics of Families Summary: Bureau of Labor Statistics, 1996; "Census Bureau Facts for Features," CB00-FF.03, February 23, 2000.
3. D'Vera Cohn and Sarah Cohen, "Census Sees Vast Change in Language, Employment: More People Work at Home, Speak Little English," *Washington Post,* August 6, 2001, p. A01.
4. See, for example, the 2001 study by the magazine *Top Sante* and the healthcare firm BUPA, in which nine out of ten working women say they often feel under stress; 75 percent of working women think their children suffer emotionally if both parents work full time; 87 percent said stress causes them to shout at and upset their children; 73 percent of working women said both parents working leads to more marriage breakdowns; 90 percent said they are expected to perform too many roles; and 80 percent said men are not much help ("Jobs and Families Don't Work for Mums," *The Express,* June 13, 2001).
5. For example, in "Women's Voices 2000," a 2000 poll conducted for Lifetime Television and the Center for Policy Alternatives, 50 percent of women with children younger than six said they found it harder to balance the demands of work and family than they had four years ago; 30 percent said it was much harder. They expressed concern about the decline in moral values in the United States, which they felt could be reversed by parents spending more time with their children. In a 2000 Nickelodeon/TIME Magazine Poll, 36 percent of kids said they wanted more time with their mothers and 45 percent said they would like more time with their fathers (Bob Herbert, "In America, FOCUS on Women," *New York Times,* September 28, 2000, p. A27.
6. Mark Dolliver, "Takes," *Adweek,* July 17, 2000.

7. The Bureau of Labor Statistics reported 440,000 male part-time workers and 3,102,000 female part-time workers in households of married people with children under six years old for 1995–1996 (Bureau of Labor Statistics, Table 5. "Employment status of persons by sex, marital status, and presence and age of own children under 18, annual averages 1995–96," last modified June 13, 1997).

8. Bond, Galinsky, and Swanberg, *The 1997 Study of the Changing Workforce,* pp. 127–30 (see chap. 9, n. 7); Ellen Galinsky et. al., *The Changing Workforce: The National Study* (New York: Families and Work Institute, 1993), p. 83.

9. Christine Hogg and Lisa Harker, *The Family Friendly Employer: Examples from Europe* (London: Daycare Trust, 1992), p. 29; Juliet Schor, *The Overworked American: The Unexpected Decline of Leisure* (New York: BasicBooks, 1992), p. 154.

10. Katherine Baker, "Flexible Work Styles in the Corporate Research Center," *Information Outlook,* January 1, 2000; "Flextime," *Controlling Law Firm Costs,* September 2001.

11. Studies have shown that the cost of replacing workers who leave ranges from 1.2 to 2 times the salary of the replaced worker, and that it takes about a year for a new employee to achieve maximum efficiency. Ellen Galinsky et al., editors, *Parental Leave and Productivity: Current Research* (New York: Families and Work Institute, 1992), p. 34.

12. Cummings and O'Reilly, "Fathers in Family Context," pp. 53–54, 59 (see chap. 6, n. 19).

13. Cummings and O'Reilly, "Fathers in Family Context," pp. 53–54, 49.

Chapter 13: LAWS THAT CAN HELP

1. Randy Gleason, "Teleconference Speaker Says: U.S. Lags Behind in Women's Benefits," *The Pantagraph,* June 6, 1997, p. A6; Tara Mack, "In Britain, Who'll Mind the Kids? Confronting a U.S.-style Crisis in Child Care," *USA Today,* July 12, 2000, p. 12A.; Leslie Dreyfous, "Mom's Delicate Balance; Back in the Workaday World," *The Record,* December 22, 1991, p. L01.

2. Hogg and Harker, *The Family Friendly Employer,* p. 18 (see chap. 12, n. 9).

3. Hogg and Harker, *The Family Friendly Employer,* p. 18.

4. Hogg and Harker, *The Family Friendly Employer,* p. 145.

5. Hogg and Harker, *The Family Friendly Employer,* p. 18.

6. Christopher J. Ruhm, "Parental Leave and Child Health," *Journal of Health Economics* (November 2000): 931–60.

7. Ruhm, "Parental Leave and Child Health," p. 19

8. Ruhm, "Parental Leave and Child Health," p. 45.
9. Robin Brown, ed., *Children in Crisis* (New York: The Reference Shelf [vol. 66, no. 1], 1994), p. 87.
10. Hogg and Harker, *The Family Friendly Employer,* p. 19.
11. Hogg and Harker, *The Family Friendly Employer,* p. 18.
12. Hogg and Harker, *The Family Friendly Employer,* p. 18
13. Michael Selmi, "The Limited Vision of the Family and Medical Leave Act," *Villanova Law Review,* vol. 44, no. 3 (1999): 406.
14. Selmi, "The Limited Vision of the Family and Medical Leave Act," p. 408; Andrew S. Hughes, "Time Off for Baby: Family and Medical Leave Act Provides Little-Used Opportunity," *South Bend Tribune,* June 10, 1997, p. D1.
15. Galinsky et al., *Parental Leave and Productivity,* p. 15 (see chap. 12, n. 11).
16. Marilyn Watkins, Ph.D., "Family Leave Insurance Frequently Asked Questions," *Economic Opportunity Institute Brochure,* Seattle, Wash., March 22, 2001.
17. Selmi, "The Limited Vision of the Family and Medical Leave Act," p. 408.
18. Lisa Bornstein, "Inclusions and Exclusions in Work-Family Policy: The Public Values and Moral Code Embedded in the Family and Medical Leave Act," *Columbia Journal of Gender and Law,* vol. 10, no. 1 (2000): 77; ("The Commission found that many workers—over forty percent— are unaware of the law, and others are unable to take advantage of the leave because of financial constraints. Employees in households with low family income levels, low levels of education, and those from Latino backgrounds are the least likely employees to work for covered employers. Further, young, part-time, low-income, and never married workers are least likely to meet the service and hours of eligibility requirements."); LEXIS, p. 9; "The fact that the leave is unpaid further exposes the myth of gender neutrality. While mothers can sometimes take disability leave following childbirth, which often allows full or partial income replacement benefits, fathers rarely can take paid leave. Without wage replacement, fathers are less likely to be able to take leave, and parental leave is likely to be used primarily by women due to their position in the workforce as compared to that of men." (LEXIS, p. 32)
19. NOW Legal Defense and Education Fund, *Pregnancy and Parental Leave, an Employment Guide* (1999): 2. For example, these include Vermont, the District of Columbia, and Oregon, which extend family leave to employees of companies with ten, twenty, and twenty-five or more employees, respectively.

20. George Donnelly, "Meet the Generous Corp.," *CFO: The Magazine for Chief Financial Officers,* vol. 15, no. 8 (August 1999): 14; "SHRM Study Reveals What's 'Hot' for Benefit Plan Offerings," *Managing Benefits Plans* (August 2001): 1. Just 18 percent of survey respondents' companies offer paid maternity leave beyond short-term disability and 14 percent offer paid paternity leave.

21. Schor, *The Overworked American,* p. 2 (see chap. 12, n. 9).

22. Schor, *The Overworked American,* pp. 29–30.

23. Schor, *The Overworked American,* pp. 2, 29–30, 80–82.

24. Galinsky et al., *Parental Leave and Productivity,* p. 34.

25. Galinsky et al., *Parental Leave and Productivity,* p. 55.

26. "Nearly 30 [percent] of the children whose mothers lack paid leave or flexibility of hours are failing in math or have behavioral problems, three times the rate of children whose mothers have these benefits, the studies found. For each hour that either parent works between 6 and 9 in the evening, their child is 17 percent more likely to do poorly in math, and for parents who work nights, their children are three times more likely to have been suspended from school" (Ronald Kotulak, "Parents in a Trap: Businesses Need to Recognize That Children Deserve More of Parents' Time," *Chicago Tribune,* May 13, 2001, Perspective, p. 1).

27. Galinsky et al., *Parental Leave and Productivity,* p. 11

28. "The recognition that caring for children is not just the mother's responsibility, and that men need financial help from the government to be able to take a bigger caring role, is significant. . . . Parents, especially women, need help to balance work and family care because otherwise they and their skills will be lost to employers and the economy—either because they will have to give up work or because they work less efficiently" (Nick Burkitt, "Analysis: Left Behind on Leave: Continental Europe Will Still Be Streets Ahead of Us on Rights for New Parents Even if the Government's Proposals Are Implemented in Full," *The Guardian,* December 18, 2000, p. 17).

29. Takashi Koyama Yomiuri, "Men Wary of Taking Leave for Child Care," *Daily Yomiuri,* May 26, 2000.

30. Hogg and Harker, *The Family Friendly Employer,* pp.107–9, 125–27. Both Dow Benelux and National Westminster Bank found it necessary to provide training to mid-level management about the benefits of family-friendly policies, as well as in how to implement such policies. Dow Benelux requires that mid-level managers report on the implementation of equal opportunities among their employees. Senior management steps in if a particular area or department does not contain

appropriate representation in the use of equal opportunities policies.

31. "Benefit Programs Are Vital Sources of Personal and Financial Stability, SHRM Says," *PR Newswire,* May 19, 1997; Society for Human Resource Management, "Work and Family Survey" January, 1997. Countries such as Sweden, France, Belgium, the Netherlands, and Spain have enforced equal entitlements for full- and part-time workers to prevent the marginalization of part-time workers and create higher-level part-time jobs. Arne L. Kalleberg, "Nonstandard Employment Relations: Part-Time, Temporary and Contract Work," *Annual Review of Sociology* 26 (January 1, 2000): 341–65.

32. "Breastfeeding is accompanied by about a 5-point higher IQ; 40 percent of that increase results from maternal bonding and 60 percent from the nutritional value of breast milk" ("Health Watch: The Week's Top Medical Stories," *Atlanta Journal and Constitution,* Reader, p. 5Q, September 26, 1999).

33. Cost, Quality & Child Outcomes Study Team, *Cost, Quality, and Child Outcomes in Child Care Centers,* p. 1 (see chap. 2, n. 14).

34. Cost, Quality & Child Outcomes Study Team, *Cost, Quality, and Child Outcomes in Child Care Centers,* p. 11.

35. Galinsky et al., *The Study of Children in Family Child Care and Relative Care,* pp. 3, 57 (see chap. 2, n. 5); Sharon L. Kagan and Nancy E. Cohen, *Not By Chance: Creating an Early Care and Education System for America's Children: Abridged Report, The Quality 2000 Initiative* (New Haven, Conn.: The Bush Center in Child Development and Social Policy at Yale University, 1997), pp. 24–27; Cost, Quality & Child Outcomes Study Team, *Cost, Quality, and Child Outcomes in Child Care Centers,* pp. 4, 10, 11–12.

RESOURCES

BEFORE GETTING MARRIED
PREPARE: www.lifeinnovation.com
FOCCUS (for Christians—some emphasis on religion): Talk to your clergy
or search on-line for closest contact point.
Susan Piver, *The Hard Questions: 100 Essential Questions to Ask before You
Say "I Do"* (New York: Putnam, 2000).

BEFORE GETTING PREGNANT OR HAVING CHILDREN
Pamela Jordan, Scott M. Stanley, and Howard J. Markman, *Becoming Par-
ents: How to Strengthen Your Marriage As Your Family Grows* (San
Francisco: Jossey-Bass, 1999). Contains an active-listening dialogue
guide, complete with steps and exercises.
For the Becoming Parents program: www.becomingparents.com.
Jay Belsky, Ph.D., and John Kelly, *The Transition to Parenthood: How a First
Child Changes a Marriage: Why Some Couples Grow Closer and Others
Apart* (New York: Delacorte Press, 1994).
Carolyn Pape Cowan and Philip A. Cowan, *The Landmark Ten-Year Study,
When Partners Become Parents: The Big Life Change for Couples* (New
York: BasicBooks, 1992).

CHILD CARE

Postpartum doulas: Check locally, or look through www.napcs.org.

National Association of Postpartum Care Services, 800 Detroit St., Denver, CO 80206, or call 1-800-45-DOULA.

Look for NAEYC (National Association for the Education of Young Children) accreditation of early-learning centers, day-care programs, and preschools; find information about quality child-care and related matters at their Web site: www.naeyc.org.

Ellen Galinsky et al., *The Study of Children in Family Child Care and Relative Care: Highlights of Findings* (New York: Families and Work Institute, 1994). To order, call the Families and Work Institute at 212-465-2044, fax 212-465-8637, or visit their Web site at www.families andwork.org.

Cost, Quality, & Child Outcomes Study Team Executive Summary (Denver: Department of Economics, University of Colorado, 1995); $10. To order, send your name and address, along with a check or money order payable to "Cost & Quality Study," to Cost, Quality, and Child Outcomes Study, Economics Department, Campus Box 159, P.O. Box 173364, University of Colorado, Denver, CO 80217-3364. Phone: 303-556-4934.

Summary of NICHD Study of Nonmaternal care: www.nichd.nih.gov/pub lications/pubs/early_child_care.htm

NEGOTIATION

Roger Fisher and William Ury, *Getting to Yes: Negotiating Agreement without Giving In,* 2nd ed. (New York: Penguin Books, 1991).

Rhona Mahony, *Kidding Ourselves: Breadwinning, Babies, and Bargaining Power* (New York: BasicBooks, 1995).

Betty Carter, M.S.W., with Joan K. Peters, *Love, Honor & Negotiate: Building Partnerships That Last a Lifetime* (New York: Pocket Books, 1996).

MARRIAGE SKILLS AND COUNSELORS

www.smartmarriages.com: information clearing house and a great starting point.

For Harville Hendrix imago certified therapists and Getting the Love You Want Workshops: www.imagotherapy.com.

Enrich (PREPARE for married couples): www.lifeinnovation.com.

REFOCCUS (if you are Christian and religious): Talk to your clergy or search on-line for closest contact point.

John Gottman, Ph.D., *Why Marriages Succeed or Fail . . . and How You Can Make Yours Last* (New York: Fireside, 1994).

Harville Hendrix, Ph.D., *Getting the Love You Want: A Guide for Couples* (New York: HarperPerennial 1988); offers exercises and guide for dialogue.

Harville Hendrix, Ph.D. *Keeping the Love You Find: A Personal Guide* (New York: Pocket Books, 1992)

MISCELLANEOUS

For information about child care, child development, and fathers' influence: www.zerotothree.org.

Check out the Household Task Analysis: www.centerforworkandfamily .com/household.htm.

For information on the Family and Medical Leave Act (FMLA): www.dol .gov/dol/esa/fmla.htm.

"A Call to Commitment: Fathers' Involvement in Children's Learning," a free U.S. Department of Education publication, outlines the benefits of and gives specific suggestions for daily paternal involvement. Available at www.ed.gov/pubs/edpubs.html.

For information and forum about Mommy Trap issues: www.mommy trap.com.

INDEX